BLADES TALES

A Collection of Memories, Stories and Anecdotes of Supporting Sheffield United Football Club

Compiled and Edited by:
Matthew Bell, Kevin Titterton, Howard Holmes and Karen Keenan.

photo: Andy Greaves

To Matthew

Christmas 2000

For all your hardwork in music.

Love mum & Dad

X

First published in 2000 by
Juma
44 Wellington Street
Sheffield S1 4HD
Tel: 0114 272 0915
Fax: 0114 278 6550
Email: MLacey5816@aol.com

ISBN 1 872204 70 8

Cover photographs: Front, top photo by Howard Duke; front, bottom photo by Kevin Titterton; back cover photo by Andy Greaves.

ACKNOWLEDGEMENTS

This collection would not have been possible without the assistance of all those Sheffield United supporters who have contributed by letting us share in their personal reminiscences of watching the Blades - their excitement, their hope, their despair, their joy, their pain and their amusement. Thank you to everyone.

We could also not have got by without the help of two men in particular, although they probably don't realise it. These fellows are, of course, Sheffield United's official historian and statistician - respectively Denis Clarebrough and Andrew Kirkham. Denis' book "Sheffield United Football Club - The First Hundred Years", and their joint publication "A Complete Record of Sheffield United Football Club 1889-1999" proved inestimable in checking various facts, figures, dates and events. We hope the contributors don't mind when we have found it necessary to 'massage' their memories to mirror what actually happened and not what they remember happening!

Finally, all the photographs in this book are the work of Sheffield United supporters. This serves two purposes: (1) It allows us to pursue our intention of portraying what it is like to be a follower of the Blades. The supporters are the ones that matter - the players and officials are transient and play just bit parts in the drama, although, of course, none of what you are about to read could have occurred without them; (2) We don't have to worry about copyright!

For this reason, then, some of the photographs may not be quite of the quality you would expect in a posh book like this, but please bear with us.

We do, though, wish to thank Martyn Harrison for his invaluable advice and practical assistance with all matters photographic.

CONTENTS

foreword

By Gary Armstrong*

Some things you just never grow out of. Quite why football support provides such a strong emotion perhaps raises many questions about belief systems and values in British society. These are big issues which nobody can provide answers for. In the absence of such explanations, fans go with the flow and simply enjoy or endure, and increasingly articulate their allegiance in print.

I'm not sure what being a Blade means. I've been one for thirty-one years now and perhaps the most important facet of my fandom is the chance it provides to share something with thousands of others. And in keeping with that, what the contributors to this volume exhibit is a willingness to share with fellow Blades a variety of emotions which range from misery to euphoria. So, expect to find yourself chuckling and also expect tinges of regret and sentimentality.

Reminiscences abound which attempt to explain various feats of becoming, being and unfortunately, due to our decades of mediocre teams, the nothingness of being a Blades supporter. A few themes stand out. The father-son thing around football is something that comes through many tales, and something that will strike a reader is that following the Blades seems to be inseparable from the consumption of beer. Those just beginning their boozing days can read with astonishment how in 1964 there were, as one contributor puts it, "twelve pints to the pound", and at the same time, try to picture his evocative detail of an eighteen-stone steel worker doing the Cossack dance on a pub table. These two themes to me encapsulate football support; at one level fandom can be terribly serious and introspective, yet at the same time in the company of likeminded fans can be ribald and carnivalesque.

As is evident from the contributors, the Bramall Lane football ground and its environs are intimately tied into the biographies of Blades fans. The games the ground has hosted provide everlasting memories. Names of players will evoke a variety of images and incidents. Even the physical structure will jog a memory. Some may well be nostalgic for the rain that would pour through holes in the corrugated iron roof of the Kop. Older readers may well include some of those who watched a game in 1946 sitting on the girders of the Kop roof. Thousands will lament the absence of the two hundred steps that were once at the back of the Kop, or the queue of young urchins awaiting 'silver disc' entry, the white railings and what became of the DJ welcoming us all throughout the 1970s to "Beautiful Downtown Bramall Lane".

The floodlight pylons that were visible from miles away have now disappeared and the low roof of the Kop illuminated in winter only by dim bulbs has lost its sinister atmosphere. The bright new shiny world of contemporary football has also done away with Wagon Wheels in flimsy yellow paper, Vimto in plastic containers, muddy pitches and army recruitment posters on the white wall of the Kop. The tannoy and the Bladettes have long since replaced the Sheffield Recreation Brass Band who played on the pitch before games between the 1940s and late 1960s.

But the pop records that replaced them can still jolt memories of the glory days of the 1970s. I wonder if the American country singer Lynn Anderson is aware of the significance to thousands of Sheffielders of her song 'Rose Garden', or whether the strangely-titled American band Limmie and the Family Cookin' realise in their old age that their hit song 'You Can Do Magic', when played on pub jukeboxes or golden oldie radio shows, can evoke so many images and provoke many a watery eye.

Most contributions are from Bramall Lane regulars from the past thirty years. As such, there is many a tale told which involves skirmishes with rival fans. Many a dad and respectable member of society may well have their memories jogged by references to bush jackets worn by the bad lads of the Shoreham End in the late 1960s. Others may remember the Barmy Army gatherings of the 1970s and whilst you, good reader, might claim to abhor hooliganism, the incidence of mass egg throwing at Wednesday's boys on their East Bank Kop in the late 1960s is one which the pious Blade might allow him or herself to abhor a little less.

Fortunately Blades have always had city rivals Wednesday to laugh at. The stereotype of the Owls fan abounds in this collection. Invariably fickle and miserable.....don't get me started. I'm lucky enough to have written a couple of books that permitted me to say my piece about that lot. I'll let the readers draw their own conclusions from what others say in this book. Some things never change.

I was quite tickled to hear that when Sheffield's first nightclub - the Penny Farthing - opened in the 1960s the Wednesday players would be quietly enjoying soft drinks, while across the dance floor complete with pints of John Smith's were Sheffield United's finest. Over the decades United players are invariably the ones on the front page of the local evening paper, having been found out for various misdemeanours. The Owls players by contrast are more usually on the inside pages presenting prizes to long-serving dinner women or in the company of misguided children.

Maybe you remember travelling to away games on Sheffield United Tours or watching youth team games at the Ball Inn ground. Possibly yours was the shapely bum pinched by Jimmy Johnstone or you were the child with the ice lolly that Alan Hodgkinson shared without your consent. On the subject of players' antics away from the pitch, I must add that the great Tony Currie once called me a pillock. I have witnesses. I was so proud.

The editors explain that this book idea arose from a meeting that questioned why the club did not sell onion bhajis and samosas as well as plotting to overthrow the then Chairman. The latter had a rationale but the former makes me ask; whoever entered Bramall Lane in search of a bhaji? The same editors apologise in advance if anything that follows causes offence. In my opinion they shouldn't be so sensitive. Part of partisan fanship is having the wherewithal to offend. A good book should leave a reader wanting more, or at least seeking answers to questions that have been provoked by the text. Personally I feel there is another volume to follow this and many a reader upon finishing should have the confidence to send their tales in to the editors.

So, who can claim to have had the longest ever away trip? Can anyone out there lay claim to the best blag to enter a match free? Who released the monkey at Weston-Super-Mare Zoo the night before the game at Bristol Rovers in 1977? Any tales out there of United's games in Algeria, Poland, Israel and Holland in the 1970s? Or has anyone ever played against a young man who went on to be famous with the Blades?

Younger fans reading what follows will possibly marvel at some of the events that happened over the previous five decades. I feel sorry for today's younger fans - will they, in thirty years' time, ever be able to gather together the tales that follow here? What will they be able to tell a reader about when nobody knows or ever sees most footballers outside of the matchday? And how can they make a reader laugh with tales of the big-gob in the crowd or the subversive song when the PA system now controls chanting and anyone who shouts advice to players faces arrest and banning from the ground? Huge elements of football fandom are gone and others are being lost. Enjoy these tales, I've a feeling they can never be replicated.

* Gary Armstrong is the author of 'Football Hooligans: Knowing the Score', 'Blade Runners: Lives in Football' and is co-editor of 'Entering the Field: New Perspectives on World Football' and 'Football Cultures and Identities'.

Introduction

I remember it clearly. It was early in 1995, during a quiet moment (probably a beer break) in a meeting of the Blades Independent Fans' Association in the upstairs room of the Railway Hotel, overlooking the South Stand, between plotting how to get rid of Reg Brealey and discussing why the club does not sell onion bhajis and samosas from its snack bars, when Howard Holmes, a veteran of two previous Blades-related publications, declared, "I've got a good idea for another book".

We were obliged to listen, and Howard must have anticipated our agreement that it was a good idea, as he had already booked a room in Sheffield Central Library and had had posters printed inviting people to turn up there one Saturday morning to tell us their stories.

So there we were, armed with tape recorders, awaiting the rush. Nobody turned up. Well, yes, they did - a couple with a young child who had little interest in football and who apparently had entered by mistake, and a scruffy-looking man who appeared to be a tramp who had come in for a warm. And he didn't like football either.

Undaunted, we advertised our intentions in the club programme, the 'Green 'Un' and the 'Flashing Blade' fanzine and over the summer of 1995 we had quite a few, mainly written, contributions.

Kev took it upon himself to type them all up and we had the beginnings of a book. But there it stalled. You know what it's like - work, family, the house and other things get in the way and you just don't have the time to finish what you started, so it gets left for another day.

It wasn't really until 1999 that we got it off the ground again and, like a deadline-day buy to boost a push for promotion, it was thanks to our own late signing (Karen Keenan) that the momentum was maintained. Karen foolishly agreed to proof-read! She also added a few stories of her own and this is what we ended up with.

We have divided the 'Tales' into sections, but these are completely arbitrary and some stories might slot just as easily into two or three differ-

ent categories. Some of them you will have read before as they have been purloined from eleven years' worth of 'Flashing Blade', but the majority are previously unpublished. Some are short and sharp, some are virtual life stories, but we hope they are all enjoyable.

The memories contained in this book are (almost) completely uncensored and are generally faithfully reported from their original wording, except where inaccurate known facts have been corrected or where original thoughts and wishes expressed have been overtaken by subsequent events. Where memories were recounted orally we have attempted to reproduce the inflexion and tone of the story-teller, thus the Queen's English may be slightly compromised in places. Therefore, although some people may be offended by occasional words used in this compilation of stories, our aim has been to report the linguistic mode and mood of each contributor accurately.

We have attempted to cross-check all the facts that appear in footnotes and 'asides' within the stories but we cannot accept responsibility for any errors made by the contributors (or ourselves), nor do we apologise if anything they say appears uncomplimentary towards anybody. They are, after all, the opinions of the contributors, who are effectively the authors of their own material. We do, though, apologise if anything in these pages causes offence and we would be pleased to hear from anybody with alternative opinions to those expressed herein, for possible inclusion in a future book.

Some contributors either submitted their tales anonymously or asked to remain anonymous, and we respect their wishes, especially where criminal proceedings were forthcoming (or might otherwise be subsequently!).

The title of each story was usually devised by the author, although some are all our own work and we are therefore sorry if they are a bit corny!

And finally, if, whilst reading this book, you think, "I know a few better stories than that!", then please write them down and send them in and we may be able to come up with a second helping in the future.

Prologue

I never actually played for United, though I think it's been quite close sometimes. I'm probably slightly too old at thirty seven for first-team football now. But I did interview Jimmy Hagan once, and saw him play, so that's all right.

When I was writing the Crucible Theatre play, 'United on a Wednesday Night' I found nobody decent to support the plan of the villain of that show that there should be one super team for one super city - not even among Sheffield Wednesday-supporting MPs who have been so triumphantly wrong about everything from the Great Mining Strike to the World Student Games and the National Curriculum.

As part of that play I did some in-depth research about how Sheffielders decide whether to be Blades or Owls. Initial evidence suggested a very slight correlation with which side of town you lived, and who your mother supported. It was also suggested that on the whole, Unitedites seem to have more moustaches.

My long experience on Radio Sheffield, however, now proves prima facie that Unitedites are much cleverer, wittier, better looking, more tolerant, a little more pretentious and rather better at football. It is also pretty certain that if you change sides and become a Blade (and it can be done - ask Derek Dooley) you do better at school, and Blades also do better in parliament (ask Richard Caborn), as well as getting bigger parts on television (ask Ray Ashcroft).

You also, if you want, become more attractive to the opposite sex (ask me).

Rony Robinson

Matchday Memories

Never Go With Your Mum

Alistair Graham

On November 16th 1996, my dad, mum, two sisters and myself set out on the short journey to Burslem, Stoke-on-Trent. Burslem is the home town of Port Vale, who were hosting the red and white wizards that day.

Arriving at our destination about an hour and a half before kick off, my mum and my sisters, who don't share the same affection for the Blades as me and my dad, disappeared to go shopping. Their plan was to go to nearby Newcastle-under-Lyme for the afternoon and pick us up from Stoke-on-Trent College after the game.

The match, a 0-0 draw, was best forgotten as both sides failed to make a breakthrough, despite United's high league position on the day. Despite a brief flutter towards the end, with United hitting the bar twice, it was a quite depressing game and with the winter weather beginning to take its toll all we wanted to do was get home.

Believing that my mum was waiting for us outside the ground we rushed through the crowds to the nearby college. We half expected her to be sitting in the car grumbling that we were late but to our surprise there was no sign of either her or the car. We were surprised at first but just put it down to the fact that there was heavy traffic all the way down the road.

We waited a while, then decided it would be a good idea to have a walk down the road to see if she was stuck in traffic. However, we reached the bottom of the road and had still not found her so we set off back to the arranged meeting place.

On the other side of Stoke, however, my mum had pulled up at the Victoria Ground, the then home of Stoke City Football Club. They had been to Newcastle-under-Lyme for an hour and had then decided to go shopping in Stoke town centre. This was the beginning of their problems: when they left the car park they found they were completely lost and had to ask for directions to the football ground. The locals, obviously believing that they were looking for the Victoria Ground, directed her there.

A policewoman waiting in lay-by near to the Stoke City ground turned out to be my mum's knight in shining armour. At her wit's end, my mum had asked here where Sheffield United were playing and an immediate rely of "the other side of Stoke" did not help the situation. Kindly, though, the policewoman offered to escort my mum and sisters to Vale Park.

Back in Burslem, however, time was ticking on and my dad and me had been up and down the road like yo-yos on overdrive. We had now waited half an hour and the road was beginning to clear of traffic. Dad was asking all sorts of questions, such as "Are we in the right place?" and "Should we get a taxi home?"

I ignored him at first because I knew they would soon arrive - wouldn't they? An hour later, though, and I started to ask the same questions. What should we do?

An hour and forty five minutes later they finally arrived and as mum drove up the road it was like a light at the end of the tunnel.

Since this trip we have come to the conclusion that it would be best in future to leave my mum and sisters at home and we have either travelled to away matches by coach or have gone in the car by ourselves. If mum does express a desire to come with us to an away match again we will probably buy the local A-to-Z and make her memorise it, or maybe even make her attend the match with us.

If you ever find yourself in the same predicament all I can suggest is that you leave your mum at home, go on the train or coach or even hitchhike, just to make sure you don't face the same daunting delay that we were forced to.

Time For Another Lads?

Handsworth Blade

There is a flip-side to leaving a match early and one that is happening all too frequently (for me) these days - that is getting in after the kick off.

Even though you don't get your full money's worth, I don't think this phenomenon is in any way as bad as missing the end of a game. It's like if you miss the start of a film; you can always pick up the storyline and get to see the conclusion, which is important. Apparently, this is very true of 'The Shining', which is supposed to be a brilliant film, but I've always watched it from the beginning then switched it off after thirty minutes, as it's a bit slow. Next time I will go to the pub, miss the first half-an-hour and probably think it is fantastic.

Anyway, back to football. This 'doing a Besty' and turning up late (and pissed) for me started as a one-off season: 1988/89, a time of promotion, Deane and Agana, Jock Bryson and Peter Duffield penalties. It began the game after the Blades had stuffed Chester 6-1. It was a Tuesday night, against Northampton. Obviously, after Saturday's performance, a few more turned up for this game - I think there was a massive crowd of 12,000. Couple this with United's matchday organisation and planning, which is as good as it is for the rest of the week, and it resulted in me having to queue to get in late - but a 4-0 victory followed.

This was September 20th 1988. United's goals came from Tony Agana, Ian Bryson 2 and Brian Deane. Graham Benstead saved a penalty.

Other games followed that season. Stuck in a traffic jam all the way to Blackpool, then stuck in a queue to get into the ground, which coincided with Pikey's first ever goal for United. Another win, this time 2-1.

This was October 15th 1988. Martin Pike and Simon Webster scored.

Worst of all was Brentford away. Ominously, the bus broke down at Woodall services, then twice more, and its death came a mile from Griffin Park. I did manage to get in at half time and for half price as well, and finally got back home at about three in the morning. A pattern was emerging though - 4-1 to the wizards.

United won 4-1 at Griffin Park on September 24th 1988. The goals were scored by Mark Todd, Tony Agana 2 and Alan Roberts.

The next few years passed by pretty much uneventfully, until the disastrous Howard Kendall took over. Lateness returns with a vengeance. West Brom away, midweek, before the bald (if only bold) one decided that Blades away matches and attacking football went hand-in-hand, like England fans and civil liberties. We set off early afternoon but I somehow managed to lose direction in Birmingham, finishing at somewhere called Bromsgrove. The lads had a few pints, I had one (driving). We parked up at the Hawthorns early doors but we couldn't find a boozer that would let us in, so we had to walk what seemed like miles to a hotel bar. We were still there at twenty to eight but managed to blag a lift off some Baggies fans. We got into the game fifteen minutes late, but it was another 2-1 victory.

This game took place on November 13th 1996. Andy Walker and Don Hutchison scored.

The following season continued in a similar fashion. Oxford and Bradford away; boozer and then getting lost. Walsall away in the League Cup; just setting off late. Stoke: piss-poor parking facilities, followed by even worse organisation at the turnstiles, resulting in missing the first forty minutes. Apparently we had to wait for tickets to be printed for unreserved seats (well, we sat anywhere when we got in). Port Vale and QPR: rolling out of the pub late. The QPR game, though, convinced me that Tony Pritchett made his match reports up or was, at very best, confused. In 'The Star' the following day he reported that after United went behind in the early minutes the crowd started chanting, "Charles Green, he sells the team......"

I can confirm for a fact that we made that song up the week before in the Old Crown, Handsworth, and we didn't get into Loftus Road until at least fifteen minutes after that early goal, which was when the song was given its first ever public airing.

This was on February 25th 1998. The game ended 2-2, with Dean Saunders and Graham Stuart scoring for United.

On to 1998/99, which also carried on along the same lines. Bolton and Vale away, Portsmouth at home: all alcohol-related lateness. In fact, at Bolton, we were in the ground at 2.45 but still managed to miss their first goal, as many others did, due to the ale on sale under the stand. Discipline for the Blades; poor. Discipline for alcohol; outstanding.

On August 29th 1998 United drew 2-2 at Bolton's new stadium after being 2-0 down. Dean Saunders and Gareth Taylor scored.

You may not have noticed, but excluding cup games (Walsall away), whenever I've got in the ground late the Blades have never lost. This is even more amazing considering nearly all the games were away when United's away form was abysmal. Overall, my lateness record reads: Played 12, Won 7, Drawn 5, Lost 0.

For this statistic alone I think United's board and management should be looking to do a deal with me - they pick up my bar tab and reduce my admission fee (as I won't be seeing a full match) and I'll guarantee to turn up late for every game.

This has got to be worth a gamble as the usual policy of pleading poverty and buying no-one is guaranteed to fail - just look at your history books. But at least I've got a successful track record.

Rome burns while Nero fiddles......or Brealey....... or Woolhouse....... or McDonald ......or .....?

Memories Of Supporting The Blades - Season 1994/95

Steve Gregory

Outstanding memory of the season - Easy. Even though we had lost 1-0 to Sunderland my most treasured moment of the season came as we were passing Hillsborough on our way home. I don't usually come this way home for obvious reasons but on this particular day I couldn't resist it. To cheer ourselves up I wound down my car window opposite the ground and whilst laughing and simultaneously swinging my Blades rattle, shouted for Forest after they had stuffed Wednesday 7-1 on their own ground (yes, it was even April Fools' Day!).

Ironically I had earlier had the rattle confiscated by a very worried-looking Sunderland steward ten minutes after entering Roker Park. He said it was an offensive weapon even though I was using it amongst a group of segregated Blades fans. I was astonished to say the least but it certainly made up for its absence passing Hillsborough. Not a Pig fan in sight; just the sound of the Blades rattle echoing round Sheffield 6! Ah, the stuff dreams are made of.

This was April 1st 1995. United lost to a late Craig Russell goal at Roker Park in relegation-threatened Sunderland's first game under the managership of Peter Reid. Wednesday were defeated 7-1 at Hillsborough, the record home loss in the Premier League until Forest themselves lost 8-1 to Manchester United in the 1998/99 season.

Best away match - This has to be Luton and an amazing 6-3 win. A couple of pints in the Lord Rodney near the ground set the scene for a great day. Wasn't very impressed with the ground and had to walk by allotments up the sides of houses that seemed to be stuck to the walls of the stand, they were so close. A long alleyway running the length of one side brought back nasty memories of being attacked by mad Portsmouth fans in a similar setting at Fratton Park in the mid-seventies.

A good viewpoint in the ground saw us go 2-0 up by half time and in the second half the score went from 4-1 to a heart-stopping 4-3. Fortunately the nerves were settled by two further goals amid some outstanding finishing to send us home happy.

This match took place on December 3rd 1994. United's scorers were Carl Veart (2), Kevin Gage (2), Andy Scott and Glyn Hodges. John Hartson, a Brian Gayle own goal and Marvin Johnson (penalty) scored for Luton.

Worst away match - Easily Bristol City, losing 2-1. Torrential rain on the way down the M5 threatened to postpone the match and after the game I was wishing it had! The coach's windscreen wipers had stopped working (full marks to the driver), Alan Kelly was injured and ruled out in the warm up, the pitch was in a terrible state, Brian Gayle scored yet another own goal and Kevin Gage was sent off for a nothing tackle. Guess it was just another one of those days. Seemed to have a lot of those that season!

This match was played on January 21st 1995. Brian Gayle scored for both sides, with Bristol City's winner coming from Mark Shail.

Daftest - Mickey Mouse. I mean the Anglo Italian Cup game against Udinese at the Lane. Lost count of the number of players (plus Dave Bassett) that got sent off. Think the referee came from Italy (he did). My only game attended in this competition, thankfully.

This was on August 24th 1994. United lost 2-1 (Adrian Littlejohn scored) but Charlie Hartfield, Glyn Hodges, Nathan Blake, a Udinese player and Dave Bassett all received red cards.

Amazing - Brian Gayle's numerous own goals - some outstanding!

Brian Gayle scored three own goals during the 1994/95 season - home and away against Luton Town and away to Bristol City. He also scored an own goal to give Leeds United victory and the Championship at Bramall Lane in the last game of the 1991/92 season.

Irritating - Goals scored against us by ex-Blades Jamie Hoyland (Burnley) and Richard Cadette (Millwall). Don't you just love it when that happens?

Jamie Hoyland scored for Burnley in a 4-2 televised defeat at Turf Moor on November 20th 1994. United's goals came from Mark Winstanley (own goal) and Andy Scott. Richard Cadette scored in the last minute as Millwall beat United 2-1 at the New Den on October 29th 1994. Nathan Blake scored for United.

Hurtful - Almost knocking myself out jumping for joy and hitting my head on the back hoarding at Bolton after Nathan Blake scored our goal. Perhaps our grittiest performance of the season against an excellent side. Lost both Brian Gayle and our way after this match.

United drew 1-1 at Burnden Park on March 22nd 1995.

Sweet Revenge - Jostein Flo's last minute equaliser against Wolves at the Lane. Earlier in the season we somehow lost a 2-0 lead in injury time at Molineux. Drove home that day stunned, wondering where the three points had gone. Can't ever remember us conceding two goals as late as that in all my life supporting the Blades.

On January 2nd 1995 United drew 2-2 at Wolves. Nathan Blake scored twice for the Blades, but John De Wolf (penalty) and Neil Emblen both scored in injury time. Then on April 22nd 1995 the return game ended 3-3. Don Goodman, Steve Bull and David Kelly scored for Wolves, with Dane Whitehouse (penalty), Mark Foran and Jostein Flo, in injury time, replying.

Funniest - Dave Bassett stripping off to his underpants at the end of the season's last match with Grimsby. One of the lads. I was wondering if this would be Dave's last game with us.

United (Dane Whitehouse, Kingsley Black, Jostein Flo) beat Grimsby Town (Steve Livingstone) on May 6th 1995. After the game Dave Bassett was stripped by fans as they invaded the pitch.

Season summing up - A largely forgettable season in which we threw away too many vital points, particularly at home and against most of the struggling teams. Overall team performances were generally poor except for a handful of games and the players let themselves down badly, especially in the final run-in for the play-offs, a time of the season when we used to finish stronger. Good job we weren't involved in a relegation struggle!

I suppose the gaping hole down John Street didn't help our cause, as didn't Reg Brealey's inability to provide vital financial help in the form of team and ground improvements. He seemed to spend most of the season in trouble with his business problems at home and abroad, as well as constantly criticising the newly-formed Blades Independent Fans' Association (BIFA).

Mystic Bob

Max Hill

The day started badly when we missed the bus to town and arrived at the Lane just as the coaches were about to leave. Had we been a minute later we would have missed the coach.

The pointers were that Bob, Dave and myself might not be in for a good day. At the turnstiles Dave voiced his disappointment at not being searched, unlike me and Bob, as he felt this to be an insult to his manhood. We arrived on the terrace at about 2.25pm and were greatly entertained by a fat bloke selling pies, a dodgy juggler and the Derby mascot dressed as a ram. The predictable chants of "Who ate all the pies?" and "Sheep shagger!" were voiced loudly by a great turnout of Blades and we hoped that the drops of water landing on our heads and backs were from the stand itself and not from the mouths of the Derby fans above us. We were annoyed that the kick-off was delayed but we were cheered by the fact that Sean Bean joined us on the terrace.

A below-strength Blades side took the lead when their keeper misjudged a bounce and Carl Veart ran round him and scored but their captain scored with a jammy free kick that hit the post and went in off Billy Mercer.

At half time the score was 1-1 and the rain carried on coming down. About ten minutes into the second half we scored again with a long-range volley from Dane Whitehouse but again they levelled about ten minutes later. It was then that Bob hit us with a bombshell. "We'll win 3-2 and we'll score in the 84th minute", he said, and we said we'd hold him to it.

After an amazing save by Mercer from Gabbiadini the chosen minute came up on the scoreboard. Dave and I jokingly said to those around us, "Brace yourselves lads, we're going to score now."

It was as if it happened in slow motion. Mercer kicked the ball upfield, Jostein Flo flicked it on and it fell for Veart. He hit it into the keeper and from the floor put the rebound in. We couldn't believe it. It is possibly the only United goal I have cheered by falling about laughing. By some fluke Bob had picked the exact minute of our winner.

For the last ten minutes or so of the game we were under attack continuously but we held out for the win. On the coach back we decided that Bob must have some kind of magical powers and since then he has been known as Mystic Bob. That night he picked my lottery numbers. Not one of them came out and to my knowledge since then he has never predicted a United score correctly but on that day he got it right and that was all important to us.

All in all we had a great day and Mystic Bob Smith, of Tapton School, we salute you.

The match was at the Baseball Ground on February 4th 1995. Derby's goals were from Paul Williams and Jason Kavanagh.

Eskimo, Willie Ward And The Rest

Pete Moxon

They were halcyon days following the Blades in the sixties, particularly when you think of fans like 'Eskimo' and Willie Ward, who usually signalled his arrival on the Kop with a favourite cry of the time: "Zigger Zagger, Zigger Zagger..!!!". Yes, Willie did seem quite a bit older than the rest of us spotty, 'bush jacket' (remember those? - 7/6 from your local army stores) clad teenagers, but with him in our midst we feared no-one.

The reason Willie arrived at three o'clock was, of course, that he had probably just downed ten or eleven pints in the hour before the match. Naturally, Willie never bothered with the toilets at the back of the Kop; he usually just did it where he stood, on the back of some lad's trousers (indeed, it was an honour to be peed on by Willie).

Our friend 'Eskimo', if my memory serves me right, was a member of a gang, known as the 'Pond Street Mob', who, not surprisingly, frequented Pond Street bus station. His loyalty to the 'Shoreham Boys' was a trifle lukewarm but there was a fellow 'Pond Street' member who went by the name of 'Butlab', who was reputedly the leader of Wednesday's Kop (which was as pathetic and unoriginal in the sixties as it is in the nineties).

Yes, those days bring back many memories but I'll limit myself to just a few, such as teaming up at away games with the 'Dronfield Lads', Ronnie Sharp, Dave Parton, Dave 'Sinny' Sinfield and Co. (do they still go to the Lane, is their hair still long, or do they even still have hair?!). Memories like:

- travelling to Manchester United on the train and borrowing the toilet rolls, and also finding fellow passengers Joe Shaw, Mick Jones, Billy Hodgson etc. in the second class carriages (United were obviously having financial difficul-

photo: Andy Greaves

ties at that time also).

- going down to Charlton, Fulham and Chelsea in the Cup in 1967 and actually going in the Skinners' Arms pub near St Pancras station at thirteen years old.

- watching the Blades look decidedly uncomfortable in red shorts as Wolves trounced us in a mid-sixties cup game.

United were beaten 3-0 by Wolves in the FA Cup fourth round on February 12th 1966.

- wondering why John Harris (and his faithful cardigan) had signed an apparently fifty-year-old left winger, only to discover it was prematurely bald Bill Punton, who turned out to be not a bad player.

- recalling some very original songs and chants from the Kop; songs about seagulls' wings and crows' black arses going over Hillsborough and pooping; songs about John Ritchie, Allan Brown and iron lungs; 'Ilkla Moor Bah T'at' of course and many more that are unprintable.

Does anyone else remember these? Yes, the sixties were a great time to be on Shoreham Street.

The Parting Of The Red And White Sea

Geoff Tilney

If Moses parting the Red Sea was a miracle, then I have also witnessed a miracle at Bramall Lane.

The date was February 18th 1959, the occasion the fifth round FA Cup replay versus Arsenal, having drawn at Highbury, two goals each. The Blades went on to win 3-0, with goals from Russell, Pace and Lewis, watched by a crowd of 48,763.

A very good result indeed, but that was not the miracle to which I am referring. My girlfriend (who was later to become my wife) and I attended the Lane that evening. The crowd was that dense that there was no room to move, so much so that I could not get my cigarettes out of my pocket. The heat was overbearing and I was most concerned about my girlfriend. In between peering through the fog that had descended I was watching Cath and, sure enough, she fainted; she could not fall down as the crowd supported her on her feet.

This is where the miracle occurred. When the people around us became aware of my plight, a 'corridor' opened up, allowing me to carry her to the back of the Kop to get some fresh air.

For the life of me, to this day, I will never know where, or how, they created that space.

Just Memories

Michael Hudson

I was first taken to the Lane by my father some time in the late forties. My first almost-complete season of home matches was the promotion year of 1952/53, to Division One of course. In that year we scored ninety seven goals in the league and were champions. We thrashed Leicester 7-2, Lincoln 6-1 and Swansea 7-1, the last named seeing the sending off of the great Jimmy Hagan. We won 2-0 at Rotherham and I sat on the pitch near the corner flag with hundreds of other lads; then Rotherham came to Bramall Lane and they beat us 4-1!

The Leicester City victory was on November 22nd 1952. United's scorers were Alf Ringstead 2, Jimmy Hagan 2, Fred Furniss (pen.), Len Browning and an own goal.

United beat Lincoln City 6-1 on September 20th 1952, with goals from Derek Hawksworth, Alf Ringstead 2, Harold Brook and Jimmy Hagan 2.

Swansea were beaten 7-1 on December 20th 1952, thanks to goals by Fred Furniss (pen.), Harold Brook, Derek Hawksworth 2, Alf Ringstead 2 and Jimmy Hagan.

The two games against Rotherham were on December 13th 1952 at Millmoor and January 1st 1953 at Bramall Lane. United won the first 2-0 (Alf Ringstead, Harold Brook) but lost the second 4-1 (own goal).

Notables that season were Ted Burgin in goal, Fred Furniss at right back (toe-ending penalties was his speciality), Harry Latham at centre half (Derek Dooley never got a look in against Harry) and a forward line of Alf Ringstead, Jimmy Hagan, Len Browning, Harold Brook and Derek Hawksworth.

There were no floodlights those days, of course, and some league matches were played on mid-week afternoons. As a good schoolboy I didn't see these matches, though I did see the last game of the season when United needed three goals for a hundred and, needless to say, lost 2-0 to Hull City, who threatened to kick them to death. As United had a tour to the Netherlands coming up nobody wanted to get hurt and anyway, all United's players were gentlemen, whereas the Hull players were all savages.

The last game of the season against Hull City took place on April 29th 1953, a Wednesday.

In the 1950s we seemed to get to the sixth round of the cup most seasons, although we did usually get knocked out then. However, when we reached the semi final it was to see who would lose to Spurs in the final, but after two 0-0 draws we lost the third match, and had to settle for promotion (again) to Division One. In the sixth round that season the Blades had won 3-1 at Newcastle with Billy Russell, the inside left, getting a hat-trick inside fifteen minutes in the first half.

United won 3-1 at Newcastle in the FA Cup sixth round on March 4th 1961.

Talking of Newcastle, I am reminded of a league match against them on New Year's Day (late fifties I think) when United won 6-2. The amazing thing was that United were leading 4-0 after eight minutes.

This 6-2 win over Newcastle was on January 1st 1955, with Alf Ringstead, Jimmy Hagan 2, Derek Hawksworth and John Spencer 2 scoring.

Thinking of players in the fifties, sixties and seventies there are so many worthies to recall. The small but great Alan Hodgkinson in goal, Cec Coldwell at right back, Graham Shaw at left back, Tommy Hoyland (Jamie's dad) at right half and the immaculate Joe Shaw taking over Harry Latham's mantle at centre half. Joe would make the very occasional mistake when trying to play the ball out of defence but his standards were so high and the quality of his football so good that these mistakes could be forgiven.

Doc Pace could be trusted to score many goals each season (he once scored three hat-tricks in three matches) and with Billy Russell at inside left and 'sixty minute' Ronnie Simpson (he got tired after an hour) on the left wing, United were always an attractive team to watch.

Memories of Willie Hamilton, a frail but extremely talented inside forward, come flooding back. He had the talent but never quite realised it. I remember walking with my father from Firth Park to Hillsborough to see United play that other team at a time when Willie was at his best. As we walked from Moonshine Lane down Herries Road towards the Five Arches it started to piss it down, with the result that dad and I were saturated. At the Five Arches we turned round and started to walk home but after a hundred yards we decided we couldn't get any wetter and turned round again, grudgingly paid out our money (we don't like giving Wednesday anything) and stood on the Kop (uncovered of course) and got pissed on for another two hours. Hamilton played a blinder, United were the best team and, you've guessed it, lost 2-0. Then we walked home and if I remember correctly (I don't) we both caught pneumonia.

This was October 4th 1958.

Those were the days, when opposing supporters used to stand together. I have stood on the Kop and chatted and joked with supporters from Manchester United, Manchester City, Leeds and Millwall and never had any trouble.

On to the early seventies: a three-sided ground with 30,000 trying to get in without having to stand near the cricket pavilion. Tactics to be adopted: turn up at the Railway at 1.30, down the occasional pint and play dominoes until till 2.00, then leave said pub and go on to the Kop to get a good position whilst having a sweep on who might score the first goal. Amongst the choice of numbers were 7.....the incomparable Alan Woodward, 9.....Mick Jones, 10...Alan Birchenall and 11....Geoff Salmons. What with Len Badger and Bernard Shaw (I saw them both make their debuts against Leyton Orient when they were both seventeen), we knew we had a great foundation to build on.

Len Badger and Bernard Shaw made their league debuts against Orient at Bramall Lane on April 26th 1962. Mick Jones and Barry Hartle scored in a 2-0 win.

Let's leave the best till last. We all know that Tony Currie was head and shoulders above the rest. Particular memories - TC's first match against Spurs when we won and he scored and we knew that John Harris had brought home the goods from Watford. Second, the match against West Ham when TC scored one of the goals of the decade, but the memory that lives with me was seeing Tony take the ball down the wing when United were attacking the Kop, push the ball around a Hammer, turn to the Terrace crowd and applaud with his hands above his head, then carry on the run - the arrogance of a genius.

United beat West Ham 3-2 on March 22nd 1975. Tony Currie 2 and Alan Woodward scored.

Another great memory was seeing TC sit on the ball as United thrashed Arsenal 5-0 in revenge for Alan Ball doing it when the Arse beat us 5-0.

More up to date, the best goal I've seen at the Lane was the one Keith Edwards scored against Bristol Rovers when United won 4-0. The ball was passed to him outside the area, Edwards dummied and sent the keeper and a defender wrong footed, ran round them both and put the ball in the net whilst saluting the Kop. It was so good that I wrote to the 'Green 'Un' about it, as Tony Pritchett had described it as "one of the easiest goals he has ever scored." That was in the days when they paid money for letters. The good news was that I won a fiver; the bad news was that they didn't send it and I had to phone and beg them for it.

United beat Bristol Rovers 4-0 on April 14th 1984 with goals from Paul Stancliffe, Paul Garner and Keith Edwards 2.

Other goal memories - Tony 'Gracie' Field running half the length of the field and beating half the Ipswich team before scoring magnificently. Of course he never did anything like it again.

This was on August 31st 1974. Tony Field 2 and Mick Mills (o.g.) scored in a 3-1 win.

Flashes of brilliance from Simon Stainrod, Steve Wigley and Alex Sabella and the goalden age of Alan Woodward, Mick Jones and Doc Pace. Close your eyes and dream.

My other memories are not so good. Rodney Marsh breaking Tom McAlister's leg and effectively putting an end to Tom's career...he would have been Scotland's goalie for many a year. In that game Mike Summerbee fell out with Marsh over the tackle and when Woodward went in goal and Marsh had hustled him, Denis Law dragged Marsh to one side and told him to lay off.

This was October 20th 1973.

West Ham coming to Bramall Lane when Moore, Hurst and Peters were in their prime. We knew we were in for a beating when four West Ham players stood in the centre circle and kicked the ball to each other. Nowt remarkable about that until you realise that the ball was spinning leg breaks and off breaks, all whilst under perfect control.

This was probably April 27th 1968. United lost 2-1. Gil Reece scored.

Now, my dad could tell you plenty more. He doesn't go to the Lane any more but he was there when United beat Cardiff 11-2 and remembers them winning the cup in 1925 and getting to Wembley in 1936 and he was there at the record attendance against Leeds and he could tell you a thing or two about........

Is This A Record?

Chris Siddall

Football is full of facts, statistics, twists and turns but I have often wondered whether my experiences in the 1983/84 Third Division promotion season are some sort of a record.

The situation was as follows. During that season I managed to attend nine away league games, of which we won three, drew one and lost five. Pretty average, and, on the face of it, not very interesting. However, what was remarkable about the games I saw was the fact that, in all nine games, including the three wins, United were only ever in the lead at any time during the matches for a total of three minutes out of the 810 minutes played!

I can't recall every detail of all the draws and losses exactly, but Burnley, a night match and a 2-1 defeat, and a 2-0 defeat at Orient, also a night match, are two that spring to mind.

The Burnley game was on November 8th 1983 (Colin Morris scored), the Orient game was on October 18th 1983.

In contrast, the three wins are all very clear in my memory and this is how they went.

The first was early in the season at Walsall (the first time I saw Paul Stancliffe play). Walsall took the lead, due to an error by the aforementioned Big Stan, United later equalised through Bob Atkins and the game stood at 1-1 as we entered the last minute of play. As we awaited the final whistle United were awarded a penalty and up stepped Colin Morris to take it. The spot kick was actually saved but Morris half hit the rebound past the keeper and the ball crawled across the line. Within sixty seconds the whistle had gone and we'd won 2-1.

This was on September 6th 1983.

The second one was late in the season away at Rotherham on a very hot sunny Saturday with a bone-hard pitch. It was 0-0 in the last minute when United got a free kick well outside the box. The kick was played up to Bob Atkins on the edge of the area. He took it on his chest, swivelled and half-volleyed the ball into the roof of the net. Within sixty seconds the whistle had gone, we had won 1-0 and everybody was on the pitch.

This was on April 21st 1984.

The third one was the following week at Southend. Again, as the game entered the ninetieth minute the score stood, as the week before, at 0-0. At this point Kevin Arnott picked up the ball about the half way line. He set off on a run towards goal which took him past what seemed like seven or eight players (it was really only three or four) and he calmly slid the ball past the advancing keeper. Within sixty seconds the whistle had gone, we had won 1-0 and just to make the day perfect, Hull City lost and we all know what that meant a few weeks later at Burnley.

This was on April 28th 1984.

So there you have it. 810 minutes of football and only ever in the lead for a total of three minutes. Is this a record?

The Swinging Sixties - A Personal Reminiscence

Len Strike

Supporting Sheffield United Football Club is akin to riding on a roller-coaster. Relatively speaking, much of the sixties was a period of stability in the club's turbulent history, and a time of nostalgia for me personally.

How times change. I still possess a One Guinea (£1.05) season ticket. That season the reserves won the Central League before crowds of up to 10,000. With no local radio reports or Teletext coverage, many went just to watch the man on the cricket scoreboard. Every fifteen minutes he would update United's and Wednesday's scores. I suffered hours of nervous tension as he moved the numbered boards to their appropriate positions. Sometimes, thinking he was being humorous, he would temporarily pretend we were losing.

The man responsible was one of the Chief Stewards, Ches Grey.

Many memories, happy, sad and traumatic, spring to mind. One of the traumatic ones occurred outside Stamford Bridge. Walking alone, a gang of Chelsea headhunters saw me as easy prey and a hot pursuit began. Contrary to popular belief, violence at football matches was far worse at that time than in the more publicised later years. In desperation for my safety I ran into a full fish and chip shop, hiding behind the queue. The barbarian throng followed me. Beside me I saw that the living quarters door was partially open. I nipped through, grabbed a chair and sat down with the family of four at their dinner table. Following my explanation they were understanding and even provided me with a cup of tea until the crowd outside had dispersed.

When not hitchhiking I travelled to London games by Sheffield United Tours coaches, which were proudly red and white striped. What value for money. Departing Pond Street at 7.30am, not leaving London until midnight, all for twelve shillings (60p) return. What excitement and adventures we provincial teenagers had in the metropolis, roaming the streets of Soho and the West End on a Saturday evening.

Less exciting was the FA Cup fifth round game at Chelsea. We were packed like sardines in a crowd of over 40,000. Behind us, in the seats, Chelsea fans, seemingly in their hundreds, began urinating on us. Unable to move and dripping wet, and not particularly wanting to turn and face them, we had to watch the match and hopefully dry out. The coach home stank. We lost the match.

The match was on March 11th 1967. United lost 2-0 in front of a crowd of 40,730.

Those days we usually congregated on the home supporters' end at away games. Trouble always ensued. United fans invariably stood their ground and had a well-respected, though grudging, reputation amongst other supporters. Battles on Villa's Holte End and Chelsea's Shed spring to mind. One of the nastiest was on Stoke's infamous Boothen End where a friend was struck on the head by an empty whisky bottle. I can still see it flying through the air before impact.

At Bolton a large gang of home fans was known to arrive after kick-off with sticks and bottles. In they came, the biggest and ugliest facing me with a plank of wood. I ducked just in time, but my mate behind me received a broken nose and St John's ambulance treatment.

Some forms of violence were quite funny, a derby at Hillsborough being an example.

Hundreds of us smuggled in eggs - the more rotten the better. Standing massed behind the Wednesdayites on the Kop, thousands of eggs were thrown at them to the accompaniment of chants of "Scrambled eggs!" Owls fans certainly had egg on their faces that game!

Unitedites have always been far more innovative, showing more humour, imagination and ideas than their friends across the city. From the famous funeral cards, issued following Wednesday's derby thrashing of the nineteenth century, through to the balloons and the flares of the 1990s, Wednesdayites have unashamedly copied our innovations.

Back to the sixties. The tastiest beer was Oldham Bitter. So good we missed the first half of the match. Talking of beer, I travelled by train to Middlesbrough only for the game to be postponed due to fog. We had to drink nasty Bass all day and night before the train home. I was well under age. Three things I remember: 1) vomiting over a full table of drinks at 10.30pm in a pub; 2) being punched hard in the face whilst sprawled on a bench at the railway station; 3) and not feeling a thing.

I've hardly mentioned football itself yet. Here goes. One of the saddest days was our 1-0 defeat to Burnley at the Lane in the sixth round of the FA Cup in front of 57,000. We were so unlucky, a fluke Ray Pointer deflected header beating us. A crush barrier gave way alongside me, resulting in a man dying of a heart attack. A bad day all round.

The match was on March 10th 1962. The crowd was recorded as exactly 57,000.

I could tell if a big crowd was imminent if the centre of the terrace was swaying by 2.20pm. To be sure of a position on the perimeter fence we sometimes had to enter the ground at 1.00pm.

Memorable goals included Ronnie Simpson's at Burnley after just eight seconds - a club record. That 2-1 win in a thrilling game put us on top of Division One.

The match was on October 26th 1963. Ronnie Simpson scored both goals.

Perhaps the most pleasing of all was Bill Punton's goal in the 1-0 defeat of Wednesday at the Lane in front of nearly 44,000. For weeks Owls fans had taken the mickey out of old, bald Bill, who looked sixty years old and wasn't much less. I was in line with the ball's trajectory and it seemed unlikely to go in. But it did. They used to laugh at Doc Pace too, but he invariably had the last laugh.

Bill Punton scored the only goal as United beat Wednesday on February 4th 1967 in front of 43,490.

Without the tactical sophistication that is evident nowadays, players would face the same combatant throughout a game. Thus, in derbies, fans would relish duels between, say, Doc Pace and Peter Swan, Joe Shaw and Bronco Layne. If Joe, my favourite, had played thirty years later he would have been brilliant in a continental-style sweeper system. What timing. What a footballer.

Players would catch a bus to the game and often stood in John Street talking to the fans, while many supporters would alternate between the Lane and Hillsborough every week. Talking of the Lane, it must be one of the most historical grounds in the world. Situated in a city that is the world's birthplace of organised football, Bramall Lane has also hosted, of course, the world's first floodlit game, and the first in which crossbars were used and penalty kicks took place. It was the home of Yorkshire cricket. The Lane has staged an amazing variety of sports and events. It has even been bombed. Typically, nothing exists at the ground to display its remarkable and unique history appropriately. It should.

Sheffield United have won nothing of importance since 1925. Have always been skint. Sell their best players. Have an unglamorous image. Yet historically they have always been one of the country's best-supported clubs. The potential, backed up by its central location, is enormous; selling their 35,000 FA Cup semi-final ticket allocation before Wednesday, Arsenal or Spurs in 1993 being an example.

So to the future. What does it hold? Will we celebrate our bicentenary at Bramall Lane? Will we remain as spectacularly unsuccessful as in modern times? Knowing United, one thing's for sure. The roller-coaster ride will continue, with all the highs and lows that that entails.

Blades, Booze and Wild Celebrations

Andy Hutch

The hole in my room ceiling, the plasterer's invoice and the Sunday morning hangover are all reminders of the joyous scenes that took place in our house after Petr Katchouro's winner at Wolves.

Having not travelled to Molineux, me and my mates decided it would be a great idea to invest in a couple of crates of lager and listen to the match on the radio. The first goal, by David White, sent us into orbit for a few seconds and once we returned back to earth it was cans of lager all round again. When the Blades play Wolves things never run smoothly though, and it wasn't long before events began to unfold.

Gareth Taylor sent off! Shit, I can't believe it. Down to ten men for the second time in two weeks. Please, please don't let Wolves score, were our thoughts, but unbelievably Wolves are awarded a penalty in injury time, which triggers loads of abusive language from my mates.

Wolves equalise and already we're praying that maybe, just maybe, we can scrape a draw against these £%&*^^&^!

Katchouro obviously had other ideas though. The man from Belarus danced through the Wolves defence like a Cossack and scored an injury-time winner, which sparked off celebrations I can only describe as ecstatic, frenzied, barmy, crazy, ballistic.......these being just a few words that spring to mind.

Although covered in plaster from the ceiling, totally legless and in full song, we somehow managed to propose a toast to Petr Katchouro, with the celebrations going on long into the night.

Petr Katchouro scored an injury-time winner, his first goal for United, at Molineux on September 21st 1996. Earlier David White put United ahead but Andy Thompson equalised with a penalty only a minute before Katchouro's strike.

It's Not Over Till John Francis Sings....

Papa Smurf

Only once have I ever missed a goal due to an early departure. I have to confess that during the memorable 6-1 romp over Chester in 1988, when Deane and Agana both scored three times, I managed to miss our sixth goal in order to get a lift home from my friend's dad. This incident caused me great annoyance and from that day on I have endeavoured to stay put until the final whistle, just in case I should miss something.

This was September 17th 1989.

The only home match I can recollect not seeing anyone leave early is the FA Cup quarter final against Blackburn that went to penalties. However, I wouldn't be surprised if a handful of people left midway through the shoot-out just so they could get home quickly! I accept that nine times out of ten the 'got to go early' brigade don't really miss anything but how can they take that risk, especially when the result is balanced on a knife-edge?

This was on March 16th 1993. The game ended 1-1 after ninety minutes and 2-2 after extra time, Mitch Ward equalising on both occasions. Ward converted the first penalty, followed by Charlie Hartfield, Alan Cork, Glyn Hodges and finally John Pemberton, while Alan Kelly saved from Jason Wilcox.

My favourite example of 'post drifter drama' is the 5-4 victory over Brighton in the 1989/90 season. United had coasted into a 3-0 lead, but they capitulated in typical fashion and were soon trailing 4-3. As soon as Brighton took the lead, hundreds of disgruntled Blades fans walked away berating the ineptitude of the team. A few moments later United made it 4-4 with an Ian Bryson penalty and the Kop bayed for a winner. Even now, fans continued to leave the ground with the result that they missed a stupendous last-minute diving header into the top corner from John Francis.

Vintage Roy of the Rovers stuff that at least a thousand 'faders' probably didn't see - although doubtless I bet most of them pretended they were there. After all, would you admit to missing such high drama so you didn't have to queue on East Bank Road?

This game was on September 9th 1989. United's goals were from John Francis (2), Brian Deane, Bob Booker and Ian Bryson (penalty). Future Blade Paul Wood scored two of Brighton's goals.

On The Buses (1)

Jamie Pigott

Between 1981/82 and 1985/86 I missed only five away games, travelling to most of them on the Sportsman's coaches.

However, such things as a wife, a mortgage and a family have put a virtual stop to my jaunts around the country, and I have to say that I miss

the days out terribly. Anyway, I digress.

In those halcyon days we always tried to avoid going on coach one because the nearest you got to a pre-match drink was a can of coke at a motorway service station. However, if you were lucky enough to be on coach two, usually stewarded by John or Pete Bramhall, then a quiet hour in a public house was sure to follow. It goes without saying that coach two usually filled up quicker than coach one.

So what memories spring to mind? Well, in no particular order, here are some incidents that may jog a few fellow passengers' memories:

1) Going to Charlton for a night match, getting off the coach and finding the game had been postponed three hours previously. However, as luck would have it, England were playing Eire at Wembley the same night and a quick dash across London saw the Wembley attendance increased by about 350 Unitedites. England won 2-0 by the way.

2) Having my coach window smashed twice in a few days, travelling home from Millwall and Middlesbrough. In fact the Middlesbrough fans boarded our coach outside Ayresome Park "looking for some boys to fight". Not pleasant.

3) Being given a police escort to Central Park, home of Wigan Rugby League club, instead of Springfield Park, home of Wigan Athletic. By this time it was 2.45 and we made it to the right ground five minutes after kick off.

4) Travelling home from Hereford on a Wednesday night and some twat had his tape recorder on full blast all night. Typically, his batteries only ran out at Low Edges.

This was February 17th 1982. Mike Trusson scored in a 1-1 draw.

5) Going to Brighton for a night match on August Bank Holiday Tuesday. The coaches left at eight in the morning and we arrived in Brighton at about one o'clock. After a stroll down the Promenade we decided to sample the delights of the local hostelries. Unfortunately, given Brighton's reputation as the gay capital of England, some of the pubs were not to our taste to say the least.

United drew 0-0 at Brighton on August 27th 1985.

6) Listening to the football results outside Priestfield Stadium, Gillingham, and realising that Brian 'Noddy' Marlow had got thirteen

scores correct on the fixed odds. There was a late result - the fourteenth he was waiting for, and if correct he stood to win about £2000. The game in question was Liverpool v Wolves, top v bottom. This was Noddy's cert result. Home win, no problem, just give me the money. Wrong! Wolves gained their only away win of the season, 1-0, and Brian was left to tear his coupon up.

7) Travelling back from Fulham one Boxing Day, the coach was hurtling up the M1 when a car in front burst into flames. On went the brakes, the coach skidded and hit the central reservation with a bang, throwing people out of their seats. Fortunately nobody was hurt but it was pretty scary all the same.

United lost 2-1 at Fulham on Boxing Day 1980. Bob Hatton scored.

8) Attending a pre-season friendly at Newcastle. The chant going round the ground was "Charlton Out!". Not wishing to appear party poopers we joined in, much to the delight of the Geordies. At the end of the game Big Jack resigned and our coach was applauded out of the city by Newcastle fans.

This was August 10th 1985. Tony Kenworthy scored in a 1-1 draw.

So there you have it! A few memories to share. I've always preferred travelling by coach rather than by car. I appreciate you don't have the freedom to go where you want but you can usually park outside the ground and be straight away after the match.

You can also build up friendships, get a card school going, and, on long journeys, watch a couple of videos. Your geography will also improve. I feel that I know Lichfield, Bury St Edmunds and Newbury like the back of my hand.

My advice to any supporter who is starting to go to away matches is to go on the coach and make a day of it.

Blades Cut A Swathe Through Leeds

Ken Cotterill

In South Yorkshire Leeds is a dirty word. From the pit head to the steel works their very name became a symbol of hatred. Distinct images of

a fiery Billy Bremner hacking an opponent or Big Jack ambling up for a corner to impede the goalkeeper spring to mind. Then the others - Norman Hunter, the original hard man; Gary Sprake, mercurial, arrogant; Allan 'Sniffer' Clarke; Eddie Gray; Terry Cooper - all class players. Don Revie's Leeds United. Hatred in white.

On Tuesday September 8th 1970 an undefeated Leeds came to Bramall Lane to play Sheffield United in the League Cup. Though the Blades were in Division Two they had assembled an entertaining side. Employing two class wingers in Alan Woodward and Gil Reece alongside Tony Currie in midfield, the Blades, unbeknown to themselves, were about to embark on one of the most successful seasons in the history of the club.

From the opening moments it was clear that Leeds were not in the same class. Brushing aside feeble tackles, John Tudor crashed a thumping volley against Sprake's crossbar. The blitzkrieg was maintained throughout, reducing Leeds to shell-shocked geriatrics. The goal, when it came, was worth the entrance money alone. A vicious drive from Tony Currie arrowed past the comatose Sprake. The trauma of years of living under the nauseating shadow of Leeds was expunged when Currie's block-buster punctured the net as Blades supporters released their frustrations that balmy autumn night.

The humiliation of Leeds was so comprehensive that one wag in the crowd (the well-known 'bloke behind me') wondered if the useless specimen in the number three shirt was really Terry Cooper, the England full back.

"Nah," came the reply from another bloke behind him, "it's Tommy Cooper."

So convincing were Sheffield United that night that not even the late, great magician could have helped Leeds.

In-Tent On Success

Rusty Old Blade

The year is 1960. As pupils of Owler Lane Intermediate School my mate David 'Ernie' Ward and myself, Geoff 'Jerry' Allen, often followed United by bicycle to save on costs.

First match of the new season was away to

Norwich, who had just been promoted from the Third Division. Setting off from Carbrook on Friday morning we cycled to around King's Lynn when, due to failing light, we looked for a site to set up our tent. Pushing through a hedge we found a patch of grass and decided that it would do.

The following morning we crawled out of the tent to find we were in the middle of a lovely manicured lawn in front of a bungalow. Luckily no-one was at home.

We arrived in Norwich late morning and pitched the tent on the outskirts of the town, and it was off to the match, played in front of almost 32,000, result 1-1.

This was on August 20th 1960. Willie Hamilton scored for United, in front of 31,972.

Back at the camp site we find the tent has been stolen, friendly locals find the culprits and return our tent. That evening we are taken in by a couple of OAPs, who give us a bed for the night. Following a cooked breakfast the next morning we are given a few shillings and we cycle back to Sheffield. 290 miles round trip to see the Blades. Those were the days.

Other cycle trips took us across the Pennines to Manchester, Blackburn and Bolton. Common sense then prevailed and we took to the supporters' coaches - remember Jeffrey's Coaches? One Saturday we stopped at traffic lights, the driver got out, ran into a nearby off-licence and came back with two crates of ale because "he was thirsty".

Season 1960/61 brings back vivid memories, such as singing 'Ilkla Moor Bah t'At' at Goodison as we beat Everton 1-0 in the third round of the FA Cup, the incredible pride in seeing Billy Russell score a hat-trick with his head at St James Park in the fifth round (what about that tangerine strip!) and the disappointment of losing to Leicester in the semi final after two replays.

Strange how the memory still holds these images when many of the more recent matches are just a blur, except 3-1 at Hillsborough, the penalty shoot-out against Blackburn, Wembley twice etc. etc.

Match Of The Season

The Cantley Critic

We hear regularly of 'match of the day' but this is a much devalued phrase. So, for a change, I thought I would reflect on my most memorable game each season. They are not all victories but each contained something to be remembered in the years ahead.

I start my file in the 1970/71 promotion season (although I could go back a little earlier):

1970/71 Cardiff City (H) 5-1 : 27.4.71
There were many memorable games but this has to be the choice in view of its importance. If we were won we were almost there; if Cardiff won they were almost there. The boys didn't fail. 40,000-plus saw Bill Dearden and John Flynn put us two up. Cardiff pulled one back to start the nerves fluttering but TC ended these and Gil Reece and Bill again rounded off a memorable night. Had a few lemonades afterwards before school the next day.

1971/72 Manchester United (A) 0-2 : 2.10.71
Yes I know we put seven past Ipswich and beat Arsenal twice but more than 70,000 people turned up for this match and 25,000 were locked out. It was, frankly, the most amazing scene I have ever witnessed. We had chances but ultimately a certain Irishman scored a goal featured often on television. The end result was disappointing but the experience was memorable.

1972/73 Manchester United (A) 2-1 : 23.4.73
Bobby Charlton's last home match and they expected to win at a canter but we didn't read the script. I went on the Stretford End and was very nearly lynched when celebrating Keith Eddy's brilliant winner.

1973/74 Arsenal (H) 5-0 : 4.9.73
Four up in next to no time, the Blades annihilated the Gunners in one of the finest first forty five minutes ever seen. It should have been ten but we let them off the hook. TC was fantastic (and sat on the ball) - what a marvellous night.

1974/75 West Ham (H) 3-2 : 22.3.75
The Everton away game ran this one close but at the end "a quality goal by quality player" swung the decision. This was a great game, well featured on the 'Match of the Day' video. TC's goal was worth the price of the season ticket.

1975/76 Leeds (A) 1-0 : 14.4.76
In a terrible season Woody's goals at Derby were

photo: Andy Greaves

Keith Edwards scores in the 4-0 win over promotion rivals Peterborough United in 1982

a great highlight but after we were relegated we went to Elland Road and Woody did them. I will never forget a young Tony Kenworthy sending Allan Clarke crashing in front of the Leeds Kop and the ref letting him off.

1977/78 Cardiff (A) 6-1 : 3.12.77
This is the only time I have seen United score six away from home in the league. Cliff Calvert, TK, Woody, Chico and Bob Campbell (2) got the goals if I remember right.

1978/79 Liverpool (H) 1-0 (League Cup) : 28.8.78
Relegated again but this match stands out. Gary Hamson scored on a great night against the almighty, and we deserved it. Pity it didn't last.

1979/80
Division Three for the first time and one match I want to forget on Boxing Day. A 4-3 win at Mansfield was the highlight of a sorry season.

This was September 22nd 1979. United's scorers were Len de Goey, Barry Butlin, Mick Speight and Jeff Bourne.

1980/81
Relegated again. I will never forget Don Givens' miss or forgive John Matthews for bottling it. There's nothing much good to remember.

1981/82
Yes I know it was Division Four but we lapped it up as United swept aside all before them. We scored ninety four goals, lost only four times and were unbeaten at home, but the only time we were on 'Match of the Day' we lost 5-2! Take your pick from 7-3 v Northampton, 4-0 twice against promotion rivals Peterborough, but maybe that last day at Darlington remains tops.

1982/83 Grimsby (H) 5-1 (League Cup) : 26.10.82
A mediocre season and nothing springs to mind of any note in the league but in this match Keith Edwards came off the bench and scored a hat trick.

1983/84
Promotion again - a marvellous season with

some marvellous games and Edwards in exhilarating form. Along with Colin Morris they tore many defences to shreds. Finding one match was hard and after soul searching it has to be Rotherham away, 1-0 and Bob Atkins' injury time winner.

1984/85
Another poor season but Portsmouth, 4-1 at home, when Pompey were near the top, stands out. Glenn Cockerill scored with a wonderful chip.

This was December 29th 1984. The other scorers were Keith Edwards, Colin Morris (pen.) and Mel Eves.

1985/86 Oldham (A) 5-1 : 9.11.85
"Blades Declare at Half Time", proclaimed the 'Green 'Un' and they were right. A brilliant performance with Keith and Colin running riot. Tremendous.

1986/87
We had high hopes but it ended in disappointment. Perhaps the most notable achievement was the first away replay victory in the FA Cup since before the war.

United beat Brighton 2-1 away after a 0-0 draw in the third round of the FA Cup on January 21st 1987. The goals were scored by Steve Foley and Peter Withe.

1987/88 Oldham (H) 0-5 : 2.1.88
McEwan out, Bassett in. Relegation first but then the revival.

1988/89 Chester (H) 6-1 : 17.9.88
They were many memorable matches this season but this was the only match I can recall when two United players scored hat tricks - one in each half (Deane and Agana).

1989/90 Leicester (A) 5-2 : 6.5.90
A marvellous season, promotion was totally unexpected and we were treated to some wonderful performances (Leeds and West Ham away excluded). Who could ever forget that fantastic afternoon in Leicester? One down, then Paul Wood, Deano, Agana, Wilf and Tony again. The M1 was a glorious sight that night and United songs rang out from all the cars. Brilliant, as was the champers afterwards.

1990/91 Forest (H) 3-2 : 22.12.90
It turned out right in the end but it wasn't until the Saturday before Christmas that we won a league game. Jock Bryson (2) and Deano scored and I went home thinking we'd just won the league, never mind the first game.

1991/92 Wednesday (A) 3-1 : 11.3.92
The Owls' revenge they said but they were never in it. It rained all night but who cared? Dane started it off and then Bobby Davison wrote himself into the history books with two on his debut. It was great walking up Herries Road afterwards. Got home at half eleven and promptly watched it again on Leeds TV.

1992/93 Wednesday 1-2 (FA Cup semi final, Wembley) : 3.4.93
The Blackburn replay ran it close but seeing the Blades at Wembley was fantastic. We didn't play well and couldn't grumble at the result but the day will live long in the memory. It might have to!

Some of you will no doubt remember these games and maybe they will have brought back memories, both good and bad.

I Don't Bloody Believe It!

Anon

When we played at Anfield in our first season back in the old First Division, none of the lads I usually travel with were going for various reasons, so I went with the Travel Club. Just before the coaches were due to set off there were some lads walking around the car park asking if anyone on coach seven would be willing to swap. One of them had a ticket for a different coach to his mates and obviously they all wanted to travel together. So I stepped in (or, with hindsight, I should say I stepped in it) and swapped. Well, it didn't matter to me, and I was helping fellow Blades and all that.

Anyway, a few miles outside Liverpool the coach I'm on breaks down and we're told that by the time a replacement gets here we'll have missed most, if not all, of the game. There were discussions on how far it would be to walk. Ridiculous! Or of walking off the motorway to civilisation, finding a pub and hope they have a radio. Sensible. While these discussions were taking place, with the latter idea on the point of being taken up by most (it was December and we were freezing), an empty coach from Salford or Rochdale or somewhere, travelling on the opposite carriageway, saw our plight and turned round at the junction we'd only just passed.

He took us to Liverpool (and took us for a ride - three quid a piece I think. He must have made himself a nice little earner, though I'm sure he'll have declared the tax. Ahem!), but we missed the beginning of the game, it cost us extra and we lost.

At half time the tannoy had announced that another coach would be available for us but football ground PAs being what they are, I couldn't hear the details. So after the match I started by walking up and down the long line of coaches outside Stanley Park but it soon turned to panicky Basil Fawlty-type running up and down through the choking smoke of revving engines.

I couldn't find any replacement coach despite asking stewards from several coaches. Still, this was Liverpool - it could have been nicked. It was probably smouldering away minus its wheels in the middle of Toxteth, just as I stood there. Or maybe it was embedded in a Wigfall's shop front just outside Bootle. Yes, all the nasty stereotype thoughts were racing through my mind as despair turned to anger.

Eventually a steward leaning out of a coach doorway asked if I was off the broken-down one. When I replied yes he said there was "room on this one." I boarded it, not caring what number it was, just so long as it took me home. I came across an empty seat and asked the lad sitting next to the window if it was spare. When he looked up and answered I realised it was the same lad I'd swapped with originally and that it was coach seven! He and his mates found it hysterical that there'd been room all along. If I'd been Basil Fawlty before, I could easily have become Victor Meldrew now, but I was too gobsmacked.

This was December 15th 1990. United lost 2-0.

Won't Get Fooled Again. West Ham. 29/2/72

Pete Furness

This match has great significance for me - I missed it. I had to make a difficult choice: follow the Blades or turn out for Jordanthorpe School against King Edward VII in the Sheffield Under-15 Cup semi-final..........at rugby.

I cursed Joe Gormley et al. for the miners' strike, which was responsible for a Tuesday afternoon kick off at the Lane. We lost 20-18, while Bill Dearden got his only hat-trick for the Blades.

On The Buses (2)

Matthew Bell

Our visit to Filbert Street in March 1996 reminded me that this was the venue (other than Hillsborough) of my first ever away match.

The date was February 21st 1976, and I saw United earn a rare away point in that dismal relegation season thanks to an Alan Woodward penalty, I think after John 'Speedy' McGeady had been fouled.

I can't really remember why I started going away. It wasn't really a conscious decision - it just happened. I'd had a season ticket for a couple of years and always went to the Lane with Shaun, Pete and Coddy. I think it was Coddy who had the idea that we should go to an away match, despite the fact that we hadn't won away all season. I seem to recall that Coddy's mum knew someone who knew Terry Moore, the bloke who used to organise the supporters' club travel, so she booked our tickets for us on the coach.

So there we were, four fourteen-year-old lads in a strange city, innocently unconcerned about the fighting in the streets and people being chucked in the canal. We must have gone straight in the ground and, rather unbelievably nowadays, the programme was included in the price of admission. We sat behind the net (in the stand to the left when you're watching on TV) with no segregation. The majority of Blades fans were crammed into the corner to our left.

And that was it - we were hooked. Two more away games followed that season - I wasn't allowed to go to Tottenham (London was too far) to see us lose 5-0 and be relegated, nor for the night match at Leeds (which we won 1-0). I did, though, go to Norwich (won 3-1) and Middlesbrough at Easter (lost 3-0). Rather predictably, those two away wins, our only ones of the season, came after relegation was confirmed. We didn't even consider not going just because we were already down, and at Carrow Road we were privileged to see Tony Currie's last goal for the Blades, and Simon Stainrod's first. Seventeen-year-old Tony Kenworthy was making his debut and the now sadly departed Steve Goulding was making a rare appearance at left back. And you know those irrelevant, meaningless, little known facts that you always associate with certain football matches? Well, here's one. The Eurovision Song Contest was won by Brotherhood of Man with 'Save Your Kisses For

Me' that night. There's something guaranteed to break the ice at parties.

Travelling by coach was the norm in the mid seventies. I certainly didn't know anybody who went by car, unlike today when I would guess that maybe only a quarter of Blades go to away matches by coach. The trip to Middlesbrough was an eventful one. This was the one and only time I have ever been on a coach when a window has been smashed by home fans. It was one of those strange events that seems to happen in slow motion. I remember having time to think that someone had thrown a tin of white paint over the window, and it was only when the glass started coming in that I realised what had actually happened. As you might expect, quite a few Blades angrily charged off the bus in search of the culprit, but he had made good his escape.

Inside the ground, as at Leicester, there was no segregation. The police tried to get all the United fans standing in one corner of the ground but they seemed to do nothing to prevent Boro fans getting in there as well. We were standing there quietly watching United succumb to a 3-0 defeat when a Boro fan took a liking to Coddy's scarf. Fortunately, Coddy's mum, who was from that part of the country herself, had came with us to the match after visiting relatives. Now, Coddy's mum was not the sort of woman you argued with. So when Coddy alerted her to the fact that this Boro fan was trying to nick his scarf, she turned on him and snarled, "If you lay a hand on my son or any of his friends you'll have me to deal with." The Boro fan didn't bother us any more.

There were very few women and girls travelled to away games then. There was Tish, who I think was Terry Moore's daughter and who was a sort of steward (not that there really were any stewards), and apart from her and Dot Pearson, who was on the Supporters' Club committee, the only other females I remember going regularly were a small blonde girl and her friend (was she called Vanessa?), who was taller with dark hair. I think Dot Pearson still watches the Blades, but I don't know if any of the others still do. Can anybody remember them, and does anybody know where they are now?

There were some other memorable trips in the next two or three seasons in the Second Division. One was coming back from yet another defeat at Bristol Rovers - we always used to lose there. As usual, we stopped at Frankley Services on the M5. All the coaches seemed to arrive at once and hundreds of United fans tried to pile into the shop together. The shop atten-

dants couldn't cope and shut the door, which left the Blades still outside not very happy. So they stormed the shop, looted as much as they could and wrecked what they couldn't carry. We stood and watched at a distance. The police were quickly on the scene and closed down the whole northbound services, ushering the United fans back on to the coaches.

There was another problem, though. Many United fans had not been able to get anything to eat from the shop or the cafe and were therefore still a bit peckish. This number included Coddy. So, without anybody noticeably taking the lead, tens of United fans, including Coddy, realised that the only place they could get some grub was in the southbound services - but there was no bridge. So what? Six lanes of speeding traffic in the dark was not a problem, so off they went, over the M5. Rather you than me, I thought. I was hungry, but not that hungry. Neither, obviously, were Shaun and Pete, as they stayed with me.

Five minutes later they all came back across, suitably nourished, some of them still carrying various chocolate bars and cans. Then we saw Coddy emerging from between the flashing headlights. In each hand was perched a cream bun, delicately balanced as he sprinted across the motorway and hurdled the central barrier. Not a crumb was spilled. "That's all they had left," he said, as if nothing was untoward. We got back on the coach and set off for home, still shaking our heads.

Coddy was also the innocent cause of the nearest I've been to a fight at a football match. This was at Forest in 1976 (we lost 6-1). The coaches, all thirty-odd of them, were parked behind the old terrace and stand where the big double decker stand is now. We were making our way to the turnstiles when this little fella jumped at Coddy and tried to pinch his scarf. Now Coddy was quite big for fourteen and he soon shook off this little Forest fan. The little fella aimed a blow, it connected but didn't hurt, Coddy threw one back and the little fella ran off whimpering. We stood there stunned, Coddy more so than the rest of us, as he couldn't believe he had actually tried to hit somebody. Trouble was the last thing we wanted.

I then spent most of the match with my back to the pitch, staring up at the roof of the stand. Not by choice, even though we were losing so badly - the terrace was so crammed that I just couldn't move. Never mind, I saw all the goals the next day on telly.

This was October 9th 1976. Chico Hamilton scored for United from the penalty spot.

Another return trip from Bristol, again involving Frankley Services, was an eventful one. Our coach coughed and spluttered up the M5 and eventually gave up at Frankley. It was a National coach, so the driver rang the nearest depot to summon a replacement to get us home. The best they could do was a single-decker service bus from Birmingham. It wouldn't go above thirty and that damn bell was rung so often in the three hours it took us to get home that I thought I was on a campanologists' outing.

The M5 had strange effects on Blades fans. Coming back from Plymouth we stopped at a service station near Taunton. Skirting the car park were four rather tall flagpoles, each with a different national flag fluttering proudly at the top. A group of daring United fans decided it would be rather a wheeze to take the Union Jack home as a souvenir of our 4-1 defeat at Home Park. First they tried merely pulling the ropes to get it down. This didn't work, so next they cut the ropes, hoping it would come down easier. No luck. There was only one thing for it - climb the pole. A volunteer stepped forward, he was given a leg up, he clasped his arms and legs round the flagpole.........and stuck there. He never moved, couldn't lift himself an inch. His mates burst out laughing and they gave up, moments before the police arrived on the scene.

This was April 19th 1980. Paul Casey scored in the 4-1 defeat.

We lost 1-0 at Blackburn in March 1977 to a last-minute goal, but this didn't spoil the Blades fans' fun. It was Silver Jubilee year and it seemed that everybody in Britain possessed a little plastic Union Jack on a stick. It was also the time that St Etienne (the French football team, not the 1990s musical foursome) were at the height of their powers and their supporters' battle cry of "Allez les Vertes" (Come on You Greens) reverberated around the football grounds of Europe. So we all took these little flags to Ewood Park and sang "Allez les Rouges!"

This was also the day that the United fans raided the groundsman's lock-up and set fire to a wheelbarrow and a ladder on the terraces, taking it in turns to climb the ladder as the flames leapt up the rungs.

The high jinks continued on the way home as well. The coaches were travelling in convoy along that windy moorland road back to the M62 when suddenly someone jumped up and started making a commotion, pointing to the coach behind us. About half a dozen Blades had climbed out of the skylights and were sitting on the roof, swaying from side to side and clinging on for grim death as the coach lurched round the bends. Somehow, nobody was killed.

This was on March 5th 1977.

Trouble was never far away, but we managed to avoid it most of the time without any problems. We were chased down the street outside Eastville once, until both groups of fans realised the others were also Blades, and everybody rather sheepishly resumed normal service.

The only time I felt in real physical danger was at Stoke City. For some inexplicable reason the coaches were always parked directly behind the Boothen End and both sets of fans were let out at the same time. There must have been mass scraps in the car park after every one of Stoke's home games. On this occasion the Stoke fans were lying in wait for us in the car park, but they had discovered a novel way of attacking the away fans. They began to rip up lumps of tarmac and loose stones from the car park surface and were throwing them with such a trajectory that they smashed against the wall of the stand and showered down on us in bits. We took refuge back inside the stand but were told in no uncertain terms by a friendly steward to get back outside. So it was coats-over-heads-and-run-for-your-life time. We made it safely back to the coaches, where the police had been standing guard, either totally oblivious or deliberately ignoring what had been going on.

There was also trouble at the Brentford away game on October 22nd 1979. It was a Monday night and United won 2-1, the last of our five successive away wins (but we never won away again that season). Mick Speight and Doug Allder were sent off for fighting in a thrilling game in which Jeff Bourne scored twice, one of them a penalty. It was rumoured that Chelsea and Millwall fans had teamed up with Brentford to take on the Blades and the streets were rather tense after the match. As we went back to the coaches, I remember a line of police at a road junction holding back a baying mob who were trying to get at the United fans. We got back safely to the buses and set off, but had made it as far as Watford Gap Services when a police car pulled us in. When we stopped we were informed that a man had died in fighting after the match and that we had to go back to London as everybody was a suspect. We arrived back at Griffin Park at about 1am, by which time it had been learned that the man had died of a heart attack and that he had not been struck by a flying brick as had at first been thought.

There was no reason to detain us but the police had to think up some excuse for bringing us seventy miles back to London so they took everybody's name, address and date of birth and let us go. I'm probably still on some police file somewhere because of that even now. We arrived back at the Lane at about five o'clock in the morning - fortunately it was half term and I didn't have to be up for school the next (same) day.

The best thing about going to away matches by coach in the last ten or so years has been the advent of 'executive travel'. In the old days, whether you were travelling by supporters' club coach or National, you were given the oldest, most unreliable buses they had available as they thought that all football supporters wanted to do was cause as much damage as possible and spread piss and sick everywhere.

Of course, this was not so (not always, anyway), and you were limited to one stop per trip, whatever its distance. There were no coffee machines, no video, and, worst of all, no toilet. When you've got a bladder as weak as mine, the last named could sometimes be a bit of a problem. Several times I was in sheer agony by the time we arrived at our destination. I'm sure many people can sympathise with this awful feeling.

One was going to Orient (lost 3-1, Peter Kitchen hat-trick, 27.3.78). The coach went all over East London looking for the ground. Walthamstow dog track, Hackney dog track, Upton Park.........everywhere except Brisbane Road. I was dying. When we finally found the correct stadium I staggered off the bus and spent the next ten minutes behind a run-down shed in a derelict factory. Bliss.

Colchester away (drew 1-1, Trenton Wiggan, 4.4.81) was nearly as bad. We stopped at Grantham Services on the A1 but I didn't want to go then...... ten miles later I thought "Why didn't I go?" and those narrow Suffolk and Essex roads were hell. This was the day Bob Champion and Aldaniti won the Grand National but that was the last thing on my mind as we eventually approached Layer Road.

But Plymouth (lost 4-1, Paul Casey, 19.4.80) was the worst. We stopped, as always, at Frankley Services but by the time we neared Taunton I was busting again. "No Services on the M5" the sign said. We saw signs to Exeter and I thought

"Not far now". The next sign we saw said "Plymouth 87 miles". I didn't realise just how far it was. My kidneys were fit to explode and I was almost unconscious when we reached Plymouth.

God, Those Were The Days.

April 15th 1989

Anon

On the day of the Hillsborough Disaster United were playing at Northampton at the old County Ground. Early in our game we heard terrace whisper that "A wall's collapsed" at Hillsborough, and further word spread that people had been badly injured.

We were unaware of the real extent of what had happened but suspected it must be something terrible as a few minutes before the end of the game there was a message over the tannoy, which said something like, "It would be appreciated if you would stay in your places at the end of the match as we have an important announcement to make regarding what has happened at Hillsborough."

At full time even all the players stayed put on the pitch and as the announcer informed us that people had been killed I remember Martin Pike going down on his haunches, hands to his face, as if he was crying.

We won 2-1, but it was a dreadfully silent journey home.

United's scorers were Brian Deane and Steve Thompson.

Is It Really Thirty-Five Years?

Pete Moxon

It came as quite a shock when I realised that thirty five years had elapsed since the day my dad took me to Bramall Lane for the very first time. In doing so, he condemned me to a lifetime of annual feelings like hope in August, despair nearly every October, fed up by Christmas, can't-wait-for-the-season-to-end by March.

So why do we football fans allow ourselves to endure the mental torture and still come back for more? Some of the thoughts that follow may give the reader a clue, as he or she may have similar stories locked away in their memories. The very nature of the atmosphere and the feelings of elation and excitement one experiences at a football match involving your team means that the memories are as clear as if they happened yesterday.

1961 - The Blades, the ball and my face

The long and often fraught road that is watching Sheffield United began for me on April 29th 1961 when the Blades, already promoted to the First Division, faced Middlesbrough at Bramall Lane in what was, I suppose, a celebration game for supporters. Strange then that only 18,868 should attend what nowadays would surely draw nearly twice that for such a match. My dad, who had so far managed to put me off my first visit to the Lane with a series of lame excuses, finally gave in to my requests of "Tek me to t'Lane, Dad!" and along with my uncle we finally made it.

My few recollections of the day are vivid and I remember we went on the John Street terrace, somewhere around the players' tunnel. My dad and uncle stood at the back and told me to stand at the front, up against the old white railings. I remember being somewhat overwhelmed by the crush of people but I nervously picked my way to the front, whilst vainly trying to keep an eye on where my dad was, just in case he tried to abandon me, as he often threatened to do when I was playing up.

As for the match itself, I recall a very sickly-looking Tony Wagstaff making his debut and Middlesbrough having a bald-headed wing half (probably known as a midfield ball winner today) who kicked most things except the ball, generally incurring the wrath of the terrace regulars.

My most abiding memory of this match includes this bald human scythe of a footballer whose name was Ray Yeomans. For once, Yeomans actually made contact with the ball of the leather sort when he and Brian Richardson clashed in midfield. The ball arrowed straight across the turf, picked up speed on the old shale track and smacked me full in the face (my father always told me to keep my eye on the ball.....I followed his advice to the letter), which, at the time, was peering attentively through the railings. A mixture of mud, red shale and water deposited itself on my face and I suddenly became the centre of attention for a few seconds as the crowd gathered round and accused Yeomans of deliberately aiming the ball at the

poor young lad who was attending his first match. Yeomans became the target of even more vociferous abuse for a few minutes until some other incident took the crowd's attention and my few moments of fame had passed.

On the way home from the match, which ended in a 4-1 victory for the Blades, I felt quite proud that Yeomans had singled me out to wreak his revenge on his detractors and, despite feeling the need to, I never shed a tear. Strangely enough, hundreds of games later, the ball has never felt the need to fly in my direction again, but every time it hurtles into the crowd and nearly decapitates someone the name Ray Yeomans invariably springs mind.

The game took place on April 29th 1961. The United scorers were Derek 'Doc' Pace (2), Billy Russell and Len Allchurch.

1967 - On the fence at Fulham

Around this time I had graduated to going to matches with my mates (most of us were Blades around lower Arbourthorne) and away matches had become the highlight of supporting United. To we thirteen-to-fifteen-year-olds it was an adventure, something to brag about to your mates at school on Monday mornings, about how six of us had run two thousand Man United fans!

This particular season saw us make three trips to London in the FA Cup, starting at Charlton, where we arrived early and 'took' their end from the nine- and ten-year-old Charlton occupants quite easily but at 2.55 around twenty or thirty rather large-looking South London chaps, brandishing what looked like machetes, soon restored what was the divine right of the home fans to occupy their end. Consolation was that we managed to scrape home 1-0 with a Mick Jones goal, with a scraggy-looking Phil Cliff making his debut for the injured legend Bill Punton.

The match against Charlton Athletic took place on January 28th 1967.

Monday dinner brought the fourth round draw and, would you believe it, another trip to London, this time to play fellow First Division team Fulham. Thanks to my paper round and my constant badgering of my mum, I was able to make the trip once again with my mates. At this point I will reflect on being able to travel to a football match in London without adult supervision at thirteen years old, with the return train not setting off until midnight. Were my parents liberal thinkers or just oblivious to what we might get up to on these jaunts?

We managed to snatch a draw, thanks again to Mick Jones, who put us in front only for Allan Clarke to earn a replay....which Bill Punton won single-handedly for us.

However, what really stands out about this trip was that after the game we did not return to Sheffield until the midnight train, so some of the time in between was spent in a back-street pub near St Pancras station, called the Skinners Arms. The landlord obviously had no qualms about serving spotty teenage adolescents with alcohol. This pub had a television and when 'Match of the Day' came on, to our delight it featured Fulham v. Sheffield United. After Mick Jones scored the camera panned behind the goal and up to the top of the open Craven Cottage terrace, where me and three of my mates were sitting on the railings at the back, celebrating the goal. The legendary Kenneth Wolstenholme remarked, "Look at those happy Sheffield United fans celebrating their goal."

We could not believe it. We were TV stars. There we were, us on TV. What a claim to fame. Had my mates at school seen it? More street cred beckoned.

In later years I often recalled this incident to my own United-crazy sons but I thought they did not take me too seriously. Then we bought the 'Sheffield United - Twenty Five Years of Match of the Day' video and the Fulham 1967 cup game was one of the featured matches. Would they let the camera pan to the top of the terrace to catch the delight of these four lads standing on the railings? Probably not but lo and behold there we were, twenty five years on, still leaping about just as I had remembered. My sons were gobsmacked. The old man hadn't been been telling tall stories, he was for real. My credibility in my own house suddenly increased; my sons realised their dad had not always been a stroppy adult, telling them what to do and what not to do. To them, all of a sudden, I was a bit of a hero!

The first match against Fulham was on February 18th 1967. The replay, at Bramall Lane was won 3-1 by United on March 1st 1967. Bill Punton (2) and Mick Jones scored.

Incredibly, London featured again in the fifth round when Chelsea and their friendly (!) fans welcomed us to Stamford Bridge and where Tony Hateley put paid to any Wembley dreams for that year, something which, although I wasn't to know at the time, was to become a bit of a habit in subsequent years.

The fifth round tie at Chelsea took place on March 11th 1967. Chelsea won 2-0.

1970 to 1990 - There in soul, but not always in body

Around the 1969/70 season a dilemma emerged in my love affair with SUFC. Should I play or should I watch the Blades on Saturday afternoons? My own football ability told me that whilst I wasn't going to make it as a pro and score the winning goal in the FA Cup final for the Blades, I still had a reasonable talent and could play to a good standard in local football. So for the next twenty years or so playing the game took precedence and I watched the Blades on any Saturday possible and every evening match. This may not qualify me as a totally dedicated supporter but I kept fully in touch with what was happening at the Lane and I read anything and everything that mentioned Sheffield United.

What incidents stand out in this period? Well, of course, the promotion season of 1970/71 when the climax began with us playing Hull City at Bramall Lane, where we literally got kicked off the park by Chris Simpkin and future piggy Ken Knighton in a 2-1 defeat. My wife (then girlfriend) came with me and was most annoyed that I became involved in a heated argument with some Hull fans and said that that was the last time she would ever go to a match with someone so immature. At the time she just didn't understand the mentality of football fans. Now she just puts up with it!

Hull City won 2-1 at Bramall Lane on March 9th 1971 after Gil Reece had given United an early lead.

From thinking after the Hull game that we had blown it, subsequent results meant a showdown with another fellow promotion contender, Cardiff City. Surely not another night of disappointment? Well, as all Blades know, this was a truly memorable night as the goals rained in with momentous regularity to give the Blades a 5-1 victory. Of course my girlfriend was with me (yes, the same one who a few weeks previously had disowned the Sheffield United part of me) and this was the first time I felt drunk with sheer happiness.....without the help of alcohol.

On April 27th 1971 United beat Cardiff City 5-1 at Bramall Lane with goals from Bill Dearden (2), John Flynn, Tony Currie and Gil Reece.

As my own playing season had finished I was also able to attend the Watford game, which we needed to win to gain promotion and in what seemed an anti-climax we duly strolled home 3-0 to clinch promotion to the First Division.

This match was on May 1st 1971. Alan Woodward (pen.) and Gil Reece (2) scored the goals.

The following five seasons contained the occasional highlight but in keeping with tradition at Bramall Lane we were only ever bit players. However, that initial burst of exhilarating attacking play that saw us top Division One at the start of the 1971/72 season still evokes a glow of pride. Funny how the goal that ended the run is still being shown on television nearly thirty years later (I still say if Ted Hemsley had been on the field instead of being injured earlier in the game, Bestie would have kissed the earth early on in that run). Seeing us go four goals up in fifteen minutes and eventually win 5-0 against the mighty Arsenal whilst standing on the Bramall Lane end amongst some very upset Arsenal fans is another highlight of this period.

After eight wins and two draws to start the 1971/72 season United finally lost 2-0 to Manchester United at Old Trafford on October 2nd 1971, with George Best and Alan Gowling scoring in the last ten minutes.

Another rare jaunt on to the John Street terrace saw me pick up the perfect ringside seat for the Eddie Colquhoun/Phil Boyer punch up - the best scrap I've ever seen in a pro football match. Colquhoun won on a stoppage and apparently finished Boyer off in the tunnel as they both went for the obligatory early bath.

These boxing and football contests were at Bramall Lane on November 12th 1974. The League Cup fourth round tie ended 2-2, with Alan Woodward and Keith Eddy (pen.) scoring for United.

The end-of-season run in 1974/75, which saw us almost make Europe, brings back memories of arriving home from work and saying to my wife, "Forget the tea. C'mon, let's go to Birmingham, we might be getting into Europe." Of course, she agreed, conveniently forgetting the night on the Kop four years earlier against Hull City. Naturally, we didn't make it into Europe and it was a downward spiral from then on, with a succession of ageing pros and maverick managers trying to revive the fortunes of the Blades.

It is my opinion that during this period United had some of the most inept performers that I have ever seen in a red and white shirt. Names such as Mick Guy, Andy Keeley, Len De Goey, John Flood, Tony Moore, Pedro Verde and Craig Renwick took us down to the depths and the man mainly responsible for most of the bad

players was 'Happy' Harry Haslam who, for me, topped this list of unfortunates with Dougie Brown, signed from none other than Clydebank reserves and who scored in the opening game of the 1979/80 season against Swindon, commanding instant hero worship from the Kop. Sadly for Dougie it was downhill all the way after that and he took to shooting from the half-way line in a desperate attempt to win back fan adulation. When he finally left United it was to go to a manual job in Scotland as no other club recognised the 'hidden' talents that Harry had seen in Dougie.

In United's first ever game in the Third Division on August 18th 1979, Ian Benjamin (pen.) and Dougie Brown scored as the Blades beat Swindon Town 2-1.

Ian Porterfield briefly revived our fortunes in the Fourth Division championship season but having been given the mandate to do what he pleased after he was awarded a ten-year contract he also brought in old pros looking for their last big payday and things deteriorated once more. My memories of this period are few and far between, probably because it was such a depressing time, save for beating Liverpool (then European Champions) and the visit of River Plate following the signing of Alex Sabella.

In consecutive matches in August 1978 United played Liverpool in a League Cup second round match and two days later met River Plate, who had many of the 1978 Argentinian World Cup winning squad in the side, in a friendly arranged as part of the Alex Sabella deal. Gary Hamson scored late on as United beat Liverpool 1-0, and Alan Woodward converted a penalty in the 2-1 defeat by River Plate.

Dave Bassett's arrival in 1988 also signalled the end of my own playing career and allowed me to take up watching Sheffield United on a full-time basis once again. This time I had allies, in the form of my two sons who, having been brought up in the correct tradition, were Blades fanatics and for most of the time since, season tickets and away games have been the order of the day.

Bassett provided memories that I am sure my children will carry with them through the topsy-turvy journey that is part of following the Blades.

Vale Of Blades

Anon

The only time I've ever been to Hillsborough other then when United were playing was in, I think, November 1975 when Port Vale played there. Being too young to have the money to go to see United at Villa Park we hit on the idea of standing on the Leppings Lane end and help support whoever Wednesday were playing. Well, we'd be heroes at school if everything went well and we could just never mention it, should it suit.

We had a pretty good time. Port Vale won 3-0 and we got on well with the Vale fans, who seemed happy enough for the extra support. We even swapped badges. It made up for not being able to travel - and for the fact that the Blades lost 5-1 that day - as well as providing ammunition for school on Monday morning.

This was November 8th 1975. Chris Guthrie scored United's lone goal at Villa Park.

John Tudor And The Gigg Lane Con Job

Ken Cotterill

One of the most popular players at the Lane during the late sixties was a tough, burly striker called John Tudor, who signed for us from Coventry City for £65,000 (then a big sum). John made his debut for United against Bury at Gigg Lane on November 16th 1968. The record books show that Tudor got both goals in a 2-0 victory. However, as an eye witness, I still claim to this day that Tudor never got anywhere near the first one.

I was standing with a friend behind the goal United were attacking in the first half. The large United support was mainly behind the other goal. As the game progressed a cross came over from a corner or a free kick (I can't recall which) and the ball bounced off a few legs, then shot into the net. It was all very quick. I recall turning to my friend and saying, "Who got that?"

He shrugged and said, "Own goal." What we did see was Tudor running back to the centre, hands raised as though he'd scored. The local press were all grouped around Hodgkinson's goal so they didn't see anything, nor would any

journalist in the stand. It was clearly an own goal yet Tudor managed to bluff all and sundry that he'd actually stuck it in.

Being a bit green and naïve in those days, I was surprised that nobody in the press challenged Tudor's claim to the goal, or even remotely questioned it. John had pulled the wool over their eyes and claimed one he shouldn't have!

Still, Tudor became a very popular Blade, scoring some great goals, including a hat-trick against poor old Bury in the return at the Lane that season. He also came off the bench to score the winner against Wednesday in a 3-2 win in October 1970. But probably his best goal in the red and white stripes was some two weeks later at Birmingham, where his stunning strike was captured by the 'Match of the Day' cameras. The goal was so good they finished the show with it. As the credits rolled up we saw Tudor score and wheel away, one arm raised, accompanied by the stirring music of the 'Match of the Day' theme tune! It felt great to be a Blade watching that!

Sadly, however - yes, here comes the down side - John Harris, United's manager in those days, was never fond of Tudor. His last goal for us was at Bolton in a 2-1 defeat. Shortly after he was off to Newcastle United in an exchange deal that brought goalkeeper John Hope and ex-Owl David Ford to the Lane. Tudor, of course, then formed a deadly partnership with Malcolm MacDonald, often outshining his more famous partner.

Alas! If only we'd kept him. Maybe, just maybe, we would have won the League title in 1975? Still, that's United. Thanks for the memories John.

The return game against Bury at Bramall Lane took place on February 1st 1969. As well as Tudor's hat-trick, Ted Hemsley and Alan Woodward also scored.

Tudor's 'Match of the Day' strike at St Andrew's was the only goal of the game on October 10th 1970, while his last goal for United in the defeat at Bolton was on January 16th 1971.

Boozy Blades On Tour

Pete Furness

Have you noticed that when you go on away trips, at five to three all the home fans are inside the ground, while the Bladesmen are only just arriving at the turnstiles, unlike those nice

photo: Kevin Titterton

Celebrating Keith Edwards' goal at Darlington

Norwich City types who once arrived at the Lane at one o'clock and wanted immediate admission.

Yes, the trusty Blade will arrive five hours before the game (and will still miss the kick off).

When other clubs' fans reminisce about away trips, they talk of great victories and triumphs. But not us. When we get nostalgic it's pubs, clubs, bars and discos, with the match relegated to a mere sideshow. How many of us, when asked about an away game, answer "Crap game but a bloody good day out...." ?

Here is a look back at some of these matches - probably not all of them were crap, but they were all good days out...........

Aston Villa 4 United 1, FA Cup fourth round, January 25th 1975
We had a coach from the local boozer and, due to the incessant rain, we did not leave until it was confirmed that the game was on. So we stopped in the pub drinking and bought more 'carry' to consume during the journey to the land of the speech impediment. On arrival we all went to the Witton Arms, where more booze flowed. Despite the drink it was a very sober crew that trooped back on to the coach after the match. The weather had been nearly as bad as the Blades. In order to alleviate the gloom the

coach stopped at Ripley so we could have a drink. It was only the following morning, with the hangover at its peak, that I wondered had it all been worth going?

Leicester City 3 United 0, FA Cup third round, January 3rd 1976
A year on and another defeat. We set off at an ungodly hour and the journey was enlivened by someone with a weak bladder peeing into an empty can of Long Life (to think we used to drink such slops).

Everard's beer - it sounds bad but we drunk it and had a good time doing so. Two Blades turned up at the ground with loads of cans of beer. The police would not let them into the ground with it and told them to sup it. We were offered some and naturally took it.

So to the game, and Keith Edwards' debut. Still level at half time we had a chance, but a Chris Garland hat-trick put paid to our chances. Some Blades tried a pitch invasion but it was all half-hearted. After the game we actually came straight back home.

Oldham Athletic 1 United 2, Division Two, December 27th 1976
A first visit to Boundary Park for most fans. Could Jimmy Squirrel (the only man to make Ian Dowie look like Richard Gere) win promo-

tion for us? No. Still, it was Christmas and probably 3500 made the trip. Seeing all the coaches stopping as we were going over Woodhead it was obvious that everyone was well into the Christmas spirit.

Oldham was wet and miserable so it was any port in a storm. The landlady was not entirely happy about serving us but she did, so we had a few. A shock came once we were in the ground. The back steps of the Kop were all wood - you could jump up and down and feel the steps move.

Oldham's afro-haired left winger, the late Alan Groves, had recently been in court for not sending his sixteen-year-old *wife* to school. It was easy to guess what the Blades were going to chant. It was easy to guess what Groves' response would be, too.

We were lucky only to be one down at half time. The second half opened with a shock - Chris Guthrie scored, which prompted some bevvied-up Blades to chant "Guthrie for England!" It got better - Alan Woodward pinched a late winner.

Blackpool 1 United 1, Division Two, November 5th 1977
Bonfire Night - we left at a very early hour for this one and arrived well before opening time. Not knowing the Statute of Limitations I cannot go into what illegalities were committed before 11am. Bobby Campbell scored for us, Bob Hatton (I think) equalised for them.

Then the fun started. All night in Blackpool to down a glass or two. Needless to say the resort was full of Blades becoming sloshed. Why is it that when you are on a pub crawl you end up further and further away from where you have to get back to? Due to a surfeit of alcohol the details of the night are a wee bit hazy. I do remember that some pubs refused to serve us as we were accused of being drunk. There was still one major shock - everyone managed to catch the coach home.

Hull City 2 United 3, Division Two, December 31st 1977
The League's computer at last got an away holiday fixture right - to Hull and back, meaning we could be home for the proper session on New Year's Eve. All the pubs near the ground were shut or were for regulars only. This may have deterred lesser mortals but fear not, the ale-detecting crew were out in force. We reacted by jumping on the nearest Hull Corporation bus. One doubts that many bus drivers have had twenty three consecutive passengers requesting

a ride to "the nearest pub that will let us in". He duly obliged, although we ended up about a mile and a half away from Boothferry Park.

The distance, plus the fact that we caught a bus back, ensured that we missed the kick off. A pleasing surprise was that we won. If memory serves, Simon Stainrod scored a couple of blinders, with Keith Edwards getting the other. After the game we rushed back home in order to get out and see in 1978.

Chesterfield 2 United 1, Division Three January 5th 1980
This was so dire it would have made Cliff Richard take up Sex, Drugs and Rock'n'Roll, let alone drink. It was also a foretaste of all the Saltergate defeats to come.

Stockport County 0 United 0, FA Cup first round, November 22nd 1980
Harry Haslam may have been happy, but we Blades were not. By now we had managed four FA Cup wins in twelve years, so a trip to one of the then Fourth Division strugglers was seen by many as another one we could win. Well, we did win (after extra time in the replay). Little did I know that I would spend my twenty fifth birthday at Edgeley Park watching us lose a Fourth Division fixture less than a year later.

The day started well. One of the lads wanted to see the racing on TV so we stopped at this pub in Hazelgrove. The pub was very nice. Mick could watch the 12.45 and there was a snooker table. When asked "how far's the ground?", our host replied "five minutes". Obviously he meant by Lear Jet. We got into the ground at 3.30.

Ah, the match. It was crap, as were most of our games that season. When fans write in and say that today's team is the worst ever, one wonders if they ever watched the Blades 1978-81 vintage. I am still scarred by having watched Dougie Brown, Phil Jones, Steve Neville, Jeff Bourne, Barry Butlin, John Ryan, Len de Goey............

Darlington 0 United 2, Division Four, May 15th 1982
Even the Blades could not blow this one. Champions, albeit of Division Four. This remains the only thing I have ever seen us win.

Only between 3pm and 5pm did we not have a glass in our hands. Younger readers may not believe this, but at the time we thought Reg Brealey was a good Chairman.

Lincoln City 0 United 0, FA Cup second round, December 19th 1983

Disaster!! The pubs in Lincoln shut at 2.30, and we did not find out until 2.20 when the first bell rang. I was the only one who had been before to Sincil Bank before and that had been a night match the previous season.

Norwich City 3 United 2, FA Cup fifth round, February 18th 1989

Note the six-year gap between this and the last trip. The later Portakabin and McEwan's Export (i.e. post-Keith Edwards) years were not good ones. Little sent the pulses racing and I only saw us at Derby, Barnsley, Huddersfield etc. I had turned thirty and was now a respectable adult. However, the old ways had been fun and the enjoyment factor was coming back.

Now aged thirty two, the trip to Carrow Road was the furthest progress in the cup that I had seen. Norwich were having their best ever season and were second in the old First Division. Bassett's Blades were not playing with the verve of early season. Could we do it? Lots of Dutch Courage was consumed in East Dereham prior to the game.

We wuz robbed. Well, Dale Gordon probably deserved to be on the winning side. Luck did not favour the brave. Still, later that night the Bladesman could hold his head up high.

Leicester City 2 United 5, Division Two, May 5th 1990

Had to put this one in. Filbert Street's second dirty dozen entry. No Blade will ever forget this one. That early goal brought all the pessimistic thoughts flooding back, but the Blades came through.

The final memory of this famous Blade day came around midnight as I was staggering home. I had got as far as Wellcarr Road and I could still hear ringing out from the Big Tree car park, "Ooh Aah Bob Bookah!!". On days such as this I can understand why I support the Blades.

Norwich City 0 United 1, Premier League, April 23rd 1994

Not St George's Day, but Nathan's Day. His goal gleaned us three points. They should have helped us stay up.

A 7am start to this one. The journey into Turner country was enlivened by some joker having brought along a couple of videos, and yes, they were not the type Mariella Frostrup normally reviews.

An advantage of an early start was that once in Norwich a serious pub crawl could be started. For once we pub-crawled towards the ground. It was noticeable how few home supporters were in the pubs. After the game our coach was blocked in so we had time for a quick drink. Back on the coach some of the lads wanted to watch the videos again, whilst we wanted Sports Report. We compromised - the videos were played with no sound and the radio on. Note to porno film makers - do not bother with a sound-track. Simply get Stuart Hall to do a voice-over; the results are hilarious.

The coach stopped at Boston for the night, so another pub crawl had to be endured. We even managed to watch 'Match of the Day' on telly. We left Boston after midnight, with a couple fewer bodies than we arrived with. A great day out.

Cooperman

Kevin Cooper

Kevin Cooper was born at Darnall on August 15th 1960. His father was at his bedside and kicked him half to death until his first words were Sheffield United.

My first game was against Chelsea in 1968, the year the Blades were relegated. Very disappointing. Cried all the way back to Darnall because I'd spent the 2d bus fare and the Blades were down.

United lost 2-1 at home to Chelsea on May 11th 1968 and were relegated to the Second Division. Mick Hill scored the United goal.

The 1969/70 season, at the second match against Charlton Athletic, I had my scarf pinched. That was it. Even the Blades won 2-0. At nine years old I was soon looking to be one of Sheffield United's legendary supporters.

On August 12th 1969 United beat Charlton Athletic 2-0 at Bramall Lane with goals by Alan Woodward and Tony Currie.

1970. Probably the pinnacle of my life. The best team then, and in my years watching the Blades. This was the dream machine. I'll never, ever forget the 3-2 victory over the hogs' heads at the Lane, when Chris Woods' grandfather, Peter Grummitt, let Tudor's back-pass straight through his legs.

United played Wednesday at Bramall Lane on

October 3rd 1970. Eddie Colquhoun and Bill Dearden gave United a 2-0 lead, Wednesday pulled it back to 2-2 but substitute John Tudor hit the winner, the ball going between 'keeper Peter Grummitt's legs.

We beat Leicester at the Lane, with David Nish scoring from forty yards into his own net. Still say to this day that that was one of the best goals I've seen at the Lane!

United beat Leicester City 2-1 on Boxing Day 1970. As well as the Nish own goal, Alan Woodward scored.

When we stuffed Cardiff City 5-1 that glorious night my father got arrested for kissing the cen-

being relegated again. Jimmy Sirrel, I believe, could have been a brilliant manager if chairman John Hassall had 'tipped up'. The best thing that happened to Hassall was his near stoning at Cambridge. Relegation again. Not bad when Cambridge's record attendance is against a team that is relegated and takes 6,000 with them.

United were relegated to the Third Division for the first time in their history after losing 1-0 to Cambridge United at the Abbey Stadium on May 5th 1979.

Enter Haslam and Peters. Enough said! Then came the season to remember. The Fourth Division championship. That season I made

Some people are on the pitch... well, nearly.
Blades fans prepare for the championship winning invasion at Darlington

photo: Kevin Titterton

tre spot - five minutes from time. And the last match against Watford, when United hadn't scored a penalty at the Lane all season, and Woodward nearly knocked the Lane end down with it, via the back of the net.

Not forgetting the best referee I've ever witnessed, in that game. Roger Kirkpatrick from Leicester. What a gentleman. Whenever he refereed the Blades we were guaranteed victory. From all our older Blades fans, may I send my regards to him (if he's still alive) and his family. They don't make them like him any more.

Just missing Europe with Ken Furphy, then

more appearances for United than Paul Richardson. My first was after a 1-1 draw with York City in the League Cup. A fortnight later at the same venue I did it again after Bob Hatton (my eyes have seen the glory of the coming of the Lord) had scored for the boys. My emotions got to me. I walked across the pitch and kissed God's second son on the cheek, to rapturous applause from the Blades singing, "Cooperman! Cooperman!"

I was gutted. I missed six more goals. United won 4-3. I was arrested, kept while Monday and fined £100. It made me a national hero, as it was in the national press.

United played York City away twice in two weeks in 1981. Bob Hatton scored as the teams finished 1-1 in a League Cup first round second leg match on September 15th, then on October 3rd United won a league game 4-3 thanks to goals from Hatton, Tony Kenworthy (pen.) and Mike Trusson 2.

I offered to take the penalty at Scunthorpe but Tony Kenworthy wouldn't let me!

Tony Kenworthy scored the penalty at Scunthorpe on February 20th 1982 but United lost 2-1.

We went on the pitch at Halifax after Steve Charles had just scored.

United beat Halifax Town 5-1 at The Shay on April 12th 1982. After Halifax took a first-minute lead the goals were scored by Tony Kenworthy 2 (1 pen.), Steve Charles and Keith Edwards 2.

Sat in the dugout at Darlington as Assistant Manager to Ian Porterfield but what gutted me the most was that I never got a championship medal for my efforts!

After that it was up and down for the Blades. I could go on and write three volumes of a book, but as Blades we all reminisce together.

The night we beat the hogs at Swillsborough 3-1, when Sir Robert Davison scored a brace, was the best thing since my son Ryan was born. Since I have been watching the Blades - since the late sixties - one thing the pigs can't say to me is that they have seen their side do the double over the Blades. I can honestly say that of them!

United and Wednesday met in the league for the first time in eleven years in the 1991/92 season and United won both games - 2-0 (Dane Whitehouse, Brian Deane) at Bramall Lane on November 17th 1991 and 3-1 (Dane Whitehouse, Bobby Davison 2 on his debut) at Hillsborough on March 11th 1992.

May I take this opportunity to say that a Bladesman is your friend for life and my life has been shared with some wonderful characters. God bless the Blades!

And also to pay respects to Roy Zide, born August 12th 1960, died 1990, aged just 29. Born in Darnall, Roy was another active member of the Barmy Army. He will always be sadly missed by all his friends and his family. Better known as Little Fat Roy. He died three days after United beat Wolves away 2-1. The year when United were promoted at Leicester and the pigs were relegated at home to the scabs of Forest. He would have loved it.

God bless Roy. RIP. Sadly missed.

United beat Wolves 2-1 at Molineux on October 7th 1990. Wilf Rostron and John Gannon scored.

Icing On The Cake

Smoz

Valentine's Day eh? Always a favourite. I mean, the Dragon spoils me, for a start (nudge, nudge, get my drift squire).

In 1993, though, we had THE match of the season to look forward to and, later that night, one of my treasured bands from the seventies, The Strawbs, were playing just down the road at the Leadmill. After we'd given Manchester United a good sorting in the FA Cup I was seriously stuck in traffic going nowhere, so I decided to park up and have a wander into the Leadmill to see if the band had arrived for a soundcheck. Sure 'nuff, the booming plink-plonk gave the game away. No sooner had I walked through the door then Don Airey, the band's keyboard player, collared me for the score. Although a Sunderland supporter himself, he has two children who are staunch Manchester United fans. We talked about the match and football in general for a while and then the conversation turned to music in football. Don asked if there was any particular song associated with Sheffield United. I cringed and explained that, yes, to Unitedites of a certain age, there was one little number that brought back that amber feeling of the golden age. I told him what the song was.

Smiles, smirks and open laughter from the other band members and road crew alike made me wish I'd never opened my gob.

All power to Don though. Half way through the set that night, when he's doing his solo 'keyboard wizard' bit, he stops what he's meant to be playing and launches into Lynn Anderson's 'Rose Garden'.

Listen.........I'm not one for this 'new man' rubbish, but my eyes were moist, I can tell you. Perfect end to a perfect day.

My Most Memorable Match

Ken Cotterill

The stadium was Hillsborough, Sheffield. The date, September 5th 1964; a glorious autumn day for the derby match: Sheffield Wednesday versus Sheffield United.

It was a hard life being a Unitedite in those days (it still is). United were the perennial underdogs. Wednesday were the glamour side in the steel city. They had the best team, the best ground and the more illustrious history. The previous season Wednesday had beaten United 3-1. Wednesday had made a confident start to the 1964/65 season; however, United had made their usual indifferent start. Moreover, they were going through a transition stage.

I had been a Unitedite since the age of nine. My dad had taken me one foggy January to see United beat a team in green (Plymouth Argyle). From then on I was a regular at the Lane. United seemed to have a permanent team in those days. Week after week the line-up was the same. There was Alan Hodgkinson in goal; Cec Coldwell and Graham Shaw at full back; Brian Richardson, Joe Shaw and Gerry Summers at half back. Of the forwards, Derek 'Doc' Pace, Ronnie Simpson and Billy Hodgson were the most dangerous and consistent. However, as we looked down on the magnificent Hillsborough stadium, most of these players were now gone.

Hodgson, the man who was great in the mud, had departed. Doc Pace was still around but he'd lost his place to a big blond youngster called Mick Jones. Alongside Jones was another youngster with similar build and looks; Alan Birchenall. Birchenall, a Londoner, had made his debut at Stoke in midweek. United had won so he kept his place in the side for the derby. He was now in at the deep end.

Wednesday, urged on by the huge crowd, began the game in fine style. They forced several early corners and would have scored but for some excellent goalkeeping from Hodgkinson. Gradually United, helped by the older hands such as Joe Shaw and Keith Kettleborough, began to get back into the game. Midway through the first half United won a corner. Jones headed against the post, Birchenall collected the rebound and slammed it past Ron Springett. United one up! The crowd, silent.

In the second half Wednesday got several more corners and it looked as though United's defence would crack. Hodgkinson and Joe Shaw were magnificent. Then United forced a rare corner. Up rose Birchenall. There was a flick of his blond head. United 2 Wednesday 0! And that was how it stayed. A great win on a beautiful day.

Alan Birchenall's midweek debut at Stoke City, on September 2nd 1964, was won 1-0, with Mick Jones scoring the goal.

A Day Out In London

John Critchley

I set the alarm to ring at the ungodly hour of 6am, or so I thought. Only I had forgotten to push the button on the clock. Must have been the excitement. Nevertheless I was awake at five and downstairs within minutes and soon frying sausages, bacon, egg and tomatoes.

Searched out the ticket for the game and then the Super Saver to Kings Cross - £40. Frosty, fog and a bit chilly but just a hint of better things to come borne in the air. Could have waited for a bus to town but had been advised by my doctor to try and walk off a back strain, so made my way on foot to Doncaster station. On platform 3A, along with a fair smattering of both Blades and Owls, most decked in club colours. I never bother - can be a hindrance.

Boarded the train, not one of the latest models, and in need of fitters' attention. I couldn't wait to get in motion. Made an unscheduled stop at Retford, then planned ones at Newark and Grantham and operating on only one engine - slowly. The conductor predicted the train would arrive at its destination at about 10.40. Incorrect, but only by around ten minutes. London at last!

Had a bit of a stroll to get a breath of air (I won't say fresh) and to exercise my slightly aching back, before purchasing a return to Wembley Park on the Metropolitan line, then sitting next to a young French couple on the tube, whose pronunciation of the station names prompted a few sly smiles - particularly Willy's den!

After alighting at Wembley Park, I had a wander past thousands of high-spirited, can-drinking supporters and one pub with police in large numbers across the road waiting to pounce. Not my scene. Kept walking until I found another boozer. Crowded but without the atmosphere of the other. Caught the eye of the barman and purchased two pints of bitter. Both for me. I wasn't going to queue again and it was all I wanted to slake my thirst.

Walked down the famous Wembley Way singing and soaking in all the atmosphere. Not as much hassle as I had feared - a few insults but no threats or fisticuffs.

Bought a programme - £4 but large, glossy and readable, despite a few glaring errors. Found entrance G then my seat. Not much of a seat and about two inches between rows. Fourteen pounds.

Millions of balloons, red and white and blue and white, some great flags and banners and no sign whatsoever of the atmosphere of sheer hatred that can happen at derby matches back in Sheffield. Can't wait for the game to start, but don't expect to be going home happy. Pessimist!

The game. A cauldron of noise and Waddle and out. I couldn't believe the lack of a defensive wall. Kelly caught cold. No-one picking up the former sausage seasoner. Too deep for Whitehouse, Hodges isn't a marker and Ward is too busy keeping tabs on Sheridan and Wilson. Could only mean trouble. A mistake! Too many class players against hopeful triers and ones not wanting to make it a war in front of the cameras.

Not the team I would have picked. Bradshaw and Hoyland would have had a game and Whitehouse would have been where Wednesday would have least liked to see him - up front. But Harry knows his players better than anyone and it's easy to pick a side that doesn't have to go out and actually play the game, isn't it?

Brilliant ball by Carr and a goal for the beard-ed Alan Cork. Hope at last! Still, I can't see the Blades going on to win the thing, despite the bloke in front of me saying they would at every opportunity. Surely the boss will change a few things at the break? He'll have the lads breath-ing fire and give a few kicks up the backside.

Nothing! Wednesday getting more on top, despite Waddle fading and Kelly shining. Ward and Gannon are working tremendously in the engine room but sadly just haven't got that something extra so badly required on the day. The Owls just can't get the ball into our net, but it isn't for the want of trying.

Extra time. Our deadly rivals look as if they've at least two more players on the most famous of turf. United ever more desperate and Deane fails to defend a corner, letting in the dangerous Bright to score the winning goal.

United just weren't good, hungry or fit enough on the afternoon. And Wednesday in two finals. They spend real money on real players and play in a style suited to Wembley. Sadly United don't but circumstances dictate at Bramall Lane, don't they?

Queuing for Wembley semi-final tickets, March 1993

A plod back to Wembley Park. A bit of banter and congratulations to Wednesdayites by the more sporting among we Unitedites. Good losers! Had to stand on the tube to Kings Cross. Joined the five o'clock train back to Donny and home by seven fifteen with a 'Green 'Un', to check the results that count now. Trust Wimbledon to have one of their off days at Oldham! Now for Leeds and Man City. The real cup finals begin on Tuesday at 7.45 and the lads will just have to win at Hillsborough again, won't they? Then all will be forgiven!

"Ee-O-lady-Marma!"

Len Strike

I remember an unusual football chant from the sixties. We sang "Ee-o-lady-marma!", which was reputedly a Zulu war chant, on Charlton's Kop throughout the FA Cup third round tie there in 1967, as well as on our S.U.T. coach. A repetitive chant, we occasionally added, "Ritchie's got no father!" to it. I had never heard it chanted before and never have done since.

Mick Jones won the tie in the last minute with a dramatic header.

Down Memory Lane

Scott Cheshire

This is a nostalgic trip by bus from Ranby Army Camp to the Lane just after the war to see United beat Liverpool 3-1. It was Monday September 8th 1947. I seem to remember it was a glorious summer evening. Certainly it had been an arduous day of square bashing for a raw recruit at Ranby Camp, Retford. Luckily, we were released that day at 4pm, well in time to escape for an evening out. The East Midland bus (orange I think) did its stuff and off to Sheffield we went.

Bramall Lane was a magic name to a cockney lad who'd watched all his football (and cricket) in London or on the south coast. I had been told by my father about Yorkshire folk stoking up the blast furnaces when the opposition was batting and I was curious to see how the ground could accommodate football as well as the other game. I knew too that the place had suffered bomb damage and that, most important of all, the Blades were playing Liverpool that evening.

The bus took an interminable time, winding its way into countless villages off the main road. Eventually houses began to replace fields and the vehicle filled with men, all in caps and wearing red and white scarves. Once in the city there was no need to ask the way! All roads led to one point.

Knowing nothing of the geography of the ground I went into the first turnstile I saw (H.M. Forces 1/6 I think) and clambered up a great many steps to reach the vast terracing behind the goal. The players were already out on the pitch and, as if awaiting my arrival, the referee blew his whistle to start the game almost at once. But who was whom? Liverpool were in white shirts and black knickers (no shorts in those days!). Cyril Sidlow was between the posts for them. Number four was a team change - in place of Taylor....Paisley. Yes, Bob Paisley, none other. Bert Stubbiness, then the most expensive player in the game, I think, and recently signed from Newcastle United, led the attack. But, disappointingly for me, Billy Liddell, the famous Scottish winger, was a last-minute absentee.

Of course it was much easier to learn who the home team were. The goalkeeper was obviously a character and firm favourite with the crowd, who cheered his every turn; he also sported a cloth cap. Jack Smith. The centre half was massive. Hair plastered down (surely with Brylcreem?), Harry Latham was a pillar of solidarity. Alec Forbes, soon to be on his way to Arsenal, was instantly recognisable with his flame-coloured hair and crunching tackles. On the left wing the long-legged Colin Collindridge was causing all sorts of problems with his great speed and trickery. But, best of all, there was peerless Jimmy Hagan directing everything with his marvellous vision and skill. The ball seemed automatically and magnetically attached to his boots, his passes were sprayed around with uncanny accuracy and I'm sure a chorus or two of "Wonderful, wonderful Jimmy Hagan" was struck up.

The programme cost 2d. Readers were invited to purchase their Wardonia blades from the sole makers, Thomas Ward. I could have had "the best meal in town" at Bert's of Charles Street (closing at 9.15pm), had time and army wages permitted. At least the entertainment from the band - the Sheffield Recreation Prize Band with its conductor Mr T.W.Green - was entirely free, as they performed just by the players' tunnel.

The Blades had made an indifferent start to the season - a draw and three defeats from the opening four games. "No need for despondence," said the programme editor. Prophetic words too. Sheffield United won 3-1 (Hagan scored one of the goals) and 33,000 departed happily (there were no visiting fans in those days). Soon it was the bus station and back to camp to face the prospect of 6.30am reveille and yet another day of torture.

No matter. I'd made it to the Lane all right and I was to repeat the excursion a half dozen or so more times before His Majesty King George VI decided I was surplus to requirements and could return to the south. By that time Ward's were offering a packet of ten razor blades for three shillings and a reduction of 4d from the time of that first visit! Quite important on a private's pay of twenty four bob a week - £1.20 to you!

United beat Liverpool 3-1 on September 8th 1947 with goals from Jimmy Hagan, Harold Brook and Dennis Thompson.

But Dad, It's Over Ninety Minutes!

Handsworth Blade

I have to hold my hand up and say foul, as in the late seventies and early eighties I used to be an early leaver. In my defence, though, it was all my dad's fault as I was only a youngster at the time and he was the one who used to take me to the match.

During the Blades' free-fall plummet from the First to the Fourth I lost count of the times I missed Conroy, Brown or Richardson picking the ball out of the back of the net as United crumbled to last-minute draws and defeats aplenty.

In fact, if the referee had blown the final whistle at the exact moment we left the ground, then I'm convinced the Blades would never have been relegated in 1979 and 1981 (both bad years for Sheffield in more ways than one). I'd even go further and say they would have been in with a realistic chance of promotion and a good outside bet for Europe. Then again, I'm sure that winters were never that discontented back then.

Crucial early-leaving games that spring immediately to mind include Cambridge, Rotherham and Huddersfield. Even in the crumbling final days of the Third Reich, no sooner had someone said "Don Givens missed penalty" than we were out of the door.

The ultimate game not to leave early around

that time had to be a season later at Crewe. For virtually all Blades present that day Crewe can only bring back brilliant memories - for me it was mixed emotions. Think back, May 1982, United 2-1 up, five minutes to go - you could almost touch promotion. At this point my dad decided it was time to go, "to avoid the traffic." We were just under the stand when a faint roar went up - 2-2. Then as we reached the car a massive roar went up - 3-2 to the Blades, a last-minute winner from Jeff King!

At times like that it is difficult to explain your emotions - because the Blades have won it in the last minute you feel elated, but you also feel absolutely gutted because you've missed it.

But the best part is yet to come - and this should happen to everyone who ever leaves early "to avoid the traffic." My old man had parked bang in the middle of a car park that was practically empty at 2pm, but by 4.45 it was bumper to bumper. The only quick way out of that car park was with the assistance of a crane. Like all the other elated Blades, it must have taken an hour to get away from Crewe, except they'd seen all the late drama and we hadn't.

A couple of years later when I started going to the matches with the lads I vowed never to leave early again (although sometimes I've got to the point where I'm vowing never to go at all again). To leave early is as nonsensical and as annoying as a Wednesdayite who thinks he's got a sense of humour.

As far as possible I've kept to that vow. The only times I've left early since have been for a totally different reason. In the last days of the great Dave Bassett, against Derby and Huddersfield, and once against Birmingham, I just had to leave early. I am of the opinion that the Blades should never be beaten at Bramall Lane, but in those three games my feelings for United were ones of dejection, helplessness, hopelessness, despair and folly and you could label the team's performances with any of those expressions. It wasn't so much the losing, it was the manner of those defeats. It was as if the team's performance in those three games reflected the shambolic, couldn't-care-less attitude of the Board. They were a beaten, dispirited team and my presence wasn't going to alter the final result. My new vow is to get so pissed before each match that I'll not get so low again and therefore have to leave early.

By the way, I lied. I have left early to avoid the traffic just once - an away game at Stoke. I don't know what possessed me. I was driving and everyone agreed. For one fleeting moment I had become my father. It could have been fifteen or twenty years earlier at some godforsaken hell-hole in the Third or Fourth Division. I got my deserved reward, though, courtesy of Deano's late leveller.

Brian Deane scored in injury time to earn United a 2-2 draw at the Britannia Stadium on Boxing Day 1997. Gareth Taylor had put United ahead but Stoke then went 2-1 up.

Scarf Ace

Steve Titterton

Sheffield United v Everton, FA Cup third round, January 3rd 1970, aged ten years.

Everton at this time were top of the First Division, while United were doing well in the Second. Myself and Uncle Mick had two tickets for the Bramall Lane Stand. This was in the early days of the hooligan problem. Uncle Mick collected me from our house that Saturday dinner time and moaned about the fact that I wanted to wear my red and white scarf. "Don't wear that, we'll only get into trouble." Not to be put off, I tucked the offending article inside my coat and off we set.

Everton, with the famous midfield trio of Kendall, Ball and Harvey, were soon in the lead with a penalty converted by the squeaky-voiced one. The second half saw a transformation. Alan Woodward ran the show down the right wing and a deep cross was met by the head of Colin Addison and sent beyond the despairing dive of Gordon West into the Everton net. This goal was met with the usual fervour and we rose as one to salute it. My scarf, which had been brought into the open once the game had started, was now held aloft, one end in my hand and one in my uncle's.

If the Blades fans thought this was good, things got even better only minutes later. Another Woodward run in front of the John Street faithful, another deep cross, this time met by the head of a diving Gil Reece. Again the net bulged, again the crowd rose, again one end of the scarf was held aloft by the raised arm of my uncle. The problem for me was that the cries of "We're gonna win the cup!" drowned out my efforts to bring my uncle's attention to the fact that the other end of the scarf that he wanted to leave at home, the scarf that he was frantically waving whilst standing on his seat, was still fastened around my neck. This meant that I was lifted bodily from my seat and swung about his head.

Death seemed imminent, either from strangulation or from being propelled at speed from the Bramall Lane Stand, probably on to the prostrate form of Gordon West. It didn't really matter. The Blades won a famous victory against the eventual champions and I never had a problem about taking my scarf again.

Wasteney Time With Memories

Dave Wasteney

It's Sunday afternoon and I'm full of Marston's Pedigree and Yorkshire pudding. No football on the telly this week so it's not long before I'm nodding off on the settee. In next to no time thoughts of the Blades fill my head, a few memories of watching United, not in any particular order of importance or relevance. I can't vouch for total accuracy - time and the Pedigree have seen to that - but here are some of the highs and lows that have meaning for me.

There was the Willie Carlin run in the derby at Hillsborough; Colin Addison's header against Everton in the FA Cup; Hodgy 'shooting' at the Kop as he ran towards it; Gil Reece's two headers at Upton Park; going to Derby where we always seemed to lose 3-0, Alan 'White Boots' Hinton scoring two of the goals; being 3-0 down at home to Bristol City before putting on John Tudor, who inspired a comeback to 3-3; travelling on the coach to Stoke when a youth two seats behind us threw up and we had to spend the rest of the journey with our feet up to keep them out of the mess; the atmosphere that night in Birmingham when Kenny Burns was reduced to rugby tackling Billy Dearden; the home game against West Ham in the early seventies when the power strike meant a Tuesday afternoon kick off and Ian Mackenzie marked Clyde Best, just about the best striker about then, completely out of the game. I wonder how many others like myself had time off work to visit the dentist that afternoon!

Gil Reece's two headers at Upton Park came in a 2-1 win over West Ham United on November 6th 1971.

United only lost 3-0 at Derby once, on November 20th 1971.

United drew 3-3 with Bristol City at Bramall Lane on September 5th 1970. Alan Woodward, Bill Dearden and John Tudor mounted the comeback.

The Tuesday afternoon game against West Ham was on February 29th 1972. Billy Dearden's hat-trick took United to a 3-0 win.

Thrashing Ipswich 7-0; Tony Field's amazing goal (I saw it live and on telly and still don't believe it); Don Givens' penalty miss; the games against Arsenal with TC and Alan Ball taking the piss out of each other; Trevor Hockey, bless him, pleading with the referee not to book a Wolves player who'd tried to kick him over the John Street Stand; class like TC, Addo, Woody, Sabella and Deano (amongst others); crap like Terry Garbett, Chris Guthrie, Phil Thompson and David Bradford (amongst many others); away at Burnley when Peter Noble, all five-foot-nothing of him, outjumped Eddie Colquhoun and co. all afternoon and Leighton James at his peak led Len Badger (sadly past his best) a tata, only to sully his reputation by refusing to accept Len's sporting handshake at the end, making gestures instead.

United hammered Ipswich Town 7-0 at Bramall Lane on November 27th 1971. Alan Woodward hit four (one a penalty) and Len Badger, Bill Dearden and Gil Reece one each.

Tony Field's amazing solo dribble was also against Ipswich Town, in a 3-1 win on August 31st 1974. He also scored another, with the third being a Mick Mills own goal.

TC for just being TC. Away at Everton when the car broke down at Heeley and we only got to Goodison minutes before the kick off. We asked a policeman which end was for away fans and followed directions on to their Kop! (I never did get a reply from the Merseyside Chief Constable about this). Anyway, anyone who's been unfortunate enough to suffer the same will know how scary that afternoon was. We were 2-0 down at half time, though Len Badger had hit the post, before Keith Eddy and Bill Dearden levelled it. There was a threat on the air but when TC slotted home the winner near the end the Evertonians went wild. I believe the coaches were stoned and cars were damaged by the mardy Merseysiders. I think we were halfway down the East Lancs Road before we dare celebrate the win!

This was on April 19th 1975.

There are, of course, many more ups and downs, funny incidents and great goals, but one I'll never forget was May 6th 1990. The scene is Manchester airport departure lounge, around midday. Dave is sitting in his Blades tracksuit, morosely watching the flight information on the screens, announcing a six-hour delay on his flight to Spain. Dave's vainly trying to shake off a hangover caused by celebrating promotion the previous day by downing a few pints of Stones.

Suddenly, into the bar area come seven or eight Sheffield Wednesday players, led by Dave Bennett, Jeff King and Nigel Worthington. All are laughing and joking, enjoying their bonus for getting relegated - a week in the sun! Dave can't resist it. as they approach he says, "Hello lads. You look a bit down!"

Seeing his tracksuit their faces drop. They stare stonily at Dave, turn and head back towards the snack bar. No laughing and joking now. Dave doesn't see them again (wonder why) but suddenly his hangover's gone and even the six-hour delay doesn't seem so bad. "There's only one David Bassett!", he sings to himself as he heads towards the bar.

Torn Between Two Lovers

Duncan Payne

"I DON'T BELIEVE IT!!", I yelled in true Victor Meldrew fashion. It was just after 6pm on Sunday November 21st 1999, twenty four hours after Ilkeston Town had been held to a 1-1 draw by Rushden and Diamonds. In the immortal words of Mary McGregor, who hollered back in 1977, in the days when Blades danced to the tunes of Alan Woodward and Keith Edwards first time around, I was Torn Between Two Lovers.

"Sheffield United versus....number 62...... Ilkeston Town or Rushden and Diamonds."

"I don't believe it!!", then the phone rang three times in the space of a minute and a half. I missed the remainder of the draw.

Let me explain. I went to live in Ilkeston in 1989. A Blade for life (© Sean Bean's tattooist), I had first ventured to Bramall Lane eighteen years earlier. Unaware to begin with of Ilkeston's finest, it wasn't until 1992 that I discovered that particular team, who also play in red, white and black.

A 2-1 win over Willenhall in the West Midlands Regional League started my affair. I didn't consider that I was being unfaithful, as after all my two teams were seven divisions apart. There was no chance they'd ever meet.

I started to get more and more involved and in 1995 I became the club's programme editor and a year later my book on the Robins' history was published. Yet I was still a Blade at heart and the 1994 relegation hit me as hard as anyone. The boardroom fiascos, however, pushed my tolerance to the limit. The way the fans have been treated, the systematic dismantling of a talented squad and the destruction of an average team makes it very hard to remain committed.

And all the while Ilkeston were on the up and up. Promotions in 1994, 1995 and 1998, plus two glorious FA Cup runs (well, that's if you count the third round draw a glorious cup run) tempted me away from my first love into the arms of a younger, more inexperienced, but very exciting lover. My first love was getting more spiteful, twisted and nasty. In the guise of Mike McDonald my loyalty was questioned by her. How dare she?

But deep in my heart the feelings remained, which is why was it so agonising, yet exciting, when my two clubs were drawn together in the FA Cup.

How would I react at the match? Would I choose one team ahead of the other? Cheer every goal regardless of who scored? Wear my Ilkeston shirt and my Blades scarf and hat? Where would I sit in the ground? And to be perfectly honest I had no idea then and I still don't know now what I would have done. Apart from feel guilty.

However, Rushden did the decent thing and knocked us (Ilkeston) out, courtesy of a very poor display of refereeing by Alan Hall of Birmingham, and I was saved the agony of being Torn Between Two Lovers.

The Best Match I Have Ever Seen

Derek Goodison

I have always thought that the term 'The Best Match I Have Ever Seen' to be somewhat misleading. Football matches lodge in the memory for a variety of reasons; not always for the outcome, but for fine individual displays, or the importance of the result. The one that sticks in my mind took place in the early part of the 1962/63 season. Why this should be I will explain.

United had achieved promotion two seasons earlier with an excellent side, built on a sound defence, perhaps overly reliant on Derek Pace for goals, but well capable of holding a high place in the top division. The visitors that day were Spurs, slightly off the boil since their double in 1960/61 but still the outstanding side in British football. United took an early lead through Billy Hodgson but against Spurs, with players like Blanchflower, Mackay and Greaves, this could only be described as fragile. Then came the killer goal, the one I can never forget.

Barry Hartle, game as a pebble, but of only delicate physique, drifted down the left wing, attacking the Kop end. Two Spurs defenders moved in, leaving him with but one option: a high, hopeful ball into the box. This must be, alas, a wasted ball. Just two players in the penalty area: one, Doc Pace, hard as nails but only 5'8"; the other, Maurice 'Mo' Norman, the 6'4" England centre half. No contest.

From my seat in John Street I saw a moment of sheer magic. The North London Goliath tensed to win what was an easy ball for him, then Pace, very gently, hand in back, eased him into premature take off. The moment I will never forget. The procession of emotions across the giant's face. First, contempt. This is my ball, and with a eight-inch advantage, nothing can stop me. Then, doubt, horror and finally pure panic, with the realisation that he had reached the apogee of his trajectory and he was nowhere near the ball. Grounded, he watched the ball sail over him and Pace and on to the instep of Len Allchurch, who almost broke the net.

Pandemonium. Norman followed the referee to the halfway line but the ref, listening to the considered judgement of over 39,000 Blades, decided the goal was legit. All that remained was another goal for United (Keith Kettleborough) and a Spurs consolation, followed by an all-out assault on London Road (twelve pints to the pound then).

This match took place on September 22nd 1962.

Thumb You Win, Thumb You Lose

Adrian Bell

Having followed United since birth (1966 - first match against Liverpool, October 1971, 1-1, Currie scored, trainspotters!), and having been a hitchhiker for the last few years, a marriage of

photo: Matthew Bell

United fans celebrate Tony Agana's second goal, and United's fifth, at Leicester

the two was bound to present some unusual experiences. Even more so considering that I live in Brackley, Northamptonshire, which means the only time I can get a bus to the match is when we play Northampton.

Adrian's first match was on October 30th 1971.

The first match I hitched to was the 3-3 FA Cup draw against Colchester in January 1989. I set off at 10am and after about ten different lifts I found myself in Sheffield by 2.30. As we all know, it was a bizarre afternoon. I can't even remember how I got back, but I assume I did.

On January 28th 1989 United played Colchester United, then bottom of the Fourth Division, in a fourth round FA Cup match at Bramall Lane. Colchester quickly went 2-0 up (one of the goals being scored by future Blade Colin Hill), before Mark Todd, Brian Deane and Ian Bryson made it 3-2 to United. In injury time Steve Hetzke headed Colchester's equaliser.

Since then, memorable events have included a rainy hitch after the 0-0 v Port Vale in 1989, a twelve-hour hitch (8am to 8pm, including four hours at Watford Gap and an unintentional sleep with my head on a table at Leicester Forest) to the Manchester United FA Cup match in 1990, hitching to the Blackburn match that

might have decided promotion and getting stuck on the M6, turning round and admitting defeat half way into the second half, with Blackburn still thirty miles away.

United drew 0-0 at home to Port Vale on February 28th 1989, and lost 1-0 to Manchester United at Bramall Lane in the quarter final of the FA Cup on March 11th 1990. United went to Blackburn for the penultimate game of the 1989/90 season on May 1st 1990 needing a win to secure promotion. The match ended 0-0.

And then my personal fave.....that day at Leicester. A little nervous after my experience on the way to Blackburn, I decided to give myself plenty of time for this one, so, with rucksacks and a tent, myself and the girlfriend set off hitching on Friday night.

We got a lift from Watford Gap to Kegworth on the strength of my girlfriend's blonde hair (so the driver said, obviously keen to impress) and in Kegworth we were driven to a campsite by our friendly driver. In the dark we set up our tent only to find in the morning that our 'campsite' was actually one of those private places full of mobile homes and we were camping in somebody's front garden. The residents were very pleased to see us (hmmm) and asked us to disappear before the site supervisor arrived. We did.

We left our gear in station lockers at Leicester and then found the ground. On the way back we got a lift with a Luton fan travelling back from their win at Derby and he was heartily congratulated on his team dumping Wednesday into the Second Division.

Since then my girlfriend has passed her driving test and got a car so the old thumb had a bit of a rest. But then, due to a lack of money (and faith in British Rail) and my girlfriend's lack of desire to travel to Burnley on a cold Tuesday night in January, the thumb was brought out of retirement. Coming back from that match was probably my most satisfying hitch ever, as the M6 at one in the morning is not very welcoming, especially when you're due at work at half past eight. Still, hearty thanks go out to the Preston Blade who got me on my way to the M6 and then the Burnley fan who stopped to pick me up before realising who I was and then didn't deposit me in the fast lane when I told him. I actually arrived in Brackley at 3.30am, being driven right up to my door in a big truck.

This was the FA Cup third round replay at Turf Moor on January 12th 1993. United won 4-2, thanks to a Brian Deane first-half hat-trick and a fourth from Adrian Littlejohn.

After this successful money-saving exercise I decided to have another bash. Unfortunately I couldn't get out of work for the Manchester United cup match (on a Sunday) so I convinced myself that the Middlesbrough match was more important and made a hasty decision to take the afternoon off work and hitch up. Remarkable timing led to me arriving at Meadowhall at seven o'clock and the Lane at 7.30. The trip home was less successful. Trowell services is quiet enough during the day, so imagine how bustling it is at gone midnight. I actually crawled in home at 4.30am and was up for work at eight (groan!).

United beat Middlesbrough 2-0 on February 9th 1993. Franz Carr and Brian Deane scored.

My next hitch followed a tip-off from my dad that people would be arriving for the last five thousand semi-final tickets in the early hours of Tuesday morning so I hastily arranged a day off and set off hitching at nine o'clock Monday night. By midnight I was at Meadowhall and at the Lane by one, having walked all the way because I was too tight to fork out for a taxi. With my feet throbbing I got out my tasteful flowery sleeping bag and slept comfortably on the pavement, surrounded by other assorted lunatics. In the morning my dad brought me a flask of soup, an apple, a banana, and bag of crisps and some cake, which did my hardened traveller image no good at all. Whilst waiting for the queue to start moving I was interviewed by Radio Hallam but I am still to meet anyone who claims to have heard me.

My final hitch of the season was to Goodison. I was on holiday and myself and my girlfriend's brother decided to spend the week hitching. He is from Pangbourne, where the nearest thing to football is Reading, but after Everton he is now a converted Blade (and Glyn Hodges' number one fan after his leisurely amble back to an onside position after one of his polite conversations with Nev the Atomic Dustbin). We arrived in Liverpool via London, Leicester and a very dodgy lift with a Scouser who took us to his 'friendly' local in Toxteth (me with my Blades shirt on too), which was fine if you wanted to pick up some swimsuits stolen from Burton's.

Thanks are due here to the driver of Travel Club coach No.6 who let us leave our rucksacks on the coach during the match and also to the kindly Blade who spotted my shirt at the start of the M62 and went out of his way to drop us at Knutsford services on the M6. Here we met some more Blades and some Stoke fans who were in high spirits, as well as some Sunderland fans who seemed a little less happy with life.

The match took place on May 4th 1993. United won 2-0 with goals from Carl Bradshaw and Glyn Hodges, the latter a follow up after Neville 'the Atomic Dustbin' Southall saved his penalty.

So to all you Blades travelling away, the next time you see a hitcher pick him up - it could be me.

Superstitious... Me?

Denis Wilkinson

I am not normally a superstitious person. Ladders hold no fear for me, I never shirk the thirteenth pint and rabbits' feet are as tasty as the rest of the beast. And yet, as I was getting ready for a match recently, I began to realise that I always follow the same routine. I started to wonder why, in one aspect of my life only, I am careful to do the 'right' things.

Pints
It all started in the mid-sixties when I used to have a couple of pints in the Lansdowne with

my father. After a while we converted another follower and the pint score went to three. It wasn't until my father didn't get to a match one day that the number of pints downed rose to four. It was the 1968 relegation season and things were not going well but with the full encouragement of four pints we beat Coventry 2-0 and superstition was awoken.

This was December 23rd 1967. The scorers were Colin Addison and Alan Woodward.

Humbugs

Despite finding the elixir of success it wasn't enough to prevent relegation and we tried various changes to our Second Division routine in an effort to recover the winning combination. By the time we had got to five pints and changed to Magnet in the Tramway around the middle of the 1969/70 season, we knew we were on the right road but promotion eluded us despite some fine performances. It took an away match at Oxford at the end of January 1971 (Trevor Hockey and John Hope's first match) for us to discover that what the Blades had been really short of wasn't a midfield destroyer or a flash new goalie; it was half a pound of Old Fashioned Mint Humbugs in addition to the statutory five pints!

Bill Dearden scored both goals in a 2-1 win at the Manor Ground on January 30th 1971.

The first season in the First Division was fabulous with the first ten games unbeaten. After that defeat at Old Trafford at the end of October things started to go downhill a bit and hopes of a top six place subsided into a very respectable mid-table finish. But we Blades are made of stern stuff and we hadn't come from two pints to five, from relegation to the top, to be satisfied with a mid-table position.

In succeeding seasons we tried various combinations trying to revive our successes. A change of venue to the Tudor Room in the old Social Club in the cricket pavilion didn't change much but it did mean we could leave the bar later. Inevitably that led to a six-pint pre-match routine. Unfortunately seats R42 to R44 in the Bramall Lane Stand were not convenient for the conveniences. We got a lot of hassle dashing back and forth; my mate was up and down so often I reckon he was the only one in the stand who saw the match standing up. Things had to change and that extra pint wasn't the way to do it.

Mintoes

So it was back to five pints, but what to do to bring back that extra magic? We tried rum and butter toffee, but even when we increased the dosage to half a pound success was still limited. Then the breakthrough came with Nuttall's Mintoes. No fancy stuff, no hypnosis or psychology - simply five pints and half a pound of Nuttall's Mintoes and we could, and did, take on and beat the best. Only a good kicking at Birmingham City in the last match of the 1974/75 season kept us out of Europe but we knew that next season would be ours; we knew how it was done.

We hadn't reckoned that for every winning combination there is an opposite; an anti-luck, as it were. In 1975/76 it took the form of the New South Stand. No matter what we tried we couldn't shake the Blades out of their disastrous run and you know what happens then. Confidence fails, new tactics are tried without success and all the time you get further away from success (sound familiar?!). We accepted relegation about three and a half stones heavier, with rotting teeth and thanks from a booming British booze and sweet industry.

Mansfield

The next few years were eminently forgettable and by the time of the switch to the new Social Club under the dreaded South Stand we thought that things couldn't get worse. As they say, every time somebody closes a window somebody else bolts the door and we were in Division Four. The change of beer to Mansfield seemed to help and by very modest standards we enjoyed a bit of success, winning our only trophy in over fifty years. By this time we had given up on all the combinations of sweets and the five pints were not to bring United luck; they were the only way to endure the match!

And so it went on for a few seasons. I had a couple of illnesses at the beginning of the 1987/88 season and a little later I moved home to 130 miles away from the Lane (for work reasons, not so I could be 130 miles away!). The net effect was that I didn't see too many matches that season but I know that I was not encouraged to see my first match of the season - a 2-1 defeat at home by Millwall, who were promoted to Division One at the end of the season. I did get to the play-off game away at Bristol City and I held out no hope for the next season in Division Three.

The Millwall match was on September 19th 1987 (Richard Cadette scored), while the Bristol City play-off first leg was at Ashton Gate on May 15th 1988. United lost 1-0, drew the second leg 1-1 and so were relegated.

Stones

In the same way that everybody can remember what they were doing when Kennedy was shot, I know that everybody says they were at the famed 6-1 defeat of Chester in September 1988. I was and I have the programme to prove it! It was the start of a new age. Five pints were out of the window, the Social Club had turned over to Stones and I found what I had been searching for for over twenty years; a guarantee of success for the Blades. Now a pair of maroon woollen socks and a pair of red checked Marks and Sparks Y-fronts may not sound like a winning combination but consider what they have done for United. In their first season we got promotion and with ten minutes to go at Molineux it seemed we would even get the win that would give us the Championship.

This was May 9th 1989. When United went to Molineux, Wolves needed a point for the Championship and the Blades needed a point to make sure of promotion. Both teams ended happy in a 2-2 draw. United's scorers were Paul Stancliffe and Tony Agana.

Underpants

Those faithful socks and underpants saw us through the following season so those who were at Leicester on that unforgettable roasting May day will at least now know where the smell was coming from! They saw us through every one of the famous battles against relegation in the early nineties and they even kept the Blades on the straight and narrow when I became fed up of a scrum-down every time I wanted a pint in the Social Club ("We haven't got no glasses luv!").

Defection to the Red Lion and to Wards were taken in their stride with barely an unnecessary defeat. Nowadays the socks are a bit like United's strikeforce - showing their age and thinning a bit. They are more darn than sock. Nevertheless they are pulled out for every match and lovingly taken off immediately afterwards so as to preserve them as long as possible.

Inside Out

At this stage you may be wondering about two things. First, what is this prat rambling on about and second, why am I reading it? Well, I was talking to a mate of mine and in a rare moment of honesty I explained to him the reasons for the Blades' (relative) success in recent years. "No chance", he told me - the reason was he always wore his underpants inside out for the match! Now that set me wondering. Perhaps if we all had five pints before the match, carried half a pound of Old Fashioned Mint Humbugs, or rum and butter toffee, or Nuttall's Mintoes and wore the same socks and underpants (inside out!) we wore for the Chester match, we might just bring enough luck to avoid relegation. It's worth a try, but somehow I don't think it would work.

Can Ya Can Can?

Matthew Bell

One of the all-time favourite Blades chants is the one that goes along to the chorus of the famous 'Can Can' - you know it..... "Na na na na, he's a Blade and he's a Blade...."

Having this song sung in your direction is the ultimate accolade for a Blades fan or player (although the player may not realise it).

Many was the time (it doesn't happen so often nowadays) when a United fan or two would be escorted round the perimeter track at an away ground back on to our end after going on the home end, remaining undetected for a while but then, during a quiet moment in the game, they would bellow at the top of their voices, "United!", or some such identifying cry. Bedlam would soon follow as the home fans realised that opponents were in their midst, the Blades would stand and fight until the coppers came and took them away to a heroes' welcome at our end of the ground.

It is usually players who show one hundred per cent commitment all the time, for whom nothing is a lost cause, who get the crowd geed up, who are recipients of the "He's a Blade and he's and Blade" chant after a crunching challenge or a swashbuckling run. It helps if you're local or have come up through the ranks (e.g. Carl Bradshaw, Dane Whitehouse, Curtis Woodhouse) but it is not exclusive, as the likes of Bob Booker and Mark Patterson have proved.

Anyway, the real reason for this is to try to discover how and where the chant started. I first recall it at a pre-season Group Cup match at Grimsby in 1981, when, for no apparent reason, a group of eight or ten Blades started jumping up and down on the terrace, pointing insanely at each other and shouting "Na na na na, he's a Blade and he's a Blade!"

Were they the inventors? We need to know.

The Group Cup match at Grimsby took place on August 18th 1981. United lost 2-0.

Blades Abroad

Missing All The Fun

Clive Porter

"What have I done to deserve this?" is a thought that must have occurred all too often to United fans, and certainly during the time I have been watching the Blades.

My time as a fan started well enough, in the Second Division at the end of the sixties. There were some great times for an enthusiastic teenager: Everton in the FA Cup, Leeds in the League Cup, and top of Division One in 1971. I remember two thirds of the city wore a happy smile that autumn. Then came the mass exodus to Man United. I was standing on the scoreboard end when Best scored That Bloody Goal....and still maintain he would never have done so had Ted Hemsley still been on the pitch.

As teenage years drew to a close success pushed United to the fore above other, more recently acquired, interests. The 3-2 win at Everton probably remains my favourite away match. Then huge crowds but no goals at Birmingham. People came from all directions. Around midnight we were rather drunk at New Street Station and had several bottles ready for the journey back to Oxford. The policeman told us to behave, as "We've got men all along the line." "Well, they'd better move or they'll get run over," replied Chris helpfully.

Then the rot set in. Relegation and promises unfulfilled in the Second Division. Watching the Blades becomes just a habit, with enthusiasm difficult to maintain. Cambridge becomes my least favourite away match. The police have to restrain Chris from beating his own head against a wall, and the car and the A1 pubs are deathly quiet on the way home.

Hope springs eternal but then comes Boxing Day, and the rest is not worth repeating. Walsall.

The World is rather more alluring than the Fourth Division so I do not renew my season ticket and make travel plans instead. I see the first few matches but a 1-0 defeat at Stockport is not a great send off. Nevertheless, Keith Edwards is signed before I leave and hope is reborn. So I miss the good times of 1981/82.

It was comparatively easy to follow the results in Australia and as United moved to the top of the table I would rush home on Sunday afternoons for the results and reports and pour over the league tables in Monday's 'Sydney Morning Herald'. Generally the news was good and I watched happily as promotion and then the championship were won. However, it was all happening thousands of miles way. My celebrations were solitary; I've only been told about the mass fun and frolics at Darlington.

Perhaps I didn't miss much the following season. I enjoyed life in Australia and I'm pleased that I didn't see Terry Curran playing for United.

During the subsequent promotion season it wasn't just that I missed the ecstasies and agonies involved - it was very hard merely to follow them. I learned of United's good start when I borrowed a paper while travelling on a boat on a Borneo river. English language papers in South East Asia carry details of English football so while I was there I could track the Blades' progress satisfactorily, if in odd circumstances. However, gaps in my knowledge developed when I ventured into more remote areas, so it became a priority when in a large city to find the British Council library to read the papers from home.

Wearing smart clothes usually made it possible to be allowed in. It was disorientating to sit beneath air conditioners discussing the Christmas results in England, only to walk out into the heat, noise and bustle of Calcutta, Bombay or Kathmandu.

Even in India I felt the tension rise as the season neared its end. I had copied a league table and tried to keep it up to date....Hull's goal difference appeared worryingly similar to United's. In the north of the country I was travelling with a Chelsea fan - a drawback that was outweighed by his short-wave radio. We tuned in to the World Service and dear old Paddy Feeney.

One evening we were staying in a spartan old castle above a deep valley. Our three hippy-type companions were somewhat stoned and very bemused as we crouched over the radio (Chelsea were also going for promotion). Both our teams won and our wild celebrations drew guffaws from our laid-back friends. They did, however, provide the means to continue our celebrations.

At the end I was on my own in Delhi. I knew everything depended on Hull's final game. By my calculations they needed to win 4-0. It was twenty four hours after the event that I finally found a sports report on World Service that mentioned Division Three. Hull had only won 2-0. I wanted to jump up and down but there was nobody there who understood. It was only when I got home that I discovered just how close it had actually been.

The next day I flew back to England. I even saw the team coach heading down the M1 for the tour of China. I'd been away two and a half years and missed two promotions.

A Season In Sweden

Mark Corbett

Having been lucky enough to be offered a work placement in Kalmar, Sweden, I was presented with a novel opportunity to follow United's progress during the 1993/94 season. The following matches remain particularly memorable (for differing reasons):-

Blackburn (A) 0-0 (18.10.93) - the game was depressingly dull, but this was no bad thing since I watched it in the pub and I was too distracted by thoughts of my impending departure to Sweden; I was due at the airport 'early doors' the following day.

Sheffield Wednesday (H) 1-1 (23.10.93) - after having only been in Sweden for a few days I quickly became concerned about the responses the Swedes gave when I told them I was from Sheffield.... "Ah, Sheffield Wednesday......Roland Nilsson". Err......no. In light of this, and being delighted that my clock radio could pick up Radio Five, I thought a draw was a fine result.

Chelsea (H) 1-0 (27.11.93) - I got invited to a meal at a colleague's house and had to catch a bus at 4.40 pm. Through the fuzziness of the radio I could just make out that we were still 1-0 up but I had to go! The meal was Japanese and I still wince at the memory of it. I had to wait until Sunday morning to be put out of my misery.

From what I can recall, there then followed a series of depressingly bad results. Every Monday morning my boss would call in to see how I was going on and the first thing he always said to me was, "So I see that you lost.......again." The run was broken by the win over Oldham. One Swedish Man Utd fan told me to "support Manchester United...they're much better than your team." Oh dear.

Christmas fixtures - I was invited to my boss's house for Christmas Eve and a colleague's for Christmas Day. She sent her son (a session musician from Stockholm) to collect me. During the drive to the house he asked, "So where in England are you from?"

I replied, expecting the usual Wednesday/Nilsson response, but instead his face lit up and he said, "Oh yes, Sheffield United! A friend of mine has gone to play for Sheffield United. He's called Jonas Wirmola. How's he doing over there?"

Manchester City (A) 0-0 (19.3.94) - I don't know how many people know this, but on a Saturday afternoon, for most of the season, Swedes have the choice between viewing live football from England or Germany. I was naturally delighted to hear this and enjoyed watching many exciting games. Although my command of the Swedish language could never be described as even passable, I managed to understand that the next live match would be Manchester City v Sheffield United. Great, I thought. The rest is (dull) history.

On Monday morning my boss told me that yes, he had watched the Sheffield United match, initially, but he had to turn over to the other channel for better entertainment, i.e. the German league match (or "Yerman", to quote him correctly). By way of consolation he told me, "Your player Blake was quite good."

West Ham (H) 3-2 (28.3.94) - This was a game we had to win and Radio Five was doing commentary. When we went 2-0 down I cursed, knocked the radio to the floor and wandered into the living room, which had a much more pleasant atmosphere. I shared accommodation with some foreign students, and the gorgeous Raquel, a Barcelona fan, was watching MTV so I told her the score and gratefully lapped up her words of condolence. Imagine my elation, then, when Paul Rogers scored the winner; I've always disliked West Ham and this was the first time in aeons that we'd beaten them.

Liverpool (A) 2-1 (2.4.94) - For an Easter break I went to Copenhagen with Raquel and her friend (another attractive Barcelona fan). I tried several times to find out the score but failed miserably. When I got back to Kalmar I saw the 'News of the World' in a newsagents and within seconds, with mouth wide open, my eyes were feasting on the scoreline. I squealed with delight, received a wary look from behind the counter and bought the paper, despite the fact that it cost £1.70. This was the most surprising United result in a very long time and I wanted to read every word!

I then did a small tour of Sweden before leaving for England (not that I wanted to leave, but my six months were up!). In Stockholm I read about United's best performance of the season (Newcastle at home, 2-0) and in Gothenburg I watched on Swedish Teletext as we drew 1-1 at Oldham. I then returned home on the Friday with Chelsea to come on Saturday. I remember listening to the local radio commentary and being dismayed when we went 3-2 down at the inordinate amount of time it took them to realise that if the scores stayed the same then we were relegated.

That Saturday night was unbelievably depressing - not only had I returned to unemployment but to heartbreaking relegation as well. On the Monday I took a bus to town to begin my quest for Income Support and I remember the clouds over Bramall Lane being frighteningly dark. It was only after Chelsea's 4-0 FA Cup final thrashing that the healing process began!

It's A Pain In Spain

Darren Reid

Growing up as a Blade in the late seventies and early eighties had its fair share of bad moments. The word 'Walsall' will always signify more than just a midlands town, the feeling of seeing the Blades lose 6-0 at Middlesbrough and 5-0 at Leeds was bad, and Boxing Day 1979 seemed the worst. But actually it isn't. It's sheer agony being stuck far away from home with nothing but a radio keeping you informed about how the Blades are doing; the situation I was in in the early nineties.

Having supported United since childhood, to be so far away was difficult to bear. From the mid seventies onwards hardly a Saturday afternoon passed when the United result was not of paramount importance. My final game before departing for Spain was the play off at Bristol City in May 1988. I never thought that training to be a catholic priest would take me so far afield, but the Bishop of Hallam saw differently, and I was sent to the city of Valladolid in northern Spain for six years.

To be asked to spend six years away from United seemed like a life sentence and it was difficult to cope with the obvious void on a Saturday afternoon, mixed with the guilt of not being at the Lane with friends who never miss, and not being able to give support to the lads.

As any true Blade far away from home knows, the agony of being isolated from one's greatest love is indescribable. Love songs and ballads begin to take on new meanings as you yearn for the afternoon at the Lane and returning home to 'Praise and Grumble' on the radio. For that corner of Spain's Castille region became my own Babylon in which I made up an ethnic minority of one.

It's a sort of illness as you are doing something trivial, such as putting the kettle one or going to the shops and you get thoughts like, "I'd be on the coach now" or "It'll be half time now". Clearly it's a sad state of affairs.

The one point of refuge is the BBC World Service, but it is quite diverse and you therefore have to suffer reports on such things as hockey and rugby before finally arriving at that important moment when the results are announced. More often than not is is the bare scoreline that is given, thus you are plunged into the mentally exhausting process of asking yourself a thousand and one questions. Who scored? What was the crowd? Did we wear our away strip even though we didn't need to? Fortunately for me, about ten days after the match these questions were answered as my granny used to send me the 'Green 'Un'.

As you can see, the life of an exiled Blade is psychologically disturbing. It's hard to describe when you're back home in the company of fellow Blades that you miss the love-hate relationship with people you know who support Barnsley, Chesterfield, Leeds and our friends from that bastion of footballing excellence across the city.

One time during the 1988/89 season I was walking down a street in Valladolid and this English bloke heard my voice and made conversation. It was good to meet someone English and on enquiring where he was from he answered he came from Wolverhampton. This evoked a response with regard to our respective positions at the top of the Third Division, as it was then. However, the look on his face gave a clear indication that my seeds for a good footballing conversation had fallen upon stony ground and we soon had to revert to polite discourse.

The frustration was hard. Previously I had never appreciated the joys that surrounded me when I was at home. A good chat with a fellow Blade is sheer joy, reminiscing over past joys and consoling each other over the many bad days, whilst a good argument with an Owls fan was something I craved for. Any exiled Blade will appreciate how desperate this situation is. Once you've experienced the pleasure of watching United regularly (particularly travelling away), life can never be the same. Part of your life is missing once you are in exile.

More and more these days people are living in a transient society, with increased mobility, so it seems that more people are living away from their homes, their beloved and their Blades. Be it on an oil rig, digging the Channel Tunnel, working as a brickie in London or studying to be a catholic priest in Spain, the feeling you get at three o'clock on a Saturday afternoon is the same - one of isolation. So to all Blades, turn out and support the lads and enjoy every minute of it, regardless of the score, but as you dip into your pre-match pint in one of the popular watering holes in the Lane's immediate proximity,

spare a thought for the many Blades far from Bramall Lane, yearning for that unique pleasure of simply being at a United match.

Fever Pitch. U.A.E.

Alan McKee

Christmas 1993 for me was three thousand miles away from Bramall Lane, in the United Arab Emirates. My ideal Christmas present would have been three points against Liverpool on Boxing Day but 'The Gulf News' informed me that I had been deprived of that by inspired goalkeeping and inept finishing.

United drew 0-0 at home to Liverpool on Boxing Day 1993.

However, I was gifted from the UK a package that contained a copy of Nick Hornby's 'Fever Pitch', quite the best book I have read on the subject of football. Regrettably it centres around Arsenal and fluctuates around their frequent Wembley appearances and their boring 0-0 draws at Highbury. It is a book to be recommended to any football fan and therein lies the lead in to my own concise version.

I was brought up to the idea that I could not be a fan but a supporter. What nonsense. I do not know who my mother was trying to kid. I can only assume she was reacting to her father, who as a Glaswegian was a fervent supporter of Third Lanark FC, and he took me to my first game - Third Lanark 1 Partick Thistle 4. Thereafter I was hooked on Scottish football until moving to Sheffield at the age of ten.

Being Scottish and living in England has its advantages. Whenever Scotland play England at football, rugby or even tiddlywinks, there can only be one team to support. However, in the wider arena of sport it leaves you with the option to support England or English teams when Scotland are not represented. Of course any knowledgeable football fan knows that the best players in British football have all been Scots - Jimmy Mason of Third Lanark, Jim Baxter, John White, Denis Law, Dave McKay, even Billy Bremner. Of course there are a few exceptions - Joe Shaw, Alan Woodward, Brian Deane and Tony Currie were all from south of the border but would have graced any Scottish team had they found Scottish ancestry.

Being Scottish also means that the first thing you do when going to a match is, having complained about the price of the programme, you immediately turn to the team biographies to determine which opposition players are Scottish - you already know that the best United players were Toner, Howitt, Colquhoun and Hamilton. Indeed, Willie Hamilton should always be included in any greats of Britain squad for some of the performances he gave at the Lane and later in his career, but all too briefly, at Villa. He exemplified Scottish footballers - skilful, visionary, temperamental, suicidal. There are of course exceptions to every rule and I am certainly not moronic enough to think that Bone, Houston and certainly Dougie Brown, the worst centre forward I ever saw, could be considered as true Scots. Perhaps they had English ancestors. To bring the argument more up to date I must have seen Tom Cowan through tartan glasses as he always looked to me to be a good competitor, but the true Scot of recent years of course has been Ian Bryson, whose contribution in the lower divisions was matched only by Deane's.

How a ten year old Third Lanark follower should come to be a Sheffield United supporter is another story. It could so easily have been Wednesday for on my first day at school in Sheffield I was set upon by a gang of youths in blue and white scarves who demanded to know which team I supported. As a born coward, and with previously acquired knowledge of who plays in what colours, I admitted that Wednesday was going to be my team. However, nobody is ever going to tell a true football fan who he is going to support. It happens. Thereafter it had to be United.

Since that day I have been faced with many situations that indicate I may have made the wrong choice but I alone know it was right. Within months of being in Sheffield I went to a scout camp and have since been told on good authority that one Roy Hattersley was a fellow camper with a troop from Walkley. I cannot remember him but no doubt he tried to convert me. Two of my contemporaries at school, who today are eminent Professors of Education and Russian, were both avid Wednesday fans. This probably indicates that the more intellectual amongst us support Wednesday but again I must have resisted their approaches. One of my wife's best friends is married to a man whose family were Wednesday directorate of the past. Bearing in mind that my English home has been in Warwickshire for more than thirty years it was probably no surprise when I went to dinner with another of my wife's friends, admitted my allegiance to United, only to be told by the host that if his father had been present I would not have been allowed through the door. His father was

Billy Frith, one time player and manager of Wednesday.

Nevertheless I have given United unwavering support through four decades, despite not having lived in the city since 1962. Nick Hornby conceived meaningful chapters around a large number of matches involving Arsenal (and Cambridge United). He has the advantage of being considerably younger than me and has probably kept all his programmes to jog his memory. All I can do is sum up the multitude of games I have seen in one paragraph.

From my first match at the Lane, which I remember as being United reserves versus Blackburn Reserves, to my last before departing for these sunny climes, the 2-2 draw with Spurs in September 1993, the sheer unpredictability of the team's performance and the wit and cynicism of supporters has made every game an experience.

The 2-2 draw against Tottenham Hotspur was at Bramall Lane on September 11th 1993. Adrian Littlejohn scored both United's goals.

The opportunity to see matches at Liverpool, Manchester United and Newcastle, as well as Aldershot, Crewe, Newport and Scunthorpe does not present itself to every football fan.

Sam Hashimi had dreams of away matches in Jeddah, Riyadh, Baghdad and probably even here in downtown Sharjah (I live within 100 yards of the Al Shaab Stadium), but thankfully he never got control.

It is impossible to conceive a conclusion to any football-related story because there is no ending. The game goes on even though some of us are not there to see it. United will survive as they have always done and we can only be thankful for the memories they have given us over the years and shout and cheer them on to further glories.

Blades On Vacation

The Cantley Critic

Holidays in my household are usually confined to June and July (i.e. out of season), so it was much to the other half's surprise when in deepest winter I came to announce that I had booked for Ibiza in October. She thought I was ill, or was looking for an excuse to spend even more time than usual watching the Blades in the months ahead.

I had to confess that, on reflection, maybe it wasn't a wise move; it could have been the weekend of the derby match or some other top Premier League action. I needn't have worried - the players saw to that on May 7th. When the fixtures came out it was Luton at home and Millwall away. A sigh of relief. Luton, full of star names such as Kerry Dixon, and a trip to the Den is as attractive as a few rounds with Frank Bruno. It was also the Fizzy Pop Cup in between; unusually we qualified for the third round. I hoped for Brighton away but typically we got a home draw against Bolton.

The build up to the holiday had not been good. Crap against Barnsley, even worse at West Brom. The excuse of the sacking of their manager was a bit thin.

United drew 0-0 at home to Barnsley on October 16th 1994 and lost 1-0 at West Brom two days later.

Anyway, as we set off down the M1 for East Midlands Airport, Harry (Bassett) comes on Radio Sheffield, spelling out the problems and his threats to the strikers if they do not perform. Hardly the way to go about things - threats are well known to be demotivating.

We are soon on our way; the flight is very comfortable in my Blades travel suit, and after the usual hotel transfer and short kip we settle by the pool in our pleasant and quiet hotel. It's almost the end of holiday season and thankfully the normal contingent of Herr Klinsmann's brethren are conspicuous by their absence. It's warm and very relaxing as I lay on the sunbed reading Linda Hoy's book, 'United on Vacation'.

"Is it good dad?" asks my eleven year old. "Aye, the guy's on Praise and Grumble", I reply.
"Can I borrow it?" he says.

I knew it, you never get much peace, despite me carting him off to the 'Big T Club' whenever I can. The day passes, I look at the watch - four o'clock. It's half time, wonder what the score is?

Wife's becoming agitated, "I knew it, you can never give it a rest."

At 5.15 it's time to get the result. The hotel entertainer, who seemed a decent bloke until he appeared in a Chelsea away strip, said he had access to satellite television and would get all the scores. My son, unable to contain his enthusiasm, dashed off to meet him (complete with his spanking new jade away kit, bought at considerable inconvenience on the first day of sale). He

returned looking glum - we've lost 3-1.

"He's winding you up", says me, "Kelly won't have let three in against **them**."

Sadly he wasn't and the Sunday paper (available in Ibiza on Sunday) confirmed that both sides had scored twice, except that Ryan Bayle, sorry, Brian Gayle, had scored for the opposition. "Useless buggers", I think. First home game I've missed since Division Three and they blow it.

United lost 3-1 at home to Luton on October 22nd 1994. Nathan Blake scored.

Two or three pints of lager later (£1 a pint!) I get over this one and start looking forward to Bolton. The clocks have changed so we are now one hour ahead. It's half nine here and I wonder if unbiased Don (even bigger Blades nut than me) is delirious or in despair. The night passes and I get roped in by the Chelsea-ite to captain a quiz team in the hotel bar. A collection of Man United, Newcastle, Liverpool and Arsenal shirts in my team but, par for the course, we lost. The other team had more questions - well, that's my excuse, but any argument with the Shed thug only results in a bonus point to the other team!

Wednesday morning and no news yet on last night. I thought about ringing the Bladesline but I'd probably be out of 100 Pesetas coins by the time they got round to the score. So it's off to play tennis against my lad. At least I won that - poor kid, all he's done so far is lose. As we come off court my eyes suddenly come across another Blade.

On approach I made the first move, "You don't support **them** do you?"

"Yes", came the reply, "I said to the wife you were a United supporter. I recognised you from the matches, you and your pal with the flat cap (unbiased Don again). We lost last night. Andy Scott own goal in the last minute."

United lost 2-1 at home to Bolton Wanderers in the third round of the Coca Cola (League) Cup on October 25th 1994.

I couldn't believe it. No, of course I could, anything is believable with United. We had a right good natter. Why we were relegated, what Bassett should have done, where he was going wrong, where the skill was in the team (?), what we would do, what the prospects were for the rest of the season etc. Not surprisingly there were more bad things than good. He filled me in on the depressing details of the Luton game; I told him about West Brom. We agreed who to sell, if anyone would buy them. We weren't going to Millwall but would be back all full of optimism at Stoke and would endeavour to seek each other out.

By now I had finished Linda Hoy's book. At least this had a happy ending after the usual ups and downs of a United supporter.

Soon be time for heading back home. Unbiased Don should have taped Ian St John's amateurish effort on Leeds TV, along with 'Your Match'. He should also have dropped in the 'Green 'Un' and the match programmes. I was looking forward to these; maybe now not very much.

Me And The Handsworth Blades

James Slack

When I was on holiday in a place called Alvor, Portugal, something magical and unusual occurred - Sheffield United consistently won football matches.

For various uninteresting reasons, I was forced to holiday mid-season and miss the matches against Norwich, Charlton, Barnsley, Bury and Huddersfield. At the time of my departure this was not an overtly depressing prospect. Five games, five defeats, no stand and a crooked (expletive) of a chairman.

Fourteen sun-drenched days later, ten points had been amassed, the might of Bury had been (temporarily) dispatched, the crooked (different expletive) of a chairman had gone and threats were being made concerning the building of the new stand. Coincidence? No.

After five consecutive defeats to start the 1995/96 season United beat Norwich City 2-1 at Bramall Lane on September 1995. Nathan Blake and Carl Veart scored. They then beat Charlton 2-0 (Blake 2), drew 2-2 at Barnsley (Blake 2), beat Bury 2-1 (Dane Whitehouse pen., Veart) in the Coca Cola Cup and won 2-1 at Huddersfield (Jostein Flo, Glyn Hodges).

Sheffield United did not start to win matches because Nathan Blake was a man possessed, it was not because Glyn Hodges decided he could give a toss, and Reg the (expletive) did not leave because Laver and Procter stopped the staff's salaries.

In September 1995 the players' and staff's salaries went unpaid. It was seen as a rebellion by Messrs Laver and Procter against the incumbent Chairman Reg Brealey, and went a long way towards finally forcing out Mr Brealey.

It was because of me and the Handsworth Blades.

The story goes like this. On the Saturday of the Norwich match I had just arrived. At 3pm I nervously made my way to the nearest Sky-brandishing pub and set about drinking a large amount of strong lager in order to dull the pain that a sixth defeat would bring. And then it happened. I looked up behind the bar and saw the old white away shirt, emblazoned with the words 'Handsworth Blades'. Only five shirts hung in that bar - England, France, Ireland, the annoyingly ubiquitous Manchester United shirt, and ours. Someone had got their priorities in order and I was in heaven. It was just a matter of time before the angels started singing. Goalflash - Carl Veart. Agonising wait. Joy.

I did the same thing for the Charlton game. Go in the juicer before kick off, look up at that shirt, and wait. More joy. Bury. Joy. Huddersfield. Joy.

It is now, however, that I must make my apologies (as I have since done) to anyone who had to watch the first half of the Barnsley match. Due to the (not unreasonable) protestations of my girlfriend, I didn't make it into the pub until half time that day. Me and the Handsworth Blades could only salvage a point. Sorry.

The purpose of this story is simple. Whilst most of you probably remain unconvinced, I know that the 'Handsworth Blades' shirt is magic. Whenever it is united with a Blade on matchday, victory will undoubtedly follow.

Should Sheffield United, unlikely as it seems, make it to a final I will be faced with a very unpleasant dilemma. Do I go to Wembley and pray that United can win the game for themselves, or do I go back to Portugal and the Handsworth Blades, thereby making victory inevitable?

The bar is called, originally enough, the 'French Bar' and it is situated at the top end of Alvor. If, as I really hope, those Handsworth Blades are reading this, your shirt is still hanging proud and is still radiating magic. I owe you all a pint. Good work fellas!

Dawn In Cornwall

Nick Davies

Anybody who has been a Blade for more than five years has a tale or two of misery to tell. In a gathering of any Blades conversation will inevitably turn to the Boxing Day Massacre, Don Givens' penalty miss, the sale of Tony Currie etc. etc.

In many ways I've been fortunate. Having started watching United in the halcyon days of Currie and Woodward I moved away from Sheffield at the end of the 1976/77 season. The first season after relegation had just been completed and the introduction of the nascent talents of Edwards, Kenworthy, Stainrod, Hamson and McGeady augured well for the future, a hideous home destruction by Blackpool in my final game notwithstanding.

United were beaten 5-1 at home by Blackpool on April 12th 1977. The only saving grace was that Keith Edwards scored for the eighth consecutive game, a post-war record for the club.

As my train pulled out of the Midland station that spring morning my heart was gladdened by the thought of my return to Sheffield in a couple of years to once more take my place on the Kop with United by then firmly re-established in the First Division. Little did I realise the length of time circumstances would contrive to keep me away from my home city, nor the horrors that would befall the club in my absence.

I didn't actually get to return until January 1990, just in time to witness the triumphant climax to that unforgettable season. Thirteen long years away! You get less than that for murder these days. And God, it must have been rough for those I left behind, having to live and work alongside gloating Wednesdayites during those dark and dismal days.

Mind you, it was no picnic for we exiles. The bulk of my time away was spent in deepest Cornwall and it was lousy spending Saturday afternoon hunched over a radio followed by a wait until Tuesday for the 'Green 'Un' and Monday's 'Star' before sense could be made of the latest tragedy. At one point I actually found myself sharing an office with four Owls fans! They were a typical bunch. Two were from Barnsley, one only followed Wednesday because her last boyfriend before she left Sheffield did and the other was Cornish born and bred. As a youngster, his favourite sporting personality was

Fred Trueman and apparently some weird Celtic logic dictated that he should support a football team from Yorkshire. He liked the name Wednesday probably because it was cattle market day in his home town, or something. To be pitied.

My only rather bitter consolation in those early days was that the sorry fact that United were relegated to Division Three resulted in visits to Home Park, that football hotbed that is the home of the mighty Plymouth Argyle, so at least I would get to see my team. Actually such a pilgrimage (sorry, couldn't resist the pun) degenerated into one of my most depressing memories of a lifetime following the Blades. At the time I was dallying with a charming young thing by the name of Dawn. As one does, I had spent many a post-coital moment extolling the wonders of the Red and White Wizards and so it was with mutual anticipation that we planned to journey up the A30 for the visit of the Blades.

A couple of weeks before the match things started to go wrong for Dawn and I. One night in the pub she announced that a friend of the family was coming to stay for a few months; an Italian called Giovanni. Being of similar age, Dawn was assigned to look after him during his stay in Blighty. One or two alarm bells rang. Dawn was nothing if not impressionable and what chance did I stand against smooth Latin charm? I needn't have worried on that score. Giovanni was a pasty, podgy looking man with a careworn face and sad demeanour. More Robert Morley than Robert de Niro. Nevertheless he definitely had designs on the soft and lustrous flesh of young Dawn. He dogged her every step with a dreamy look in his eyes and gifts were showered upon her. We never seemed to get a minute alone (not a happy set of circumstances in my testosterone-fuelled youth) and he made it very plain that he wasn't fond of me, his perceived rival, either. Within a week I was beginning to find him downright bloody irritating and I am thoroughly ashamed to relate that a latent xenophobia burst to the surface, viz.:

Giovanni: "For why Neek call me Wop?"
Dawn's dad: "Just the English being ignorant son."

Considering the burgeoning mutual hatred I was surprised one evening when my bedroom door opened to reveal Giovanni. I moved away nervously, scanning the hall behind him for violin cases and horses' heads, and fearing a kiss on the cheek. We stared mutely at each other until he broke the silence in hesitant tones. "Neek,

Tony Kenworthy

Paul Casey

photos: Andy Greaves

can I see your sweeming trunks?" Startled, I searched the room for a blunt instrument. But it turned out that he fancied a dip and he wished to examine my swimwear with a view to borrowing it. Cheeky salad-dodging git, he had a good four stones on me.

The week before the match he whisked Dawn off to London for a few days. Despite her protestations that she found him as attractive as a cold lasagne, I brooded darkly during their absence. They returned from London and I brooded further. A chasm was developing between Dawn and I, measured by her swift termination of our embraces and the forced nature of our conversations. And Giovanni was looking smug.

The parlous state of my love life was briefly forgotten as we caught the train to Plymouth for the eagerly awaited day. Dawn, Giovanni and I were accompanied by Malc, a fellow exile from Mansfield who had no particular interest in the match but who was keen to hear some northern voices. I even achieved an uneasy rapport with Giovanni as I attempted to explain to him the wonders of supporting the Blades and all that it entailed. He smiled politely and uncomprehendingly.

The match was an unmitigated bloody disaster. Plymouth stuffed four goals past a woeful United side and memories of childhood walks back to Pond Street with tears in my eyes and murder in my heart sprang readily to mind. Yet again the Blades had betrayed me.

This was on April 19th 1980. United lost 4-1, Paul Casey scoring the goal. Tony Kenworthy had a penalty saved.

The other three were embarrassingly silent as we trudged from the ground and then suddenly the day got even worse.

Anybody familiar with Home Park will be aware that the ground is situated on top of a hill with an enormous park running down to the railway station about a mile and a half away. We had just begun the descent when I heard a commotion behind us and turned to see about twenty of Shoreham Street's finest running towards us. Their demeanour didn't suggest that they wanted to ask us the quickest route to the station and this was further evidenced by their informing us loudly that we were going to get our effing heads kicked in. A dilemma! Did I hold my ground and explain that I was a Blade or did I run like buggery? The sight of Dawn and Malc already halfway down the hill decided the issue and off I set. I don't know what made me look back but there was Giovanni, rooted to the spot, haplessly fumbling through his pockets. Every instinct screamed that I should leave the bastard there but after wrestling with my conscience I couldn't do it. Maybe it was something to do with the picture of hopeless innocence he presented but I found myself going back and screaming at him to run. He just stood there looking forlorn and muttering something about his ticket, but the hordes were now only about fifty yards away. With the aid of sign language I managed to explain that these gentlemen were going to kick us to a pulp and that did it. He was off like a greyhound and for a fat lad he was really swift. Must have trained in the Italian army I suppose. We got away and arrived back at the station. Dawn went into conference with the hapless Giovanni who, it had transpired, had lost his train ticket. "The stupid bastard", said Dawn, "he did this in London as well. He wants you to explain to them that he's Italian so they will let him on the train."

I paid for another ticket for Giovanni and we made a very subdued journey home. A few days later Dawn came to see me. She explained that she had fallen for Giovanni and that when she finished her A-levels in a few months she would be going back to Rome with him. And that was the last I ever saw of the pair of them.

A Meeting With Sheffield United - New South Wales. May 1994

Mickey Brock

It's taken a bit of arranging but we're finally going to meet up with Dave Bassett and the boys at long last. I feel quite honoured to see them as their schedule has been a punishing one to say the least. Hardly have they had time to think about the jet lag, let alone get over it, and they are playing a series of matches against teams they know nothing whatsoever about.

The meeting is still three and a half hours away but everything is in readiness. I've got one of our exclusive 'UK Soccer Supporters Downunder' T-shirts to present to Dave Bassett and another that we are hoping to get signed by the players. I have my camera for those all-important photos of events and an extra little surprise that I am hoping to spring on Mr Bassett at some stage of the evening.

Stuart is to pick Dylan and myself up and we are hoping that 'The Mars Bar Kid' Dylan is on time for once as time is something we are short of. We are to meet Clint at Mickey 'West Ham's' place at 5.30 and then it's off to the Mitre 10 Stadium in Newcastle for the big rendezvous. To say that Clint is a little excited about meeting his beloved Sheffield United team is like saying that I suppose I would put up with winning the Lotto! I only hope that he does not curtsey or start dribbling at the mouth.

Everything is now ready: directions to Mickey's place at hand, Rupert Bear scarf ready to wear to show neutrality. All I have to do now is wait for the guys to show and we will be on our merry way. The best thing is we are going to see an English side playing in our own backyard.

Mind you, I wouldn't have minded if it were a Scottish team that was playing. I'd even go to see Banbury United if they came out. Well, I did spend years watching them as a boy.

Both the lads are on time and I have to admit that Stuart and myself are a little taken aback at the Mars Bar Kid's punctual arrival. Most unusual for the boy. Off we go into the wild and windy May afternoon and the topic of conversation for the entire trip is........football. We do come up with a few jokes about United especially for Clint's pleasure but he would hear none of it. I did like Mickey's one about the Blades keeping their balls in the fridge to condition them for the long, high ball tactics they employ. Unfortunately United did not use these tactics during the game and all the geeing up beforehand was wasted. Well done to Dave and the boys.

Whilst waiting for Clint, Mickey's delightful wife Veronica made us all a cuppa and his daughter kept us amused with her painting and her renditions of 'The Hammers'. Beautiful little girl, if somewhat misguided by her father.

Clint duly arrived and we set off to the Mitre 10 Stadium - or so we thought. I had arranged to meet up with Dave and the team before the game but, as things transpired, it was to be a private meeting afterwards. Mickey took the co-driver's seat because he is a big lad and he knew where the Mitre 10 Stadium was. So we arrived at the home of the Newcastle Knights - the Marathon Stadium - about five minutes before the time we were supposed to be at Mitre 10. It did cross our minds as we pulled into the empty car park that this might not be the correct venue and the big fella apologised and muttered something about "thinking it was here."

A quick about-turn, cross the road to the 'servo' for directions (which Mickey and Stuart managed to totally confuse between them) and it was off again for a tour of ALL the lovely roundabouts Newcastle has to offer before finding a taxi driver to ask for further directions. Apparently we had been on the right road about half a dozen times already! It was close to 7pm when we finally got to the stadium and we were an hour behind schedule and there was nowhere to park. Straight up to the guy in charge of VIP parking and after explaining the story to him he allowed us to park right outside the ground. Terrific! Now to find Gary Williams - he is the organiser of the entire tour and a more helpful person you could not wish to meet, and ranking as highly in that department are Dave Bassett and the entire Sheffield United team. Mr

Williams let Clint and myself in but as it was close to game time he suggested that we come back after the match and he would see what he could do.

The match itself was entertaining enough with all those watching deciding that Northern N.S.W. probably shaded the first half after some fine moves by the Blades early on. Due to a bad error at the back the Blades went in to half time 1-0 down. The half-time entertainment included two vehicles being driven on to the pitch and a bevy of dancing beauties disgorging themselves from the innards, much to the pleasure of the United substitutes who were (supposed to be) warming up, but who spent a great deal of time watching the girls and even trying some of their moves. One can only hope that Mr B was not watching. Credit where it's due though - Nathan Blake is a natty little mover.

United were far more imposing in the second half and the introduction of Blake and Glyn Hodges seemed to improve the flair of the side. Nat had three half chances that all missed by a fraction but on any other day could have netted him at least one. It looked like being one of those nights until a free kick was awarded just to the right of the box. As the players jostled in the area up strode Hodges and planted the ball into the top left hand corner of the net with a sweetly-struck shot that was worth the admission fee alone. Hodges turned out to be a little bit of a larrikin and he even offered Mickey one of the balls because it was a tad flat although the ball boy would not let him keep it. The score remained at 1-1 but it was a most entertaining game and it was great to have the chance to see a team from the UK out here after so long a wait.

Time to present Dave with the shirt now and try to get the other one signed and once again Gary Williams was on hand to help us out. Clint was busy collecting autographs while I waited for Dave to finish an interview with the local reporters. Gary suggested going into the dressing rooms to meet the players and it was an invitation that neither of us needed to be asked twice about. I have to say that Sheffield United are often referred to as 'The Family Club' and that is an opinion that I would most certainly back up without reservation. They could not have been kinder or nicer to everyone and that includes about twenty five children who were already there. They happily signed autographs for all and not once did they refuse even though there were an awful lot of people wanting to collect them. Fantastic bunch of lads and a credit to their club.

Dave Bassett entered the room and we finally got the chance to speak to him and to get that all-important picture of him holding up his latest prized possession - a 'UK Soccer Supporters Downunder' T-shirt. At first he thought we wanted him to sign it but after reassuring him that it was for his good self he seemed quite happy with it. I got a photo of Clint with the great man and with a couple of other players and eventually felt cheeky enough to ask for a favour. Dave listened patiently and then invited us back to their private reception to get the other shirt signed by the team. This was not something that we were expecting but we gratefully accepted. This also shows what an extremely nice man Dave is and the Blades are as a whole. Nothing at all is too much bother or trouble for them. I had a self addressed envelope containing some pages that I hoped to have signed by the team at some stage and asked if it would be possible, perhaps at some later date, for it to be posted back from anywhere in Australia. Dave called somebody over and I thought I had gone too far this time but he explained the situation to the man who who casually replied, "I'll get the boys to do it on the bus in the morning and pop it into a post box. Not a problem."

What a dynamic bunch of blokes and not one of them too big for his boots.

Inside the reception area it was friendly and pleasant but these two words do not go far enough in their expression. Dylan wanted Nathan Blake's autograph, which was the first one I managed to get and he signed the shirt as well. The rest of the team were only too happy to contribute their signatures to it and it was then that Glyn Hodges said to me, "Did you get your ball?" and I had to reply that we did not but it shows that the players do actually take notice of people round the pitch and, more to the point, remember them! Be warned the next time you are having a go at a player because they will know who you are afterwards.

Having collected all the autographs I thanked Dave and the lads and their reply was with one voice; "Any time and thanks for coming." As I was about to leave I bumped into Clint who was completing his set of autographs, Stuart was getting photos of himself and the players and I realised just what a privilege it had been for us to be allowed into what is in all senses the players' relaxation time. Did it bother them? Not one little bit! Unfortunately I did not get chance to thank Gary Williams before leaving but rest assured that this has now been done.

A great night was had by all concerned and I haven't even mentioned that Clint was presented with a Sheffield United badge by none other than Dave Bassett himself and was he pleased or what!

All that remains to be said is many thanks to Dave and the playing staff of the Blades and a massive thank you to Gary Williams for his help in making it all possible. It most certainly was a real pleasure for us all.

The Blades In Sweden

Matthew Bell

When in summer 1988 fellow Blade Bob Hukin asked me, "How about going to Sweden to watch United?", my first reaction was "What?!".

Then I realised it wasn't such a daft idea after all - what could be better than combining a holiday with watching the Blades? After several phone calls and visits to the Lane we finally got hold of a fixture list and, assured that all the games would be within sixty miles of Stockholm, we flew from Manchester aiming to see the first two matches of the tour.

Our first task on arriving in Stockholm was to find a hotel and after being installed in a £35-a-night doss house we set out on Saturday morning to find out where in the locality IK Hugh and Ljusdals IF had their homes. "They'll know at the tourist office," we thought, so off there we went. The man at the tourist office could not have been more helpful but he had a shock in store for us. He looked at our fixture list and said, "This team (IK Hugh) I've never heard of but this team (Ljusdals IF) is three hundred kilometres north of Stockholm." Thanks very much United - sixty miles indeed.

Now, Sweden is unlike England in that everything is shut on Saturdays. Our friend rang the Swedish FA and several newspapers in an attempt to find the whereabouts of IK Hugh but there was nobody at home anywhere. "Come back this afternoon," he said, "I'll find out by then."

So now we had to find a way of getting to Ljusdals. The station proved a dead loss as trains to Ljusdals were about as frequent as Wednesday's victories and there was no way we could get back to Stockholm for Tuesday morning, when we were to fly home. The only other option was to hire a car and the only one we could get hold of was an enormous Volvo 740 at £68 per day. We hadn't come all this way to let a few quid stop us seeing the Blades so we paid up and drove our first few tentative yards in our left-hand-drive limo.

So come the afternoon we went back to the tourist office to be greeted by, "Good news and bad news." The good news was that the Ljusdals match was definitely on and that he'd found out where IK Hugh played; the bad news was that that match was off. But he did tell us that another minor event was taking place in Stockholm that night - Sweden v Brazil, so to our intense disappointment we had to make do with a poor substitute for watching the Blades - we were forced to suffer the skills of Taffarel, Jorginho, Andre Cruz, Romario, Bebeto, Muller, Roland Nilsson, Jonas Thern and Martin Dahlin in a 1-1 draw (and in the Sweden v Denmark youth game that preceded the main event, Coventry City keeper Magnus Hedman was playing).

We set off north for Ljusdals after the match, kipped in the car Sunday night and arrived in the one-horse town of Ljusdals on Monday. We drove around for a while then headed back into town and who should we see walking down the main street, beer cans in hands? Yes, it was good old Andy Jowett, a well-known face on the Kop, with three other Blades. So we weren't the only loonies.

We got down to the small stadium in good time for the match and I can't imagine a more pleasant setting for a football ground. There was a lake literally only feet behind the small main stand and beyond the lake was a pine-covered hillside. The first thing we saw was a Union Jack alongside a Swedish flag fluttering behind one goal. It seemed that the locals were treating this as seriously as an international match.

After a few minutes the players started coming out to warm up. The first to appear was Chris Wilder, and when Bob shouted "All right Chris!", he looked up, quite bewildered. I asked someone where the toilets were and we were directed towards a wooden hut in the corner of the stadium, in the area where the players were coming from on to the pitch. I walked in the door to be greeted by Martin Pike wearing only a jockstrap. We had been directed to United's dressing room! I thought better of it and went to relieve myself behind a bush by the lakeside.

Meanwhile the ever-increasing crowd was being kept amused by the antics of Jowett and friends as they joined in the players' warm up, beer cans still in their grasp. Ten minutes before kick off the teams entered side by side and lined up in front of the stand and were introduced one by one (including our new triallist, Iron Bryson, as the announcer said it). This was also our first sight of Brian Deane and the first thing that struck me was the length of his legs. After all the players had been introduced we then stood while the national anthems were played! The United team seemed just as surprised as we were.

So now to the match. The game was only two minutes old when we saw something close to a miracle. It appeared that in the three months since May Paul Williams

Ljusdals IF versus Sheffield United, Sweden, August 1988

photo: Matthew Bell

had learned how to control the ball with his chest! He did it not once or twice, but three times in the first few minutes. And then, after Deano had put us in front, he scored! We were stunned.

Ljusdals pulled one back but Webbo put United 3-1 up with a header from a corner. The second half saw Cliff Powell and Peter Duffield on for Pike and Deane and Ian Bryson soon made it 4-1 after a strong run down the left. Deane and Pike then came back on again for Williams and Wilder and the match drifted aimlessly to full time.

We found out during the second half that we were sitting in front of the local press, who seemed quite knowledgeable about United. They knew all about Billy McEwan and Dave Bassett, and knew that we had lost to Bristol City in the play-offs. One thing they didn't know, though, was why United are "The Blades" and they seemed a bit disappointed when we explained that it was nothing more sinister than a link with Sheffield's cutlery industry.

So it was back to our plush hotel after the match but Andy Jowett and friends had no such luxury. We gave them a lift back to the station, where they intended to spend the night, only to get booted out. Jowett's response was, "Let's kip in t'forest!", but I don't know whether they actually did so. They were staying in Sweden for the rest of the tour but we had to drive back to Stockholm the next morning.

The rest of the results showed that we had seen United's toughest match as we won the other three by nine, seven and twelve goals, but it seemed it was ideal preparation considering the way United played in the 1988/89 season.

Peeing at Pompey. Toilet facilities are not always what they might be at some grounds!

photo: Andy Greaves

Heroes And Villains

The Barracking Boys

Ken Cotterill

Many players over the years have been picked out by the crowd as subjects of abuse. One player who deserved a good old-fashioned barracking was a slightly built, crop-headed outside right from Glasgow, John Docherty. John came to United from Brentford for a £6000 fee in March 1961 but had trouble securing a first-team place in his early days due to the presence of Len Allchurch. Yet once Len began to fade Docherty made the No.7 shirt his own.

He was a mercurial and frustrating player, jogging down the right wing in an inflated shirt that made him look like the Hunchback of Notre Dame. His performances could at best be described as lethargic, yet somehow he seemed immune to criticism. For a short period he even managed to keep a young Alan Woodward out of the side, but Docherty's Waterloo was not long in coming.

In the early stages of the 1965/66 season Docherty's career reached great heights and dredged great depths. Against West Ham in early September he scored a good goal and set up a number of others as the rampaging Blades pounded Jim Standen's goal. For the first time in memory the stirring, emotional cry of "Docherty! Docherty!" reverberated around the ground. This game was the high point of Docherty's United career. Then came the low, about six weeks later, in a home game against Chelsea.

Docherty was having a stinker and the crowd, particularly at the John Street side of the ground, was letting him know it. However, in the second half, as United attacked the Bramall Lane end, Docherty found himself with the ball at his feet facing an empty Chelsea goal. Whether this was all too much for him I don't know, as he simply froze. The incident was like a film in freeze-frame; the open goal, no Chelsea players within a hundred miles, Docherty and the ball six yards out. Fortunately, a Chelsea defender, thinking Docherty was about to score, launched himself Superman-like at Docherty, sending him crashing to the ground. Relief oozed from the crowd as the referee pointed to the penalty spot, but delight turned to horror as it became obvious who was going to take the kick - Docherty!

Quick-witted Yorkshire wags were rendered gaga as our hero placed the ball in a funereal atmosphere. Docherty placed his kick well to Peter Bonetti's right but the keeper threw himself, stretching low for a save. Somehow the ball brushed Bonetti's fingertips to plop like a jelly into the Chelsea net. United 1 Chelsea 0! Of course this was to good to be true on an ominous afternoon. Tommy Docherty's young side hit back with two fine goals, with the winner coming from a very raw Peter Osgood.

And John Docherty? As far as I know he never played in the first team again, returning to Brentford in 1966.

The West Ham game was on September 4th 1965. United won 5-3 with goals from Mick Jones 2, Alan Birchenall, Docherty and Keith Kettleborough. The Chelsea defeat took place on October 30th.

One United player from the 1960s who was badly affected by merciless barracking was Keith Kettleborough. Keith was often the architect behind the Jones-Birchenall scoring machine and although he was not in the Tony Currie class (who was?!) he could win a game with an accurate defence-splitting pass or a thumping volley. When Ket was on song so were the Blades, and his midfield skills earned him England 'B' recognition. Sadly, for some unfathomable reason, he became a target of the blockheads. This became so vicious that Kettleborough stated in the press that he actually preferred playing away than at the Lane. Not surprisingly he left to join Newcastle early in 1966.

Besides Kettleborough, the one-brain-cell minds also gave some stick to a baggy-shorted little left winger called Barry Hartle, who came into the team somewhere between the demise of Ronnie Simpson and the signing of Gil Reece. Barry had the knack of frustrating the 'experts' by banging in the odd goal and turning out some worthy performances that delayed the signing of Reece. It was often confusing to a young supporter, as I was then, to hear the crowd barrack players who gave everything, like Kettleborough and Hartle, whilst a player like Docherty, who was allergic to sweat and who often sent out a cardboard cut-out of himself, got away with doing little or nothing.

Finally, another player from that era who came under fire was Bernard Shaw. Bernard, who like his elder brother Graham, played at left back, became a target for the John Street side of the ground. Clearly Bernard was going through a rough patch and his tackling deteriorated to such an extent that the invisible man would have made a better full back. However, the crowd's endless criticism did nothing to help Bernard regain his confidence and once he left United he turned in some excellent performances for Wolves, who were then a force in Division One.

Hutch Broke My Washing Machine

Anon

This Blade (let's call him Jon, although that obviously isn't his real name) who lived in Beighton got a job that took him out of South Yorkshire, resulting in a change of abode. He didn't wish to sell his house so he decided to rent it out - and who should he find to be his tenant but one Donald Hutchison.

When Don moved to Everton he had to vacate Jon's house so when Jon returned to see what sort of state Hutch had left it in, he was pleasantly surprised to find that everything seemed okay - until his wife tried to use the washing machine, without success.

I wonder if Don washed his boots in it?

Brian Degree-ne

Jamie Pigott

In late 1991 I was standing on the steps outside the City Hall, wearing cap and gown, awaiting the Sheffield Polytechnic Degree Ceremony when who should amble past but Brian Deane. My wife, busy taking photographs, chased after him and asked if he'd have his photo taken with "your greatest fan".

He agreed, and whilst wating for my wife to change the film he showed genuine interest in asking what course I'd taken. Three photos later Deano was on his way blissfully unaware that he'd turned a totally boring day into a memorable one.

Come And Sit With Us Beesley!

Angie Harper

While all the country went mad about the David Beckham sending off in the World Cup and every pundit, journalist and manager plead for the boy's forgiveness, the ordinary fan was looking forward to the start of the season so they could have their pound of flesh. Whether he would be able to hear what the fans were shouting was discussed at great length.

This reminded me of an incident that happened a few years ago when Paul Beesley once charged up and down the hallowed turf of Bramall Lane. Beesley was having a particularly poor game, United being one down after only ten minutes. Three rather large, vocal men, jovial from their pre-match pint, took it upon themselves to inform Beesley that he would be better off sitting next to them as he was worse than useless down on the pitch.

Our Paul, for obvious reasons, took offence to these well-meaning suggestions. Not to be outdone, he spent the rest of the first half, which was more than thirty minutes, exchanging verbal abuse with the three said men. I, for one, was torn between amusement and amazement at this verbal passing game. Meanwhile, United were hanging on, reduced to ten men, as Beesley was now completely determined to have his say.

It all came to an abrupt stand-off when the referee blew for half time, but Beesley could be seen making full use of his index and middle finger in the direction of our stand.

Whether Dave Bassett saw what went on we will never know, but Paul Beesley will always be known to me as "Come and sit with us Beesley". There must be many more footballers out there totally unaware of their nicknames. But as to not hearing the crowd, who's kidding whom?

Medal Blade

Tim Surr

My interest in United was first started in the mists of time by my late grandfather. My dad had no real interest in football so me and grandad used to make the trip to Bramall Lane. This was in the days before all-seater stadia and crowd control had even been a twinkle in Justice Taylor's eye.

We used to stand on the Bramall Lane end during the heady days of Woodward and Currie (what a great side that was). During one particular game we were standing next to an old man, wrapped up in a huge overcoat and muffler, who, to my young eyes, made even my grandad look young. As the match progressed we got into conversation with this old gentleman and at half time he reached into the depths of his pocket, saying, "I bet I have something that neither of you two have ever seen," and with this he produced a small box. When he opened the box, there in all its glory was an FA Cup winner's medal from when Barnsley won the cup in 1912.

I wonder, will this be the closest I ever get to seeing a cup winner's medal again?

Mumble Jumble

Ruth McFall

When I was at school I lived just off Carterknowle Road. Living near me at the time were Blades heroes Bill Dearden, Trevor Hockey and Len Badger. Many was the time when we would call at one of their houses on the pretext of collecting jumble (for jumble sales that obviously never existed!), only to be greeted by one of their children turning back into the house and shouting, "Dad! It's for you!"

We never collected any jumble.

No Curran, No Cry

Anon

There's a Blade named Ian who's one of those supporters who is a devoted follower, inasmuch as he has missed very few games, home or away, for years. Along with a few others they'll travel and attend the Lane to see all manner of competitions, friendlies and testimonials as well as the league and cup games. They're also regulars of reserve and youth team games and even travelling to these away games is not unknown.

However, on Monday November 17th 1980, Ian felt he had to miss a game. Played at the Lane, it was a benefit match for John Flynn, and it was a United side versus a Select XI. The United side won 8-4 but two of those goals came from the very reason Ian couldn't bring himself to go. That reason was that Terry Curran guested for the Blades in their line-up.

The other goals for the United XI were scored by Phil Jones 2, John MacPhail, Steve Charles, Steve Neville and Gary Marrow

The thought of Curran, then still with Wednesday, wearing a United shirt so angered and disgusted this loyal Blade that he felt he had to voluntarily miss a game - not an easy thing for him to do. He did, however, write to John Flynn explaining that he had not attended and the reason why and he even sent him the cost of the match admission to boost the testimonial fund!

Incidentally, along with many Blades, Ian never wanted, enjoyed or accepted Curran's later spell with United. Can you remember the subdued response from the crowd, even when he scored for us? My brother delights in remembering how, after Curran scored one of his two goals against Huddersfield in 1982, he ran towards the Kop, jumped on to an advertising hoarding and fell off, thus bringing one of the biggest cheers of all from the Blades fans.

I also heard a tale from one of Ian's mates relating to this particular game. After the game, as they were all making their way back to the pub, someone in the street asked Ian how United had gone on, to which he replied "Nil nil."

When his mates said to him, "What about Curran's goals?" he grudgingly replied that they didn't count!

Terry Curran, a former Wednesday favourite who scored in each of the two derby games against United in the 1979/80 season, controversially signed for United for £100,000 in the summer of 1982. The game referred to above took place on September 7th 1982, when Curran scored his first goals for United in a 2-0 win.

Noddy

John Critchley

My first encounter with Brian "Noddy" Marlow was many, many seasons ago when he attempted to sell me something. I cannot remember just what, but I didn't buy it or them, but I do remember Noddy claiming to be the Blades' number one fan, something that instantly put me off - number one idiot is probably what I thought at the time.

I did not articulate what I thought; others standing outside the old Shoreham Street Kop did so, however. Not that their replies seemed to bother the man from Woodlands East; in fact if anything they inspired him to continue to make outrageous claims. He was not someone I knew or particularly desired to know at the time, yet we became good friends through the years.

I got to know Brian soon after moving to Doncaster as we both travelled to Sheffield by train with many other Donny Blades. I have also travelled to and from many away grounds with Brian. I still remember and laugh about one particular trip to Mansfield when he emptied the upper deck of the bus, apart from we Donny Blades, with his hilariously awful impressions of Cilla Black and Elvis Presley. A character he certainly was and hopefully still is.

I believe he worked at Butlin's for a short time, though not as an entertainer - his dream. Brian was also once employed as a miner, though he seldom talked about that period of his life, to me anyhow, United being his chief subject of conversation.

There were a few other jobs, but none that lasted any length of time or meant as much as Sheffield United to that particular vicar's son. He could swear like a trooper, or collier if you prefer, be crude and tell filthy stories and be as nosey as hell, but it was hard not to like the man once you got to know him. He was always good for a laugh, often at his own expense. He was always good for something to eat too, as he seldom travelled without an ample supply of food for before, during and after games.

He was not a drinking man - I only saw him drunk once; when we went to watch Frickley play, the game was called off and I refused to buy halves when it was my round....... Somebody asked if Noddy was my father in one of the pubs we visited.

The other big love of his life was some woman from South Kirkby called Avril - he had a tattoo with her name on his arm, if I remember correctly. It didn't work out, but that he still thought about her was obvious.

It's a while since we last met - we used to bump into each other quite often, usually in Doncaster town centre, always talking football but usually respecting but not agreeing with each other's views. He was having some health problems and was not looking very well at all the last time I saw him, but I felt it better not to say anything as he had not seen me and seemed to be in a hurry to get somewhere - probably the Gents knowing Brian.

A Blade through and through, no longer an active one maybe, but I wouldn't bet against him having a couple of letters in the 'Green 'Un', or even turning up at Bramall Lane either.

I, for one, hope so, as there simply aren't enough characters about.

The Night I Slept With Jamie Hoyland...

Anon

For four years in the mid-eighties I worked for an establishment that specialised in research into and maintenance of pitches and surfaces, both natural and artificial turf, for all types of sports.

Naturally, football pitches were my main area of interest and I was working on a project funded by the Sports Council. Briefly, it involved going to pitches of all standards (from Wembley to Concord Park) all over the country to do tests on the grass - seeing how high the ball bounces and how fast it rolls, measuring how much grip a player can get from the turf, and various other 'player related' tests.

But we needed a method of interpreting the results (this was science after all - sorry if it's boring you), so the Sports Council organised for a squad of professional players, under the guidance of an FA Coach, to come round with us, play and train on the pitches and then fill in a questionnaire concerning the overall quality of the surface they had just played on.

The players were mainly youngsters, including a few who went on to play league football in the late eighties (Geoff Lomax, full back for Manchester City and Carlisle, Steve Perks, goalkeeper at Shrewsbury, Nigel Adkins, Wigan's keeper, Ray Woods, a winger who had a spell at Coventry, Alex Jones, centre half for Oldham), and a couple who made more of a name for themselves in later years.

Both of the latter were 'supplied' by Manchester City - one of them, Paul Simpson, played for several clubs including Oxford United, Derby County and Wolves, and had a spell on loan at United, while the other was our very own Jamie Hoyland.

Knowing that Jamie, who must only have been about eighteen at the time, was a Blade, I wasted no time in making his acquaintance. Jamie was quick to show me his Sheffield United key ring (!) and assured me that he got over to Sheffield to watch the Blades as often as possible.

I remember hurtling across Birmingham in Jamie's banged-up Fiat one day, and I also remember he and Simmo fiddling their expenses (I didn't say anything) after a session at Wigan, or was it Rochdale? Simmo claimed he had driven from his home town, Carlisle, while Jamie reckoned he had been visiting relatives or a girlfriend or something in Cardiff (!), when, of course, they had come together direct from Manchester! If you're reading this, Jamie, sorry to uncover this particular skeleton in your cupboard!

But the main topic of this story is the time we were visiting a couple of artificial turf pitches in London - Willesden, if I remember rightly, and Loftus Road, home of QPR, who at the time boasted their infamous 'Omniturf' pitch. It was the night Tommy Cooper died on stage (literally) and Frank Bruno lost his first pro fight, to 'Bonecrusher' Smith.......and the night I slept with Jamie Hoyland.

The Sports Council had booked a grotty hotel somewhere in London but there had been a mix-up - not enough rooms for us all. We couldn't let these prima-donna footballers (even if they were only kids) kip on the couch so me and my colleague agreed to doss down where we could.

I can't recall where my colleague ended up, but there just happened to be a foldaway bed-chair in Jamie and Simmo's room......

Jamie, being a Blade, did not hesitate to offer me their hospitality, so there I was, all tucked up with two future football stars......I hope I didn't snore......

I saw the two of them a couple of months later in the Red Lion on Charles Street and I bought them a pint (each) for putting up with me.

Anyway, that's how I remember it.....

A Proper Charlie

Pete Moxon

There was something about Charles Green that struck me as familiar when he was appointed as Chief Executive at Sheffield United. The trouble was I just couldn't pin it down.

The first impression was of a cold, hard-headed businessman brought in to untangle the web of deceit spun by Reg Brealey and generally kick a few butts. This feeling was reinforced after attending the BIFA meeting at the City Hall when Mr Green sat impassively as Mike McDonald and his lieutenants answered questions from the floor. I watched him closely and not once did I see a flicker of emotion cross his face, nor a word pass his lips, yet he seemed as though he was in total control of proceedings.

Was he at the helm of the apparent backroom revolution taking place within Bramall Lane, with more goings than comings taking place? The distinct impression was yes.

Still the feeling persisted that I had crossed Mr

Green's path at some point in time, but not many Charleses had figured too much in my life, so still the mystery prevailed.

It was a feature in the 'Sheffield Telegraph' that finally cracked the code and turned Charles into 'Charlie'. The article focused on his background as a local South Yorkshire footballer who might even have played for the Blades given a bit of luck. It went on to chart his engineering career and his subsequent link up with the Mike McDonald empire, but it was the football bit that solved it for me. After consulting my own football career memorabilia, Charles Green, Business Executive, became Charlie Green, a dark, handsome, well-built inside forward (yes, they still called them that in 1970 - today I think he'd be a striker!).

I was considered able enough at football to be invited to attend trials for the Sheffield and Hallamshire County Football Association Youth Team, and after all the players who were not connected with Football League clubs had gone through a selection procedure, a squad was selected to take on the S&HCFA area League club youth teams to have a look at their non-professional players who would be eligible for selection.

It was when we played Doncaster Rovers at Belle Vue one cool October evening that I first encountered Charlie. He quite simply stood out for Rovers in a team that contained several young professionals and apprentices, and afterwards we were surprised and delighted to learn that Charlie was only on amateur forms and was therefore available to join our squad. Doncaster beat us 4-1 that evening and I think Charlie scored a hat-trick.

It seemed only a matter of time before he signed full-time, but in the meantime he played for Sheffield and Hallamshire against a Rotherham United youth team (mainly full timers) and ran amok in a convincing 3-0 victory, which set us up nicely for the FA County Youth Cup game against the West Riding FA at Leeds.

By this time, as well as being a player of considerable talent, Charlie had revealed himself to be a bit of a character who liked to have a laugh and a joke, and on the coach journey up to Leeds he was on the back seat, where all the 'Jack the Lads' sat, cracking jokes and generally entertaining everyone around him.

Unfortunately we were soundly beaten in Leeds, with Charlie hardly getting a kick (of the legal sort anyway), and that meant that the team no

longer stayed together and Charlie went off back to his home town of Mexborough to what we all thought would be a professional career. But it was not to be, and soon Charlie's name began to appear in Mexborough Town's line up. They were one of South Yorkshire's better non-league teams at the time and I followed his career via the 'Green 'Un' for a short time, before he seemed to disappear........until he surfaced at Bramall Lane twenty five years later.

Despite our paths only crossing briefly, what is intriguing is when did 'Charlie' become 'Charles'? Charlie was definitely the appropriate handle back in 1970 and Charles appeared to fit the bill in later life. It's strange what two small letters in a name can do for a person's image - Charles Green, Chief Executive of a professional football club........ Charlie Green, waggish local footballer with an eye for goal and other things.........which one is for real?

Bobby's Got His Hat On

Matthew Bell

My favourite memories of Bob Hatton are threefold. He was never one to celebrate wildly after he scored a goal and when he netted the two hundredth of his career against Altrincham in the FA Cup he acknowledged the milestone with his usual simple 'arms in the air' salute as he jogged back to the half way line.

This was the first round of the FA Cup at Bramall Lane on November 21st 1981. The game ended 2-2. United's other scorer was Keith Edwards.

Then there was the time at Bootham Crescent, York, when he had just scored in United's 4-3 win. On to the field came that famous Blade Kevin 'Cooperman' Cooper, who planted a great big smacker straight on Bobby's forehead. Poor Cooperman got himself arrested for his 'lip service', while, ever the pro, Bob carried on as if nothing had happened. I know if I had seen Cooperman's lips approaching my face from short range I'd have run a mile, but not Bob.

Finally, who remembers the 'Hatton Turn'? Cruyff's had nothing on this. It's difficult to describe in words, but try to imagine this. Bob has the ball with his back to goal out on the left wing, near the touchline, ten yards from the corner flag with a defender right behind him. Bob lifts his right foot forward over the ball and places it on the ground straight in front of his left so that the ball is now between the toes of his left foot and the heel of his right. All right so far? Quickly he takes all his weight on his right foot and spins 180 degrees to his left, at the same time dragging the ball away with the outside of his left foot. The defender wonders where he's gone as Bob, now clear, is approaching the by-line and is able to send in a cross with his left foot. Wonderful stuff.

Two Get Over-Excited

Anon

Depending on your musical taste and opinion, me and my cousin could make our claim to fame of once singing with The Housemartins. Not for us, though, helping Paul Heaton and the lads with the acappella version of 'Caravan of Love', nor doing the wacky dance to accompany a rendition of 'Happy Hour'.

No, it's just that we happened to find ourselves standing next to three of them on the terracing at Portman Road, versus Ipswich in October 1987, singing 'The Greasy Chip Buttie'.

Please, no fan mail.

United lost 1-0 to an injury time David Lowe goal on October 24th 1987.

Men For All Seasons

Peter Sharpe

One Saturday afternoon I sat down in the changing rooms at Castle Dyke playing fields along with players of my cricket team, Sheffield Deaf, preparing for a match against Woodseats Social in the Norton League.

It was the first time we had played Woodseats Social as they had been relegated to our division the season before, so their players were unknown to us. Woodseats Social's captain popped into our dressing room to tell us that they did not have a full team. Their captain was none other than Chris Wilder!

I got changed and as we walked over to the pitch I realised that there were two more ex-Blades playing for Woodseats Social - Mark Todd and David Frain.

As Woodseats were four players short, our captain agreed to let two of our reserves field for them. Our captain is a Wednesdayite - I'm sure he would have been more generous if he were a

Blade!

We won the toss and elected to field. Our opening bowler, Peter Wood, who is a season ticket holder at Bramall Lane, was very keen to impress the Blades trio. He has the potential to be a good fast bowler but instead of concentrating on line and length he let rip and two of his deliveries whistled past David Frain's ear, and as a result of Peter's eagerness, several byes were conceded as the ball sailed out of our wicket-keeper's reach.

When Chris Wilder came in to bat, Peter became even more enthusiastic because he always admired Chris when he was at United. Chris punished Peter's keenness by hooking a couple of bouncers for fours. I was called upon to bowl and my ghastly first ball gave Frain an easy hit for a boundary but a few balls later I had him caught in the covers. Meanwhile, Chris was hitting my bowling all over the field but he was out after smashing 49 off about 30 balls. Woodseats finished on a total of 94 all out.

During the interval, Peter Wood's father Frank (a non-player) was telling Chris that he was the best right back during his first spell at the Lane and that many United supporters were mystified at his continual non-selection by Dave Bassett.

Frank umpired our innings along with me (until it was my turn to bat). Mark Todd fielded a ball and in his attempt to throw the ball back to the bowler he accidentally hit one of our batsmen, who unfortunately has a hot temper and is a Wednesdayite too! Mark apologised immediately, indicating that it was an accident, but it took our batsman ages to cool down, causing our players to have a quiet chuckle.

Chris Wilder came on to bowl and the ball hit the batsman's pad without a stroke being offered. A run was taken and Frank signalled a leg bye. For those of you who aren't familiar with the intricacies of cricket, you can't run a leg bye unless you have attempted to hit the ball with the bat. Chris politely told Frank that he shouldn't have allowed the leg bye, but Frank misunderstood. I came over from square leg to explain and Frank realised his mistake and offered to take a run off our total but Chris sportingly allowed it to stand.

The whole game was played in a good sporting manner (apart from our batsman's hot temper) and none of the footballers made a kung-fu attack on the umpire! We won by four wickets, despite my being bowled for a duck by David Frain. After the game I reminded David of his last-minute winner against Sunderland in the 1986/87 season. I also told Chris that I was pleasantly surprised to see him sitting with the United fans at Everton in May 1993 cheering with the rest of us, despite the fact that he had been transferred to Rotherham.

David Frain scored his last-minute winner against Sunderland on November 1st 1986. Peter Beagrie got the first in a 2-1 win.

Chris Wilder, Mark Todd and David Frain were all happy to communicate with us despite our hearing and speech difficulties - thanks for a great day! And Peter Wood then obtained Chris and Mark's autographs even though he had been trying to terrorise them with his fast bowling all day!

Sorry Jim

Peter Hawes

I can't remember the year except it was in the fifties and we (Brentford) won. Sheffield United were the visitors and they were riding high at the top of the division. Any team that wears red and white stripes has to be something special and this day they were more so because little Jimmy Hagan was playing for them.

Mention Jimmy's name to older fans and they are guaranteed to go misty-eyed. He was one of those rare English players who, like Matthews and Finney, stood out above their fellow pros not just for his ability - he could bring down a ball on the end of his toe and move off all in one smooth movement - but for his aura of 'Gentlemanliness'. No late night binges, no histrionics on the field, no preposterous posturings in front of a camera. Jimmy just did the business with his feet, and both were lethal. Five feet two and nothing of him except for two spindly legs that could unleash a shot from thirty yards that would stun the crowd. We've all seen Bobby Charlton's thunderbolts on TV, first-timers into the top corner; well, Jimmy was his predecessor.

It was one of those cool days when a buzz and an air of expectancy hung over the crowd with all eyes on danger man Hagan. I remember it was one of those ding-dongers played to a background of an endless roar from the fans. Two incidents I shall never forget. Firstly, Fred Monk, one of the craftiest players ever to pull on a Brentford shirt, and his runaway goal hit with his left from somewhere near the half-way line that left the goalkeeper clawing the air as it screamed over him. Secondly, I remember the agony of Jimmy Hagan.

The Bees were on song that season, with a side built around a half-back line including a certain Jimmy Hill at left half - all chin, knees and elbows, but he could play a bit. Centre half was Ron Greenwood, later to become England's manager, a most accomplished touch player who pocketed every opposing centre forward, until he came up against John Charles. But that's another story.

At right half was a granite-hard tackler called Tony Harper, a ball-winner in modern idioms. Every team tried to develop a hard man as a wing half then, and Tony's arrival at Griffin Park was an instant success with the fans. I often think that Nobby Stiles modelled himself on Tony's shin-biting and all-action style. Tony's ministrations, if you'll forgive the word, were usually accompanied by a toothy grin, which is where the analogy with Nobby ends, because, as we all know, Nobby played with his teeth out.

The second incident I mentioned earlier could have been scripted before the game. Given Jimmy's creative skills, it wasn't surprising that he enjoyed a lot of possession in midfield and, this being where Tony had marked out his territory, something had to give. It wasn't long in coming. Jimmy, who liked the ball close to his feet, was dancing his way through the middle when a flying bundle of knotted muscle and sinew scythed in at ground level. The ball was played, but so was the leg behind it, and Jimmy hit the turf. When a football crowd goes silent the way they did that afternoon you know something serious has happened. On this occasion, every fan knew that Jimmy's glittering career was over. The stretcher that bore him was one of the saddest sights I can recall and there was hardly a dry eye to be seen. The Bees, as I have said, went on to win the game and just missed out on promotion to Division One that season.

End of story? Not quite. Some twenty years later, in Portugal, I was introduced to a little white haired gentleman at a party who turned out to be Jimmy Hagan, recently arrived back from a footballing appointment in Kuwait. Naturally we got talking football but I couldn't quite bring myself to mention that fateful afternoon at Griffin Park.

Brentford beat United 4-1 on November 17th 1951. It wasn't the end of Jimmy Hagan's career, but in the days before substitutes he was 'a passenger for seventy minutes'. Harry Hitchen scored United's goal.

Vinnie-Dictive

Anon

One thing that springs to mind about Vinnie Jones is that once, when we were selling 'Flashing Blade' on Shoreham Street, this old Blade came up to us and after purchasing a copy, looked at me and waving his FB said, "'Ere, kiss o' death your lot. Whenever your sponsor a player they sell the bugger!"

It made me smile and I replied, "Aye, you're right. Never thought about it like that before."

The old Blade's smile faded and as he walked away he said, "Well why dunt tha sponsor that twat Jones then?"

It left me in hysterics anyway.

Another Vinnie snippet, this time in his favour, occurred one day in the Lane car park after I'd been to the Lane shop and had a quick gander at the pitch. At the top of the car park was a contractor's van with two baseball-hatted youths sitting eating their snap. They were obviously working at the Lane and were parked outside the training gym facing the back of the South Stand. They were dead in line with the Social Club entrance. I was just walking back from the pitch when Vinnie Jones came out of the Social Club and stood taking in a bit of sun before slowly walking back towards the players' entrance. On seeing him one of these lads leaned out of the cab and, with a mouthful of sarnie, shouted, "Vinnie!"

Vincent looked up and waved acknowledgement but the lad had just wanted him to play into his hands because he then added, "Why don't yer get back ter fuckin' Leeds!?"

And before he could sit back feeling pleased with himself, Jones, quick as a flash (unusual I know!), replied in a brilliant mock Yorkshire 'thick get' accent; "And why dunt tha get back ter fuckin' work!"

The other lad burst out laughing and, shouting a loud, "Aaaaargh!" at his embarrassed workmate, gave him a push, knocking his tea all down him. Vinnie Jones merely went about his business unperturbed, leaving these two arguing!

The Birch

Matthew Bell

Younger Blades fans (me included, might I add) will not remember Alan Birchenall playing for United in the mid-sixties. He formed a formidable attacking partnership with Mick Jones and it was the sale of both of them, for £100,000 each, in the 1967/68 season, that condemned United to relegation.

The Birch, as he was known, had a reputation for being 'a bit of a lad'. He continued in this vein at at Leicester City in the seventies (just look at the famous kissing incident with Tony Currie!), and his appropriately titled 'Over the Bar' column in Leicester's match programme shows he is still a great character. In the programme for our game at Filbert Street in March 1996, Birch was reminiscing about his time at the Lane. Apart from saying that United's training ground at the time, the Ball Inn Ground, was ideally situated next to a pub, he added,

"Off the field, too, things got exciting. Believe it or not, the first night club in Sheffield opened while I was a young pro. It was called the Penny Farthing Club and, needless to say, the lads became permanent fixtures there. In one corner of the club would be the Sheffield Wednesday lads with their glasses of coke, and on the other side would be us United guys with our pints of John Smith's bitter."

Apart from United selling their best players and getting relegated, the Birch informs us that something else hasn't changed in the last thirty years. That is, that United players, like the fans, were, back then and still are today, more fun-loving, and far less serious individuals than their Wednesday counterparts. All in all, it's much more fun being a Blade.

Curtis Is Our Hero

Anon

As usual we were in Yates's at about half past ten on a Saturday night. It was the night of the cup replay win at Notts County. There we were at the bar when just to our left we noticed two familiar-looking chaps. "Hey, it's Quinny and Curtis," said I to Scout and Helen. Helen swooned. Quinny didn't look too unhappy considering he'd just been (unjustly) sent off for the first time in his career. Meanwhile, our non-football fan mate Alan (he used to watch Wednesday ages ago, which explains it) goes, "Who?"

Now, Alan always asks us to point out to him any footballers we see in town on a Saturday night but he is usually not impressed by former United players (sorry Toddy), or ex-Leicester City, Hereford United and Plymouth Argyle men (apologies to Tony James). Only the fact that I say hello to Chris Wilder has ever brought any acknowledgement from Alan, but then he wasn't there when Dougie Hodgson tried to convince these two girls he was chatting up that I worked for 'The Sun'.

Anyway, we directed Alan's gaze in the direction of these two Blades icons and proudly explained to him who they were. Alan nodded towards the hero who is Curtis and somewhat took the wind out of our sails by proclaiming, "Whey, he looks like he's still at skoil!" We assured Alan that he isn't and that if he came face to face with him on a football pitch he might hold a different view.

This was January 23rd 1999 and United had come back from 3-1 down with five minutes to go in the fourth round replay of the FA Cup at Notts County to win 4-3 in extra time. United's scorers were Vassilis Borbokis, David Holdsworth and Marcelo 2.

Hey! Glyn Can Do That!

Sean O'Brien

Or he could. Did anyone else watching Dennis Bergkamp's superb goal against Argentina in France '98 think, seeing him skin that defender, of a certain Glyn Hodges, whose goal away to Forest in 1993 was even better than the Dutchman's?

To refresh your memory, Glyn, looking resplendent in white shirt and black shorts, approached the right side of Forest's penalty area. He sent the ball around a defender, knocking it round the right side of him with his left foot, then ran round the left side of the defender, meeting the ball with his left foot to carry it into the Forest net. United won 2-0, Forest were relegated - a world class goal had sent them down.

This was at the City Ground on May 1st 1993. Brian Gayle headed the second goal.

Big Mac And Little John

Steve Haythorne

Whilst serving his suspension after being sent off in the FA Cup game against Burnley, Adrian Littlejohn was spotted in the queue of a well-known burger chain restaurant at Meadowhall. The pocket dynamo tucked two Chicken McNuggets and a Quarter Pounder into his tracksuit (oo-er missus) and, like the true Blade he was, he got stuck in, with relish.

How do I know it was Aidie? Simple. He used the same grip on the burger that he used on Adrian Heath's throat......

United and Burnley drew 2-2 in the FA Cup third round at Bramall Lane on January 2nd 1993. Future United manager Adrian Heath put Burnley two up but then he and Adrian Littlejohn were sent off for fighting. Glyn Hodges pulled one back and Paul Beesley equalised in injury time. United went on to reach the semi final.

Currie Favour

Steve Haythorne

In August 1989 I, along with thousands of others, attended an open day at Bramall Lane. During my visit I purchased a copy of Denis Clarebrough's excellent book, 'The First One Hundred Years', which, when autographed by the man himself, various players, our illustrious manager and the chairman, I believe will become a family heirloom. I wandered aimlessly through the crowds that day in pursuit of one particular signature but either Tony Currie wasn't there or he didn't cross my path.

I read somewhere that everyone needs a hero. Well, TC was, and still is, mine. My wife suggested writing to him at the Lane requesting his signature on my book and, despite being a 31-year-old father of two, my schoolboy hero worship got the better of me and the missive was despatched. By return of post I received a reply from our Lord, saying that any time I was passing the Lane I could just pop in and he'd grant my wish. Armed with the book and numerous pens (I was taking no chances) my wife and I jumped in the old jalopy and began the long journey from Chapeltown (well, it's long in my car). Enquiring upon my arrival the whereabouts of Mr Currie I was informed that he was in the Social Club attending a leaving party. Not to be deterred I introduced myself to TC and was immediately made to feel welcome. We had a short chat, he signed my book and, not wishing to impose further on the party, I thanked him and left.

There is, I suppose, not much point to this story other than to say that Tony Currie was not just a very gifted footballer but he is a thoroughly nice bloke as well.

Thanks Harry

Lee Stevenson

Some Blades out there, particularly those who only witnessed Dave Bassett's last days, probably won't appreciate what Bassett meant to older fogeys like me, but I'd like to give my view anyhow.

It was the start of the 1982/83 season and United were in the old Third Division. I was ten years old and my dad, due to having alternate weekends off work, decided it was time, and I was old enough, to start going to matches at the Lane. Now, at the time my family was living in Liverpool (and still does) so going to a Blades match was a new experience to me - more like an away match to be honest but still an amazing experience.

I've lived in Liverpool since I was two and have had to grow up with all my school friends being Liverpool supporters, except the odd few who preferred the blue half, but things were great back then, playing football all night till it went dark, me pretending to be Keith Edwards, my mates being Kenny Dalglish and Ian Rush.

Now it is 1983/84 and I'm in the big school. United are still in the Third Division and it's my first ever P.E. lesson at my new school, with a group of kids I'd only known a few days. There I was in a red and white striped top that I thought was an old Blades shirt but was in reality just a top my mum had picked up thinking I wouldn't know the difference.

At this time Liverpool were the power-house of football and Everton were just challenging at the top, so as a Blade it wasn't the best time to be growing up, especially when you sound like someone out of Brookside. Anyway, everyone wanted to know "Why Sheffield United?" and who exactly they were. To be honest, nobody had heard of them apart from a teacher who remembered Tony Currie and Woody, but didn't know what division they were in at the time.

This went on for five years non-stop: "Sheffield who?", "Support a good team" and the ultimate insult of "Wednesday". I would argue back that Keith Edwards was better than Ian Rush and Sammy Lee was fatter than their mother, but the abuse would still come in from all angles; all good natured but at that age still hurtful.

Then it happened. For a year or so I'd been telling everyone that Dave Bassett was the Messiah and he would take the Blades to the First Division where we belonged. They had all laughed, but not now. I was in the sixth form now and Harry had taken us up. It was my turn now to dosh out the abuse and I was loving it. I told all my friends what we would do to them at the Lane and how Deano would run rings round Hansen and the rest of the defence. They said we would go down first season, then they said we were just long ball, but we were still there and Liverpool and Everton were fading all the time.

So I'd like to thank Harry for all those years at the top. We might not have played football like Brazil, we might have played long ball sometimes but we also played some bloody good stuff at times (I'll never forget the six we put past Spurs at the Lane). Football was exciting then and I was part of it. You gave us some great times Harry but most of all you gave me and the Blades parity, you gave us respect and equality. No longer were we a joke.

There's only one Dave Bassett.

Tom, Tom The Heffernan

Anon

I once gave Tom Heffernan a lift in the firm's van. I was passing the Lane and saw him at the bus stop just past Bri and Irene's. Heffernan couldn't drive and used to catch the bus when there were no fellow players to give him a lift. I think he said he was sharing digs with another player, although it was hard to tell what he was saying, what with his strong Irish accent and trying to hold a conversation above the noise of the heap of crap I was driving.

He seemed a really genuine and nice bloke and I seem to remember dropping him off somewhere up Meadowhead (I was miles off route). He thanked me, dead chuffed that a supporter would stop, give him a lift and talk about the game.

Anyway, then, as now, you're not allowed to carry 'unofficial personnel'. Still, if there's owt worth losing your job over....

Hodgy Ate My Lolly

Malcolm Foster

It was a hard life living in the Walkley area in the fifties. It was not the living in a box - that was uncomfortable - but supporting United in Sheffield 6. It was like being an outcast or a leper. At school it was me against the rest of the boys in class, who were of a different persuasion. Kickabouts in the street consisted of me against everyone else, except if Robert's mum let him out. He would play in goal. After all, he was only three years old.

It did help having a football fanatic as a dad. he would take me to Bramall Lane one week and Hillsborough the next, so at least I got to see football once a fortnight. The two grounds looked different in those days. At the Lane, with the cricket pitch, we stood at the Bramall Lane end and at Hillsborough, without the North Stand, we would stand at the now infamous Leppings Lane end. At both grounds kids stood at the front with their rattles (football ones, although some Wednesdayites would have been better off with the baby variety) and to make sure you got a good spot you were in the ground an hour and a half before kick-off time.

It is this fact that leads me to recollect one of the highlights of my football memories. Checking in my SUFC centenary book, it must have been on February 3rd 1962, during United's first season in the First Division, when we played the old enemy at Hillsborough. We were in the 50,761 crowd, standing in our usual spot behind the Leppings Lane goal. After standing there for over an hour I got thirsty and decided to spend a tanner, out of my half a crown spending money, on a refreshing orange lolly. I bought one from one of the many ice cream sellers who used to walk round the pitch before and during the match and was just taking my first lick when United came out for a kickabout. The best goal-keeper I have ever seen for the Blades, Alan Hodgkinson, came to our end. As the United forwards tried to beat Hodgy, I think it was Ron Simpson who hit a cracking left-foot shot that just flashed past the post, hit the wall, rebounded against the back of the netting and fell in front of me. I stood there wanting to grab the ball but what can you do with a rattle in one hand and a lolly in the other? Before you could

say "Joe Shaw", help was at hand. Hodgy, as he came to retrieve the ball, relieved me of the lolly, took a big bite out of it, thanked me, picked up the ball and returned to the pitch.

I stood there mesmerised. "Dad, Hodgy bit my lolly!". I'm going to save it, I thought, so I took the wrapper out of my coat pocket and carefully placed the remainder of the lolly in it. Unfortunately, before the game got underway it started to melt and reluctantly I had to finish eating it. I don't remember much of the match, except that United won 2-1 with both goals scored by Doc Pace. All I could think of was that Hodgy had bitten my lolly. I couldn't wait to tell my mum and brag about it to whoever would listen.

Years later I was at a cricket dinner when Hodgy was guest of honour. After partaking of a few drinks I plucked up the courage to remind him of this important incident in my life. After five minutes of me rabbiting to him he must have thought, "Who is this drunken idiot and what's he talking about?", but I didn't care, I had spoken to one of my United heroes.

Jimmy Johnstone Pinched My Bum!

Clive Porter

In the mid seventies Ruth was seventeen and a keen Unitedite. So keen that she became a programme seller with a regular spot in the newly opened South Stand. Through selling programmes she met a girl called Liz who helped tidy the dressing rooms. For about a season Ruth also lent a hand. In those days the dressing rooms were still beneath the John Street Stand. After the game the girls would wait with the ballboys in a passageway. When the players had changed and moved to their lounge, they (but not the ballboys) were allowed into the dressing room area. It was never officially approved, but accepted. They did some tidying up; dirty kit was lying around and the large bath was always mucky. Dressing room chores were also done by the apprentices and young players; in those days these would include Keith Edwards, Simon Stainrod and Tony Kenworthy. Ruth recalls that Liz fancied Steve Conroy.

After a bit of work (but not much), the girls went to the players' lounge to claim their reward of......a bottle of fizzy orange, and to watch television. There wasn't much direct conversation with the players, who tended to be in the bar, but some people and incidents remain in Ruth's memory. She can't have gone entirely unnoticed as Ted Hemsley once said hello as they passed on The Moor. One day she went into the away team's dressing room where Ray Clemence was tying his tie. He was effing and blinding but, on seeing a girl enter, his language quickly changed and he apologised to Ruth for swearing. Brian Clough, however, refused to let her in, saying that it was disgusting that young girls should be allowed into the dressing rooms.

Tony Currie was United's big star at that time. Ruth saw him being interviewed for radio and remembers him as seeming rather shy. Sadly she can't claim to have wrung sweat from his jockstrap.

Jimmy Johnstone was once standing with a group in the lounge when Ruth walked past. Her slim figure and long blonde hair must have been an obvious attraction to the wee Scot. As she went by an arm shot out at a speed that would have amazed those that saw Johnstone on the pitch for United, and showing more control over his hand than he ever did over the ball, he deftly pinched her bum. She looked down, shocked and angry, but most of all embarrassed, not knowing what to do. In fact she ignored the not-so-subtle approach and walked on: "It's not as if he'd been playing well at the time. Now, if it had been Geoff Salmons....."

Waiting For Frank

Karen Keenan

Walking along John Street recently, something I had not done for quite some time, brought back memories of the pre-match ritual carried out by me and my friends in the early seventies. Prior to the game we would have assessed the visiting team and earmarked any players we considered handsome enough to stand and wait for as they arrived and got off their team coach. Leicester City were one of our favourite teams as around this time they boasted several (by our fourteen-year-old standards) 'hunks'; Alan Birchenall, Jon Sammels and Frank Worthington spring readily to mind, and it was the last named who, on December 16th 1972, after a 2-0 victory for United (goals from Woodward and Hockey), was to get us into trouble, so to speak.

Whilst I can't exactly recall seeing the players get off the coach that day, I certainly remember them getting back on it because it must have been nearly half past six in the evening and we girls had clearly taken leave of our collective senses. On leaving the John Street Terrace shortly after 4.40pm, we had made our way to the players' entrance and waited there, hell-bent on getting Frank's autograph before he left Sheffield. Normally we were expected to walk up to the bottom of Midhill Road to meet my Dad and to be taken home by car, so you can imagine the trouble I got into once Dad found me.

I seem to recall that he eventually came all the way back to John Street from Midhill Road spitting feathers. However, by that time we had achieved our goal - Frank and teammates had emerged from the ground, he had signed our autograph books and - joy of joys - wished us all a Happy Christmas. It was worth the A1 telling off that followed.

I'm ashamed to say I never ever waited until nearly 6.30 for a United player.

Mixing With The Stars

Matthew Bell

It's not every day you get invited to the World Premiere of a major new film, so when, out of the blue, I received a phone call from Sean Bean enquiring whether I would like to attend the first showing of 'When Saturday Comes' I didn't need much persuading.

Now I wouldn't call myself one of Sean's biggest pals; I think the last time I spoke to him at length was outside the bogs that fateful day at Stamford Bridge (it's amazing where you bump into film stars). I do, though, always send him a copy of 'Flashing Blade' (one issue apparently found its way to the Ukraine where he was making a series of 'Sharpe') and it was because of this that I assumed he had seen fit to invite me.

The call came a fortnight before the Premiere, to be held at the Warner Brothers cinema complex at Meadowhall on Tuesday February 27th 1996. "It'll be about a week before I can get the tickets sent out", said Sean.

A week passed by, then ten days. He must have forgotten, I thought. Well, he's a busy man. All those interviews to take care of between watching the Blades at Palace and Charlton. But I arrived home from work one evening to find a message on my answerphone from Don McBlade (one of Sean's mates from Handsworth), informing me he had my ticket and could I ring him back? A rendezvous was hastily arranged in the car park of the White Rose at Handsworth.

Now in possession of a ticket just twenty four hours before the event, I was concerned to find that guests were asked to don a 'Lounge Suit'. Now, not being a veteran of these glitzy affairs, I had no idea what a lounge suit was. Dressing gown and carpet slippers? Tuxedo? Top hat and tails? With no time to even find out, never mind avail myself of suitable attire, I had to do the best I could. I don't possess a suit of any kind, let alone a lounge one, so my faithful jacket and tie had to suffice. I thought I wouldn't get in.

It also said on the ticket, "Due to strict security arrangements, guests are asked to proceed to their seats in the auditorium immediately on arrival at the cinema."

Tuesday night's 'Star' also claimed that tight security would be present. No riff-raff would be allowed anywhere near the cinema. Imagine my surprise then, when I waltzed unchallenged through the Oasis, floated up the escalator, fought my way through the massed ranks of the star-gazers and the paparazzi (although no flash-guns popped as I passed and no autograph books were thrust forward in my direction), breezed across the cinema foyer and strolled up to the entrance of Screen Two without so much as a by your leave. Security? Not that I saw, and with all those famous people around as well!

Once inside the cinema, I spotted Mick Rooker and David Capper near the front, and went down for a word. There was no "Alreight Matt" or anything from Mr Rooker. As tactful as ever, his first words were "How did you get in here?" Good old Mick.

After a delay caused by the organisers, Guild Entertainment, who had tickets printed for seats that didn't exist (they'd do well in the football business), Sean Bean and Producer Jimmy Daly paid a fleeting visit to greet everybody, adding that they hoped we would "enjoy t'film."

After the film it was down to the Oasis for the party - free beer, free wine, free food. After a quick chat with the United contingent present (no players - they had already gone to Norwich - but apart from Mick Rooker and David Capper, Mike McDonald, Tony Currie and Andy Daykin were also there), I watched local band Big Wide World (they have a couple of songs on the soundtrack) for a while and then went in search of 'Flashing Blade' contributor Gary Armstrong.

The place was thronging with blokes who looked as though they could afford a thousand times more than the £40 they paid for a ticket (unless it was just for show), and women who were trying to make themselves appear younger than they actually were (you know the type, make-up slapped on with a cement trowel), but there were one or two stunners around, as well as a few ordinary Blades.

I eventually found Gary and his good lady Hani and several cans later it was suddenly after two o'clock. We'd been joined by a couple of others (John and Julie) and before I knew it we were in taxis and on our way to the private party at York's in town (honoured guests only - Hell knows how I got in). The problem was we had to pay for our drinks here but I was by now in, shall we say, a 'relaxed' state so I didn't worry about that.

Sean was doing the rounds (pity he wasn't buying the rounds!), mingling with the guests and basically being an all round good chap - what a professional! He sympathised when I told him I would be driving to Norwich in a few hours......

We left at around 4.30am and tried to find a taxi. Have you ever looked for a taxi at half past four on a Wednesday morning in the middle of Sheffield? I wouldn't recommend it. Now if you want a milk float, you're on to a winner. We eventually found one in Fitzalan Square and I rolled in home at ten past five. The drive to Norwich did not look in the teensiest bit appealing as the first glimpses of light began to show in the sky......but up I was at 12.30 none the worse for wear (apart from a slight headache!) and at 1.30 we were off.....

United drew 0-0 at Carrow Road on Wednesday February 28th 1996.

Oh Bodinog We love You!

Nigel Truswell

A couple of years ago, when United played Swindon away over Christmas, we followed the game on Teletext and to our amusement, our younger son (aged eight at the time), thought United must have signed a new player as we regained the lead through "Bodin og". We explained the 'og' abbreviation and that the unlucky Welsh international, better known for missing penalties in World Cup qualifiers, had simply put through his own net.

Somehow the name stuck and he's been known in our house ever since (not that he's a frequent topic of conversation), as Bodinog. We've used the -og suffix joke often, usually at other teams' expense, though it wore thin recently with Holdsworthog two weeks in succession. It was good to see that two seasons on at a different club, Bodinog was still doing the business, as he put United into the lead against Reading and he could claim (but probably won't), that he doubled his scoring lead for United over Roger Nilsen.

Bodin's first 'og' put United 2-1 ahead at the County Ground on December 27th 1994, after John Reed had equalised future Blade Jan Aage Fjortoft's openber. Adrian Littlejohn got a third as United won 3-1.

Bodin's second 'og' was on March 29th 1997 as United beat Reading 2-0 at Bramall Lane. Andy Walker got the second.

David Holdsworth scored own goals in consecutive games in February 1997: in a 2-1 defeat at Swindon (he also scored United's goal), and then Norwich's winner at Bramall Lane. This game ended 3-2, with Petr Katchouro and Andy Walker scoring for United.

photo: Andy Greaves

In the early nineties it was said that United could only win matches after Christmas, therefore the team, the manager and these rather warm supporters celebrated Christmas on the first day of the 1992/93 season.

photo: Andy Greaves

Grounds for Change

Whatever Happened To...?

Matthew Bell

Bramall Lane has undergone considerable changes over the years, with many of those alterations coming only in the past few seasons as a result of the seating of the Kop and the building of the new John Street Stand. Now, this isn't a outbreak of nostalgia here by someone lamenting that "it's not like the old days" and I'm certainly not mourning the loss of everything listed below, but just see how many of them you can remember......

Smoking Chimneys
I don't remember these, but look at any pre-War photographs of Bramall Lane and they will be seen dominating the background. In fact, the agent of the Duke of Norfolk (who owned the land on which the Lane was built), once said that Bramall Lane had "the advantage of being free from smoke", although its surroundings hardly were. And as late as 1952, Norman Yardley and J.M.Kilburn wrote in their book 'Homes of Sport' that "a brewery chimney periodically pours smoke and soot into the air." The area between Bramall Lane and the city centre used to be packed with small factories, steel and cutlery works and the odd brewery, which all exhausted this and that into the atmosphere, but today I don't think one industrial chimney can be seen from the Lane.

Transferring from the Kop to the Terrace
There was a time when you could walk all the way round the ground but even I can't remember that. What I do remember though is a turnstile inside the ground in the wall of the end of the old John Street Stand, at the Kop end. There may well have been one at the other end as well. You could enter the ground through the Kop turnstiles and then, should you wish, pay a bit extra to pass through this turnstile on to the East Terrace, with the amount you paid being the difference between normal Kop and Terrace admission.

My dad took me and my brother to a night match against Leeds in 1971 when United were unbeaten and riding high at the top of the old First Division. The crowd was massive and the Kop was packed. My dad told us to wait in the bottom corner of the Kop while he paid (I think it was 10p) to go on to the terrace to see if there was space there, in which case he'd call us through and pay the extra for us as well. There wasn't room there either and I recall him vaulting back over the turnstile to rejoin us. We watched the match right at the front by the corner flag and United won 3-0 to begin a trio of consecutive victories against the previous three League Champions (Everton and Arsenal were both defeated 1-0 away from home in the following seven days). I don't know when this transfer turnstile ceased to operate but I guess it it would have been only three or four years later when the police and the ground authorities were becoming more conscious of the need to know exactly how many people were in each part of the ground.

United's scorers against Leeds on August 17th 1971 were John Flynn, Bill Dearden and Eddie Colquhoun. The crowd was 40,725.

photo: Andy Greaves

Look closely and you can see the White Wall and the Army posters

Away Fans on the John Street Terrace

Total segregation of fans did not come into effect until the late seventies, even though away supporters generally tended to congregate mainly on the Bramall Lane end. However, attempts to 'take the Kop', usually by Manchester United or Leeds United fans, were not uncommon and away supporters also found themselves in other parts of the ground, either by accident or design. One such group of Birmingham City supporters, six or eight strong, was standing near us on the East Terrace (it was probably the 1974/75 season), exchanging abuse and threats over the fence with some Blades fans in the bottom corner of the Kop. The United fans made as if to scale the fence and come over for a scrap, at which point my dad said something along the lines of, "If they come over here and my lads get hurt you'll have me to deal with."

Now, my dad is only 5'5" and offered the Birmingham fans no real threat but his intervention encouraged others to join in and before long the commotion caused the police to arrive and move the Birmingham fans on.

On October 26th 1974 United beat Birmingham City 3-2 at Bramall Lane. United's scorers were Bill Dearden, Alan Woodward and Keith Eddy (pen.).

The White Wall with Army Posters

While we're in the John Street/Kop corner, in that area of the ground, but on the Kop, stood a high white wall retaining the Kop steps as they curved round the John Street corner at the back. This was a prime spot and you had to arrive early in order to obtain a position standing at the top of this wall, as it afforded a fine, elevated, panoramic view of the whole ground and there was no-one in front of you - in fact, the people standing in front of you were about fifteen feet below at the foot of the White Wall. As well as its being a great vantage point from which to watch the match, the White Wall had another unusual feature - on its face hung, for years, four posters in wooden frames. At least one of the posters invited readers to join the army - perhaps the others were recruitment notices for the navy and RAF, I can't remember. Just what deal, if any, United had struck with the armed forces for these posters I can't say. They also made you wonder about the wisdom of the Army trying to recruit people from United's Kop, although maybe they thought that the Shoreham End was just the place to find potential trained killers.

The Spiral Staircase

The Spiral Staircase stood right at the back of the Kop, in the John Street corner. It wasn't strictly a spiral as it was a square tower rather than a round one, but several flights of steps, turning continually to the right, took you from the top corner of the Kop down to street level and an exit on to John Street. If you were late for the match, ascending these steps was a good, quick way to get to the Kop, but you had to be fit and you also had to hope that you weren't held up by someone not quite so fit. The Spiral Staircase, as well as the White Wall, lasted even after the Kop was demolished and rebuilt, as United originally intended to seat this corner as well. However, both departed with the old John Street Stand in the summer of 1994.

The Floodlight Pylons

Bramall Lane used to have five floodlight pylons (why five I don't don't know, but I think it was unique in the Football League) - one in each corner and a smaller one on top of the old John Street Stand roof. Again, I don't know why this one was shorter than the others - perhaps it was something to do with safety. This one went with the John Street Stand in 1994 but the others survived until extra-powerful lights were hung from the roofs of the three remaining stands. This was in the summer of 1996 when the new John Street Stand finally began to grow out of Fred West's garden.

The Players' Tunnel on John Street

The John Street Stand was always considered to be the 'nerve centre' of Bramall Lane, as it contained the dressing rooms, despite the fact that all the club offices were in the cricket pavilion at the other side of the ground. The South Stand was erected in 1975 with the intention of housing all these facilities and more but it remained more or less a shell as there was not enough money to complete the internals - that is until Reg Brealey came along. One of his forgotten achievements is that it was Reg who found the funding for and oversaw the fitting out of the South Stand, meaning that all the administrative side of the club, and the all-important dressing rooms, moved over to the other side lock, stock and barrel. The new South Stand tunnel was used for the first time for the Fourth Division match against Stockport County on Tuesday February 9th 1982. United won 4-0.

Goalscorers for United in this game were John Matthews, Jeff King, Keith Edwards 2.

The Cricket Pavilion

Even though Yorkshire County Cricket Club were evicted from Bramall Lane after the 1973 season and the new South Stand was completed in 1975, the cricket pavilion remained, now surrounded on three sides by the tarmac of the car park, until it was finally demolished in 1982. I'm not sure whether or not the pavilion was used for anything during the intervening period but it was certainly derelict and boarded up in the last few months of its life.

Only for the biggest games did the pavilion house any football supporters (although I did once watch a game from the balcony as my mate's dad, a policeman, let us in for nothing) when the crowd was forced to stand 'round the bends' to watch the game another football pitch's width away from the action. It was from here that I watched Hull City's Chris Simpkin and Ken Knighton kick United to defeat in the 1970/71 promotion season (we got in late and there was no room at all on the Kop).

This match took place on March 9th 1971; United lost 2-1, Gil Reece the scorer. The attendance was 40,227.

The Fifteen Minute Change of Scores

The pavilion balcony was where the old (football) scoreboard used to be housed. A lot of grounds had them - each letter on the board designated a match, but you had to buy a programme to know which game corresponded with which letter - apart from one. Letter 'A' was always Wednesday and their score was the only one that was updated whenever a goal was scored, or every fifteen minutes; all the others were only put up at half time. The scoreboard had later reincarnations on the front fence of the Bramall Lane end and on the front wall of the South Stand, before being usurped by the electronic scoreboard we have today.

The White Railings

There was mention in the previous bit about the fence in front of the Bramall Lane end. In fact, before the erection of the tall perimeter fences in 1979 to prevent pitch invasions there were only low white railings to keep people off the pitch. Prior to the building of the South Stand these railings used to encircle the whole ground and at one time were not even covered up by advertising hoardings, which only came into being in the early seventies. The railings disappeared bit by bit as first the Kop was demolished, then the John Street Stand went and finally the lower tier of the Bramall Lane end was seated.

The Shop on John Street

United's first souvenir shop was in a terraced house, purchased by the club, on the corner of John Street and Countess Road in the early seventies and was opened, according to Gary Armstrong's book 'Blade Runners', by "the mini-skirted, white-booted blonde babe and lead singer of Pickety Witch", although others claim it was singer Karen Young from Dronfield.

The house is no longer there, and the shop moved to the South Stand in 1981 or 1982 (but did it have a short period in the cabin on the corner of John Street and Shoreham Street?).

Ilkley Moor Bah T'At
Long before the days of whatever piece of classical music it is and the theme tune of 'The Professionals', way before 'United' by Judas Priest and Sham 69's 'The Kids Are United' and whatever other awful clichÈd rock songs the players have run out to, they used to do it to 'Ilkley Moor Bah T'At'. This is an old traditional Yorkshire folk song, which tells the story of a wayward fellow who courts a girl, Mary Jane. By doing so he is told he will catch his death of cold, and have to be buried. Then the worms will come and eat him up, and the worms will consequently be eaten up by the ducks. The people telling the wayward fellow what will happen to him if he continues to court Mary Jane inform him that they will then eat the ducks, so the last verse of the song, rather gorily, says, "Then we shall all have etten thee!" Poor fellow.

What this has to do with the Blades is difficult to say, but at least it was different.

Ian Ramsay
Ian Ramsay was the DJ who used to play 'Ilkley Moor Bah T'At' and all the other records. He was resident at the Lane for what must have been twenty five years and only packed it in a few seasons ago, since when we have had Gary Sinclair, who is an acceptable replacement as at least he has a sense of humour. I presume it was Ian Ramsay who coined the phrase 'Beautiful Downtown Bramall Lane', something that we don't hear enough of nowadays. How about reviving it, Gary?

The Cabin on the John Street Roof
Before the South Stand was built, Ian Ramsay used to play his records from a little cabin stuck on top of the John Street Stand roof. I remember going in there during a club open day in about 1975. It must have been a bit draughty in the middle of winter. Ramsay subsequently moved to the press box at the back of the South Stand.

Rose Garden/You Can Do Magic
Two of the most famous records Ian Ramsay ever played were during the 1970/71 promotion season and thereafter. 'Rose Garden', a rather naff country/pop song by Lynn Anderson, was United's lucky record during that promotion season. Whenever United were losing or playing badly Ian Ramsay would play 'Rose Garden' at half time and we would then go on to win. Every time.

'You Can Do Magic', by Limmie and the Family Cookin' was dedicated to TC. No, not Terry Curran. Not that we needed it, but the regular playing of this record reminded us that, indeed, Tony Currie could do magic.

'Rose Garden' by Lynn Anderson entered the UK charts on February 20th 1971, eventually climbing to number three during a twenty-week run.

'You Can Do Magic' by Limmie and the Family Cookin' entered the charts on July 21st 1973, also reaching number three during a thirteen-week run.

The Lights Gone Outta Me Life

Anon

I'll not forget the Saturday I was driving my dad's car around St Mary's roundabout. I was lucky not to crash, if not from having my attention wrenched from the road, then at least from having impaired vision due to trying to see through a veil of tears.

The last bastion of my obsession with nostalgia relating to all things United was being torn out - words chosen for dramatic effect as 'dismantled' doesn't seem enough somehow. They were taking the floodlights down. The last two remaining that is.

The floodlights were a symbol, both of a horizon-marker of football ground location and, in this instance, a memory of childhood. Happier, innocent times. When such as Bosnia, mortgages, worries of parenthood, heartburn, Tory governments, football club chairmen and a strong wish that you'd tried harder at school were things of an unknown and distant future.

My dad and uncle had been taking my brother to the Lane for some time before I was honoured with such a baptism. Unlike many I can't recollect my first ever game, I just remember bits of matches from that era. And although I don't recall, either, the exact first night match, they do, nevertheless, stick in the mind, not just

photo: Kevin Titterton

experiencing all this wonderment I was encroaching on to what had been his alone until now. Just "one of those territorial things" a psychologist would probably tell you, though he used to hit me a lot, so it was probably more like one of those "dislike for my shitty little brother" things I'd say. Then again he did grow up to join the police so maybe it was destiny! (only joking, our kid).

For Christmas 1976 I received Martin Tyler's book (I wonder if he ever noticed it missing!?). If I found the book itself excellent, then the cover was a dream. It showed Bill Dearden, a hero of mine anyway, jumping for the ball with the Burnley keeper, Alan Stevenson, and Bill was embla-zoned in the glare of the Bramall Lane floodlights (or so it stated on the inner sleeve). It remains one of my all-time favourite football pictures and that owes as much to the inclusion of the starburst effect of the glory of those lights as it does to the awe-inspiring, rising, majestic form of Billy Dearden (bloody hell, I'm beginning to sound like Stuart Hall!).

Sadly, the demise of the floodlight pylon will inevitably pass with acceptance, just as the loss of ter-racing eventually has, but it will equally stay in the memory as a part of the football tradition. Just think back to as recently as those 'heady' days in the Fourth Division when, for many, some of the grounds were being visited for the first time. Apart from the fact that more Blades spilled out of the pubs (such were the numbers travelling) the closer you got to the ground, the other identifying factor of your eventual desti-nation when entering these small towns was spotting the floodlights.

Admittedly that had its problems - after all, some scrapyards and railway sidings have bigger floodlighting than some smaller clubs of the lower divisions, and there has been more than one coach driver who has taken followers of the beautiful game to the old rugby ground at Wigan.

for the fact that they mark the milestone of reaching equal footing with my brother in being allowed to go to a match at night, but in the superb experiences they were.

The thing is, one of my most vivid memories of those first nocturnal treats is the floodlights. The sheer brilliance. The incredible light mixed with the noise from the Kop. The smell of grass and liniment in the crisp night air. The sight of your breath in the beams of those lights and the fact that you could pretend you were smoking. Hands gripping the white iron fencing in front of the West Terrace. Muffled up with your scarf but too excited to notice the cold, until all the red and white held aloft on the Kop dispersed at the end of 'You'll Never Walk Alone', and you realised you were shivering. Temperature or emotion?

Either way I'd be brought back to reality when my brother twatted me round the head for no apparent reason. Well, perhaps it was because I was creasing his programme or maybe that by

Still, I lost more than several yards of rubber from me dad's tyres that sad Saturday in ques-tion. It was as if another little piece of me, inside, was removed as well. The lights were removed in large sections, and the uppermost piece that housed all the lighting was swaying a little when the crane first began to turn away from the main pylon. The thought flashed across my mind of whether this section would fit in someone's garden, but as it descended its size became apparent and I knew that planning permission would be a problem, as well as the divorce settlement.

Even the suggestion of trying to cadge one of the actual lights for the patio was met with marital cynicism. Though, on reflection, I have to admit she was right about the occupants of the houses opposite being a tad upset were we ever to illuminate it. As well as complaints of blindness, there could be claims for sunburn also. Mind you, if it were to be wired up to one of those intruder warning devices, it'd certainly make any would-be burglar crap himself.

It never seems the same somehow now, whether you're approaching the city from Norton, Norfolk Park, Chesterfield Road, Arbourthorne, in fact any direction from where a quick glance across the panoramic view of the city allowed your gaze to fall upon those once-proud pylons. And if you're approaching from Bramall Lane or going round St Mary's roundabout, the sight of the church silhouetted against the sky doesn't seem as impressive or meaningful without sharing its outline with the precise network of girder engineering.

Of course the modern lighting does indeed illuminate the pitch well, but we're going to miss those five beams that began sharply some two thirds above the height of the stands, and gradually widened until they merged into an illuminated bowl that drew you in like moths to those ever-optimistic night games.

The Ball Inn Ground

Silent Blade

After renewing my season ticket at Bramall Lane, I decided to drive up and see what the old Ball Inn ground looks like now. My only visit there was back in 1975 and I could not remember exactly where the ground was. Driving up Myrtle Road I found the Ball Inn pub, parked my car there and asked someone who was doing some work outside the pub where the training ground used to be. He pointed out that it was

All that remains of United's former Ball Inn training ground

photo: Kevin Titterton

Bramall Lane, minus the John Street Stand, from the top of St. Mary's Church tower

right next to the pub.

I noticed a gate with bars on so I decided to go in to see if it was the place I was looking for. The entrance was not that wide for a park entrance and you could see some litter and concrete debris there. Walking up a slight hill I could see a large area of field that had been left to grow over for quite a few years. I asked two elderly people walking their dogs (they tried to avoid me at first because to them I must have looked a 'dodgy' stranger!) if the field was the former Ball Inn ground. One of them said, "Yes, this was the place where United trained and I used to watch them frequently". He pointed out an 'empty' area where the changing rooms once stood.

I remember that United stopped using the ground in the early 1980s (not long after our young goalkeeper Keith Solomon had died tragically there) because the club was fed up with having to repair the continual damage to the changing rooms caused by vandalism. I wonder when we first started using the ground for training? I know that pre-season team photographs were taken at the ground between 1966/67 and 1969/70.

Seeing that the unused field is quite extensive, I wondered if it might be large enough for the club to use it as a training ground again?

Traditionalists Or Trainspotters?

Kevin Titterton

In the summer of 1994 I nipped out of work one dinner and went down to the Lane with my camera. I wanted to get some shots of the John Street side before they built on it again. What a naïve fool - I thought I'd better get in quick before they began putting the new stand up! I should have known better with our club really. As it turned out I would have had time to capture the bloody scene on canvas, with versions from all four seasons of the year.

The John Street Stand was always synonymous with old men, tartan leg blankets, dew-drop noses and thermos flasks. On the terrace (the west side especially), from the early eighties onwards, the 'nutters', 'casuals', away fan baiters and barmy army recruits emerged from defending the Kop in the sixties and seventies.

To me it will always be fondly remembered as the place where I was 'born again'. Yes, it was on the West Terrace, before its dark reputation days, that I began watching the Blades, following on in a tradition with my dad and uncle who'd been taking my older brother for two or three years already. I remember the coppers telling you to get down from the white railings. Red and white stripes, the awe-inspiring Kop to the

The new John Street Stand finally begins to emerge from what for two years
had been a frozen wasteland

left. Dearden, Woodward, Currie, Hockey, bar scarves, Ipswich 7-0......excuse me, I've just got something in my eye (sniff).

Of course, knowing what it's like to follow the Blades, you have to wonder whether adults who sway their kids into the fold should be honoured or pilloried for their actions. When you think of some of the suffering we've had to endure over the years you could understand Esther Rantzen setting up a help line for young Blades alone. But then knowing what it means to be a Blade you continue it with your own offspring.

Anyway, back to this particular dinner time. I went into the South Stand and up the steps of gangway B to survey the scene. I'd been down months before, taking pictures of the old stand before it went, including different vantage points: on the terracing, inside the exits and tunnel, so I also thought I'd record the scene post-demolition. I did the same with the Kop before its sad demise. As I began to take the camera out of its case a voice said, "Another sad bastard!"

I turned round to see a Blade called Bill Brealey sitting with a grin on his face. There was a bloke to his left and one or two others dotted around the stand, all doing the same. Apparently Bill had done the same, pre-demolition. And with the Kop. He'd even done it in the mid seventies with the very stand we were sitting in. He told me he had albums full of the stuff.

If the love of your club is linked strongly with tradition then these kinds of records are great to keep for the future. Still, we had a laugh at ourselves and the stuff we collect but still struggled with the question: why?

The Demise Of John Street

Matthew Bell

The John Street Stand didn't quite make its century. Built in 1899/1900, it was then probably the latest in modern design but time eventually caught up with it as seats were removed for safety reasons over the last decade and finally it was the fire and safety officers, rather than German bombers or Lord Justice Taylor, who pronounced the death sentence.

Half the stand, including its splendid gable, was destroyed in December 1940 and, after the war, it took another eight years to rebuild completely, although its replacement gable was not quite so imposing.

John Street arguably presided over more memorable cricket matches than football contests. Known to followers of the summer game as the 'Grinders' Stand', it saw Australia beat England in a Test Match in 1902, Hedley Verity's 15 for 38 against Kent in 1936 and Yorkshire's innings defeat of the touring Australians in 1968.

Many fans will probably have far greater memories of John Street than me, for I have never been a great watcher of football from the side. I first remember going there in the early seventies to watch the reserves on the Saturdays that the first team was playing away. After the game I'd stand outside the players' entrance on John Street itself to get a few autographs, many of them from players I'd never heard of and who would never even play first team football. Footballing greats such as Peter Hardcastle, Paul Hallows, Doug George and Mike Hoban scribbled their names in my book on John Street. But I also got some of United's better-known reserves, like Alan Ogden, Mick (sorry, "Michael") Speight, Steve Cammack and the late Steve Goulding, and the odd more famous signature - Gordon Banks, Tony Currie and Wednesday's returning Peter Swan and 'Bronco' Layne. And I was once introduced to Martin Conroy who probably thought, "Who's this little oik?", while I was overcome at meeting a FOOTBALLER. Martin Conroy, where are you now?

I can't honestly recall the last time I sat in the John Street Stand or even stood on the Terrace. It might have been a reserve match against Wednesday in about 1981 when Trenton Wiggan scored the winner but I couldn't be sure.

So John Street doesn't really hold any abiding memories for me and I can't say I was sorry to see it demolished. It looked quite homely from inside the ground but outside it was, quite honestly, an eyesore. It was ugly, ramshackle and decaying, with the red-painted corrugated iron long since faded to an insipid pink. It was hardly a good first impression for anybody coming from the city centre.

Probably what I'll miss most about the John Street Stand is the graffiti on the outside wall. Still visible right up to its final hours, daubed in blue paint (with a brush - before the days of spray cans) on the brickwork were the words "OWLS", "FANTHAM" and "FORD".

Those twenty-five-year-old brush strokes summed up, for me, the John Street Stand - out of date, out of time, out of place. It had to go.

A View From The Past

Ken Cotterill

With the levelling of the old John Street Stand, Bramall Lane changed completely from the ground that my father took me to. In those days the bulk of the support gathered on the Kop at Shoreham Street, with the John Street Stand and Terrace being the next most popular viewing points.

I watched most of my early games from the high wall that used to be in the corner of the Kop. Little kids could lean over this and swing their rattles without endangering the lives of the elderly in flat caps. As I grew I moved closer to the goal. In those days (early sixties), young kids could roam wherever they liked, free of intimidation. This seemed to change dramatically in the mid sixties when the hooligan element entered the game. My dad always said it was because they had cancelled National Service.

I also watched a few games from the old Bramall Lane end before the stand was built. I don't ever recall watching a full game from this end but many a second half when United were kicking in that direction. Usually, away supporters gathered here on this bleak piece of tundra that was only partly protected from the elements. I recall standing with some Fulham supporters before a third round cup tie and thinking what hope had they got of winning the cup, but since then they have at least played in a Wembley cup final.

I also watched a couple of games from the cricket pavilion. One was against Leeds in 1965 when the congestion on the Kop was such that there was a spill-over to the pavilion. For some inexplicable reason I also remember watching a County Cup match against Barnsley from there. We were playing so badly (we were in the First Division, Barnsley were in the Fourth) that to retreat to the pavilion to play with the big numbers held there was more interesting than the game.

I never watched many games from the John Street side of the ground, mainly because it was expensive to go in the stand and congested on the terrace. We would often delight on the Kop at the push and sway from the John Street Terrace as more and more people squeezed in.

The games I recall witnessing from the terrace all ended up with United getting thrashed. There was a 5-1 home defeat by Bolton and a 2-0 football lesson by Aston Villa in 1992.

With regard to the John Street Stand, I did manage a couple of games there, although I can't remember why I was there and not on the Kop. One game was a thrilling 2-2 draw with Leicester City. We were 1-0 down at half time then, in a storming second half, we went 2-1 up only for Jackie Sinclair to score a late, but deserved, equaliser.

Bramall Lane has now completely changed. Gone is the dark, satanic terracing of the Kop, the cow shed at the Lane end, the crowded, windswept terracing on John Street and the oddity of a cricket pavilion. Times change and United move on, but it's the old, not the new, that will be remembered by this Blade.

The half demolished John Street Stand

photo: Andy Greaves

The FA Cup third round tie against Fulham was on January 22nd 1966. United won 3-1 with goals from Alan Birchenall 2 and Alan Woodward.

The game against Leeds in 1965 was probably the final match of the 1964/65 season played on April 24th. Leeds won 3-0 in front of 32,028.

United lost 5-1 at home to Bolton Wanderers on January 14th 1978, the second of three consecutive games in which five goals were conceded. Alan Woodward scored United's consolation in this match.

Garry Parker scored both goals as Aston Villa beat United 2-0 at Bramall Lane on August 29th 1992.

The 2-2 draw with Leicester City was on September 25th 1965. Gil Reece and Mick Jones scored for United.

Portraits Of Promotion

Where Were You When....? (1)

Andrew Calow

You may recall the evening in question. Promotion from the Third Division was at stake. United had finished their programme with a win on the Saturday. Only Hull City could pip them but to do so it would mean winning by three clear goals. A lot of Sheffielders went to Burnley that night; others clustered round the radio sets listening in. I was in Leeds that night and didn't fancy either. I went for a meal and then tuned in to the last agonising minutes on the car radio. The commentary came over loud and clear.

Now you may be one of those experts who knows so much about the opposing team that you can name the reserve goalkeeper's wife's maiden name. I am not, and here I was with two teams on the radio and I knew neither.

Ten past nine and still no news of the score. Suddenly a corner was given. My stomach churned. "One last chance to get the goal they need." My legs turned to jelly.

"Smith takes it. It's a long one to the far post. The heads go up and it's there! They've done it! They've got the goal they needed...... Northwich Victoria have won the FA Vase!"

The match between Burnley and Hull City took place on May 15th 1984. Hull needed to win by three goals to deny United promotion on goal difference. They won 2-0 (future Blade Brian Marwood scored both goals), so United won promotion on goals scored.

Where Were You When....? (2)

Clive Baggley

The night Burnley played Hull City in the match that won United promotion to the old Second Division in May 1984 I went with three mates (all Iron fans) to Millmoor to see Rotherham v Scunthorpe.

Scunny had the impossible task of winning 7-0 to avoid relegation to Division Four, so my friends were in a rather sombre mood, resigned to the drop. I, on the other hand, had only one match on my mind - the one being played at Turf Moor.

Early on the tannoy announced Burnley 0 Hull 1 and I feared the worst. Quite a few Scunthorpe fans knew I was a Blade and kept winding me up by telling me it was 2-0, 3-0, 4-0 etc. etc. But I heard on the tannoy early in the second half that it was 2-0 to Hull. I waited and paced up and down, up and down, taking no notice of the game being played in front of me (Scunthorpe were actually getting stuffed) but I heard no more score and felt so tense it was unbelievable.

The match at Millmoor finished 3-0 to the Millers and Scunthorpe were relegated but there was no score in yet from Burnley. The Scunny fans were obviously very quiet and pissed off.

As they waited to file out into Millmoor Lane,

there's me still standing on my own in the corner of the away end when on comes the tannoy, "Here is the final score from Turf Moor - Burnley 0 ....long pause (or so it seemed) Hull City 2." Yeeeeesssssss! THE BLADES ARE GOING UP!!

As you may have guessed I was rather pleased (ecstatic more like), so pleased, in fact, that I didn't charge my three buddies any petrol money for taking them to Rotherham. They, after all, had seen their team relegated but I was the one going through hell until that final score came through from Turf Moor.

Where Were
You When....? (3)

Jeff West

Where were you when Burnley played Hull City? Pacing up and down in my wee tenement flat in Aberdeen tuning into BBC radio and hearing the result and thinking that Hull had won promotion on goal average, only to realise the truth a few moments later, to my obvious joy, when the sports news broadcast it was goal difference that determined promotion. That's where I was.

So much for being out of touch with the Canon League (as it was then) and being cut off in the north of Scotland is a poor excuse. Nevertheless, cut off from English football is how it seemed at times.

Two years previously I had been working in Dundee and celebrated alone when the Peterborough result came through and confirmed United's promotion from the old Division Four. "Sheffield who?" most of the pub queried when they asked why I was jumping for joy and thinking of buying everyone a drink!

Ironically, a few days later I received my first major culture shock for an Englishman living abroad in Scotland and subsequently my first unsavoury experience of that football fan known affectionately, in half of Scotland at least, as 'The Hun.' The occasion was Cup Final day, my last day in Dundee before returning south temporarily to Manchester (the vagaries of the itinerant welder). I settled down to watch the Spurs v QPR final only to discover to my embarrassment that in Scotland they show the Scottish Cup Final, which, on this occasion, featured Rangers v Aberdeen. I could only watch the first half before leaving for Glasgow and at this juncture the scores were level at 1-1.

I wasn't that interested in the result, being more concerned with the score from Wembley and the next day when I left Glasgow for Manchester I swear I still didn't know the result. I did know something of the reputation of the Rangers fans, however, and when at Glasgow Central I witnessed a group heading down the same platform as myself I swiftly headed for the front of the train as far away from them as possible. Imagine my horror when, a few minutes later, strutting down the aisle and sitting down alongside me was a member of 'The Hun.'

"Are you a Fenian bastard?", he politely enquired as he relaxed into his chair and pulled out his flute and started to play 'The Sash.'

"No!", I replied, "I'm English!". My cultural naïveté probably saved me because I said it in all innocence and not at all as a threat.

A strange animal is The Hun, especially when half-drunk on a Sunday afternoon and I still did not know what to do - carry on making small conversation or turn to my book? Before I knew it I started talking to him about yesterday's match. "It was a good goal that Gordon Dalziel (Rangers) scored, wasn't it? What was the final score?"

I honestly didn't know and I almost crawled under my seat when he told me that Aberdeen had won 4-1. 1982 was the beginning of the period of Aberdeen's ascendancy in Scottish football and also signalled Rangers' temporary decline. If this episode was bad enough, worse was to come.

Swinging down the aisle of the open carriage was a virile-looking youth dressed in a blue and white shirt; a skinhead, the sort you avoid at all costs, especially when you know his team has just been beaten 4-1 by Aberdeen. But it was obviously not my day and this predator clearly detected my nervousness and swooped in for the kill.

"Are you an Aberdeen fan?", he asked as he flopped down beside me, brandishing a threatening Rangers tattoo down his right arm. "No, not me. I'm a Sheffield United fan. We've just got promoted to the English Division Three, you know." Surely he would realise that neither I, nor my team, was a threat to him.

He just turned to me and laughed and at the same time brandished his left arm towards me. Tattooed along this arm was.....you've guessed it.....Sheffield Wednesday! My fears were totally unfounded. I was not thrown from the train, nor tormented about my affiliations. I did, however, keep very quiet about my opinions on Scottish football.

A few days later when I returned to Aberdeen and Scotland I vowed to become better informed about Scottish football and all other aspects of Scottish culture. To borrow a line from 'Flower of Scotland', they had "sent him homewards to think again".

Where Were You When....? (4)

Matthew Bell

When Burnley played Hull in May 1984 I was working in Bingley, near Bradford. I wanted to go to Turf Moor but I didn't have a car and there was no bus or train connection (despite Burnley being only twenty five miles away over the hills). I did know, though, that Radio Sheffield was having live commentary of the match - unfortunately I couldn't receive Radio Sheffield in Bingley.

However, all was not lost. I also knew that there was a number you could ring to get Radio Sheffield's broadcast down the phone line, so that had to be it. Of course I couldn't carry enough ten pence pieces to ensure ninety minutes of continuous commentary, and nor could I afford it, but I gathered together all the change I could carry and went on a tour of Bingley's telephone boxes. I had to ration the calls to make sure my cash lasted till full time and in between I just walked aimlessly looking for the next phone box. I must have trudged around the streets of Bingley for miles.

I felt just how every other Blade must have felt when Brian Marwood scored early, then again before half time. The second half just dragged and dragged, and I kept phoning Radio Sheffield full of apprehension. But eventually the whistle came and I had timed it just right, with just enough money left to make it to the end.

When that whistle blew to send the Blades up I swear I leapt so high I banged my head on the roof of the phone box.

Adolf Hitler And The Nun

Len Strike

They were great days in the old Fourth Division, especially the one at Darlington in 1982. In a championship-winning season United gained ninety six points and scored ninety four league goals. Our final away game was against a club that we had never scored a league goal against, but it was only the second ever league fixture between the clubs.

I knew things would be a little different when I spotted a policeman in the middle of Darlington High Street directing Blades fans into an adjacent hostelry. Unfortunately the real police attended and arrested him for impersonating a police officer.

Inside the pub, next to me, a Church of England vicar ordered a round of eight pints of bitter. I began to worry, though, when a 6' 2" fairy with cauliflower ears followed me to the gents. I made a quick U-turn back to the bar for another pint. As I pushed my way past Adolf Hitler and a nun, who were laughing over a pint together, I thought I'd either gone crazy or would wake up soon.

The ground was packed on all four sides by ten thousand Blades, most of whom appeared to be in fancy dress. I literally never saw a home fan. The teams ran out, followed by three referees. I couldn't believe it, especially when two began doing cartwheels.

During the match I was tightly pressed up against a French maid. As the match progressed I was beginning to take a fancy to her. If only she'd had a shave.

We won 2-0.

This was May 15th 1982. United's scorers were Bob Hatton and Keith Edwards.

Blades Glory, Owls Down

Joe Morris

May 5th 1990. United needed to win at Leicester to be sure of promotion; Wednesday would go down if they lost at home and Luton won away.

Confident of both our teams being successful, me and my mate Dave, a Wednesdayite, had

photo: Matthew Bell

Dave Bassett's in there somewhere. Blades fans sing Mr. Bassett's praises after promotion is gained at Leicester.

bought tickets for a concert at the NEC in Birmingham that night, anticipating that both of us would be happy at our own team's result, if not the other's.

Dave was to pick me up at Leicester station at about seven o'clock, regardless of the results....... but after our day of pure joy and what for Dave must have been sheer despair, would he still come?

Amazingly, he did - and he had even brought a 'Green 'Un', which he had so kindly bought as soon as it came out. There it was, laid on the front seat, front page down. I turned it over to see that wonderful, famous headline; "BLADES GLORY. OWLS DOWN".

The journey to Birmingham was surprisingly harmonious, as I am not one to gloat (much) and Dave was suffering Wednesday's fate surprisingly philosophically (or he was hiding his pain well). The concert was okay, but the NEC is an awful place and we were so far back it could have been anybody up there on stage. But so what, United were up, Wednesday were down.

We got back to Sheffield at past midnight but it was still warm so we had the windows down. Just coming past the bottom of Cobnar Road at Woodseats we could hear and see a bit of a commotion, and there, still drinking outside the Big Tree, dancing on the tables and singing in the streets, were dozens of Blades, still celebrating, still chanting, "Ooh Aah Bob Bookah!!"

Dave said nothing as we drove between the revellers, but at least he didn't run any of them down!

Where Were You At Molineux? (1)

Clive Porter

At 9.00pm on Tuesday May 9th 1989 I leaned back in my seat and drank the last of my coffee at the end of a good meal in a hotel outside Fort William.

In the north of Scotland dusk comes slowly in the summer. The last rays of sun had just left the slopes of Ben Nevis; on its rounded summit the snow had faded from pale gold to white. Through the window I could watch the ripples swaying gently on Loch Linnie. All was so peaceful.

It was hard to believe that full time was approaching at Molineux, where tense and anxious United supporters would be either baying for the final whistle or urging the team forward and praying for more injury time. The climax to the long season seemed ten times four hundred miles away. Allowing time for 'Bladesline' to gather its information I strolled along the loch shore, soothed further by the cool air and the gulls' lazy flight.

Later I looked through my bedroom window at the silvery water and the mountain rising beyond as, tension rendered impossible by the setting, I rang 'Bladesline'. They'd drawn 2-2 and were promoted. "That's nice," I thought, and stood a while at the window, smiling happily.

Where Were You At Molineux? (2)

David Glen

The only occasion I came close to being arrested on match day was on Tuesday May 9th 1989. Being unable to obtain a ticket for the game with Wolves I glued a radio to my right ear and prepared for ninety minutes of tension. Having worn out the dining room carpet in a first half that saw Steve Bull give Wolves the lead, I was instructed to relax. So, taking the radio upstairs, I laid back and looked forward to an even tenser second half. Paul Stancliffe's goal had me jumping round the room. When Tony Agana put the Blades in front I was up again, prancing along the landing.

It took my wife to bring me back down to earth by shouting that the woman next door was threatening to call the police, having seen me through the landing window wearing nothing but a grin.

I have forgotten to mention that the 'relaxing' was being done in the bath and the neighbours (Wednesdayites) were unaccustomed to such celebrations.

United and Wolves met at Molineux in the last game of the 1988/89 Third Division season. Wolves, already promoted, needed a point for the champi-onship; United needed a point to join them. Steve Bull put Wolves ahead, Paul Stancliffe headed the equaliser, Tony Agana gave United the lead, then Robbie Dennison levelled at 2-2 from a free kick. The last twenty minutes were played at walking pace as both teams were happy to settle for the draw.

Memories Of The Fourth Division

Matthew Bell

WIGAN - a hot, sunny day. Wigan's player-manager Larry Lloyd vacates the wall to allow Tony Kenworthy's free kick through and into the net.

HULL - That Keith Edwards. I hate him. Scores against us as we lose 2-1.

STOCKPORT - Monday night. George Tyson is the ref. So what if Tommy Sword barges Keith Waugh into the net without touching the ball? It's still a goal. The Blades' lowest point ever. Ever. Fifteenth in Division Four. Never mind - Cooperman walks through the crowd assuring everybody that Keith Edwards will be playing for us on Saturday. I'll believe it when I see it.

YORK - 3-2 down. A hero is needed. No, it's not Keith Edwards (I love him now), it's Mike Trusson! Truss heads two spectacular goals and we win 4-3. Cooperman wanders on to the pitch to kiss Bobby Hatton. After the match, we see a Blade urinating in the gutter in full view of everybody. So what, we won and Wednesday lost 3-0 at home to Wrexham.

PORT VALE - We were in a queue of traffic after the match in one of those terraced side streets around Vale Park when a group of Vale fans came down a back alley and attacked a Transit van full of Blades just in front of us. Our car doors remained locked but several Blades leapt out of the back of the Transit. It must have been a firm's van as one Blade emerged armed with a can of brown paint, the contents of which ended up deposited all over a Vale fan.........

This was October 10th 1981. United won 2-0 and Keith Edwards scored both goals.

BRADFORD - On TV for the second time, and the second successive away win. Keith Edwards, complete with kit-matching yellow bandage on his arm after falling through a plate glass door at home, scores. He was offside, but who cares? On the divided Kop at Valley Parade, battle ensued over the fence, mainly consisting of an assortment of missiles. An old fellow in front of me is saved possible serious injury as a stone hits his glasses instead of his temple.

United repeated the 2-0 Vale Park win two weeks later at Valley Parade. Keith Edwards and Steve Neville scored.

NORTHAMPTON - 1-0 down, eight minutes past nine. "We can still win this!", claims Tweedie. "Of course we can.....what are you on?", we reply as one. Five minutes later, Trusson again, we've won 2-1!! We believed you all along Tweedie.

TORQUAY - England bowled out for 102 by India. We got to the ground at 10.05 - in the morning. I was dropped off at Woodseats at 9.05 pm. He could drive, that Rick. I wonder what he's doing now.

United drew this game 1-1 with a goal from Edwards; attendance 4,962.

BOURNEMOUTH - Tweedie and Dave do the 'dead fly' in the middle of the main road. I'm not brave enough. A good 0-0 draw that could have been 3-3.

ROCHDALE - We go on the A-road over the moors in bright sunshine while the M62 below is shrouded in thick fog. Can't believe the match is still on on the ice-bound pitch. We win 1-0 (Edwards again) so the conditions don't matter.

COLCHESTER - Match of the Day, and we can't wear our kit because it's got the sponsors' name on it, so we have to wear theirs. 3-0 down after nine minutes and a 5-2 defeat, but we've bought Colin Morris, so the train ride back is bearable.

HEREFORD - I'm on the train from University in Nottingham, having arranged a lift back to Nottingham after the match. However, a breakdown in communication means Dave's car is full. I can't go back on the train - there isn't one - and they're on strike the next day so kipping on the station will be no use. So there I am, laid amongst the tool kit, spare wheel and jack in the back of Dave's Chevette.........and it's snowing. Six of us in the car but somehow Dave makes it and drops me off at Junction 25 on the M1 at about one in the morning, and it's still snowing. Only three miles to walk now.........

United drew 1-1 at Hereford on Wednesday February 17th 1982. Mike Trusson scored.

SCUNTHORPE - The Blades mass on the Kop and a battle commences. We watch from the other end as the home fans run, but suddenly a big fat lass in a white jumper turns and holds off the Blades on her own. The Blades are taken aback, but normality is soon restored as the Blades have all four sides of the ground. In the following Monday night's 'Star' there is the headline "United fans smash up pub after being barred", alongside which is a photograph of a house destroyed in a gas explosion. Totally unrelated stories, but it looks impressive.......

United lost 2-1 at Scunthorpe on February 20th 1982. Tony Kenworthy got the goal from the penalty spot.

HARTLEPOOL - We're driving towards the ground and pass a pub full of Blades, then we see a group of monkey hangers obviously looking for a scrap. Carl opens the car window, points to the pub and shouts "They're in there!"

Later, we hear the Blades have been attacked and the pub has been wrecked. Carl is distraught, "It was me, I caused it....."

This was on March 6th 1982. United won 3-2 with goals from Mike Trusson, Keith Edwards and Bob Hatton.

MANSFIELD - Me, Rushie and Godber drive the short distance from Nottingham to see Tony Kenworthy's rare penalty miss but he makes amends with the equaliser later.

BLACKPOOL - Dave's Chevette packs in on the motorway somewhere near Rochdale, so I hitch a lift and get picked up by some Blades in a battered Austin Maxi. We get to the ground at 3.15 but it's still in time to see Keith Edwards' winner. I find out later that Dave, Bob and Carl didn't get a lift and ended up seeing Rochdale beating somebody or other 5-3.

TRANMERE - Tweedie is scared stiff as we've parked behind their Kop and he reckons we'll get beaten up after the match.......needless to say we didn't, although Keith Waugh nearly did by a Tranmere player after saving a last-minute penalty.

United drew 2-2 at Prenton Park on March 27th 1982. Tony Kenworthy scored both goals, both penalties.

HALIFAX - A wall collapses and Mr Doyle, from Leicester, is stretchered away. Fortunately he isn't badly hurt. We're 1-0 down after a minute but cruise through 5-1.

ALDERSHOT - "Come and see Sheffield United - surely the biggest attraction in the Fourth Division" implore the placards on the railings of Aldershot's public park pitch. The locals didn't need to, as we fill the ground anyway. A poor display, but Colin Morris earns a 1-1 draw in the sunshine.

PETERBOROUGH - The third away game on the trot, and the winners will be in pole position for the run-in to promotion. We manage to rustle up a mini-bus full from Nottingham University and Trent Polytechnic - twelve Blades and one Peterborough fan. He is brave enough to return with us after our devastating 4-0 win - credit the lad. We didn't give him too much of a bad time on the way back!

United beat Peterborough 4-0 on April 21st 1982. The scorers were Jeff King, Keith Edwards 2 and Colin Morris.

BURY - Godber drives me, Rushie and future 'Flashing Blade' contributor Antony Davenport from Nottingham. He is the only one of us poor students who has a car. The tension in the ground is unbearable as United batter Bury who have somehow scraped a 1-0 lead. When Edwards heads a last-minute equaliser the noise generated almost brings the ground falling down round our ears.

CREWE - Me and Rushie get the train to Crewe and are among the first in the ground, standing on the long side-terrace. An old dear is sitting at the back on a fold-up stool. No doubt she always sits there and has an unobstructed view of the pitch. Soon she begins to look concerned as the Blades fans pile into the ground, packing three sides. I don't think she stayed very long.

United won 3-2 at Crewe on May 1st 1982. The goals came from Jeff King 2 and Keith Edwards.

DARLINGTON - Six of us - me, Bob, Dave, Carl, Stuart and Ray - go in two cars. None of us have what you would call perfect eyesight and all rely on artificial visual aids - hence, we christen ourselves 'The Glasses Mob'.

We soon realise what kind of day it will be when we pass a coachload of referees on the A1. On arriving in Darlington we enter a pub in the Market Place. As it's so hot we decide to stand outside and as we make for the exit three gorillas come through the door and immediately rip off their heads to reveal dripping-wet human forms beneath.

We are standing outside the pub when about twenty home fans (the only ones we see all day) run up the street punching and kicking out at any Blades they pass. We cowards stand well back but Carl, who is a bit daft, chases after one and gives him a kick up the backside as he flees. Unfortunately the coppers are on the scene by now and Carl is nabbed, losing his glasses in the process. Our pleading that he was only retaliating after being attacked cuts no ice with the lawmen, but at least they don't cart him off until we retrieve his specs from a shoe shop doorway.

Blades fans enjoy the Fourth Division championship at Darlington

photo: Matthew Bell

Of course Carl misses all the fun of the game....the pink panther, a 6'4" baby in a pram, several referees shaking hands with the captains, bogus policemen controlling the crowd and going as mental as the rest of the Blades when we score, dozens climbing the floodlight pylons, Blades spilling over on to the pitch surrounds as the match nears its end, and encroaching closer and closer to the lines, the linesman running the line five yards on the pitch, the ball never going out of play as the Blades on the lines kick it back in, Cooperman joining Ian Porterfield in the dug-out, the real referee sensibly getting all the players (apart from the two poor goalkeepers) near the tunnel before blowing the final whistle but it does no good as the pitch is covered before any of the players can get off (John Matthews is a bit cleverer - he doesn't attempt to get to the tun-

photo: Andy Greaves

Blades fans doing what they do best - drinking - this time outside a pub at Charlton

nel, he runs round the back of the stand and gets to the sanctuary of the dressing room that way)....meanwhile many United players are stripped as they struggle through....Colin Morris, dressed in only a jock-strap, is last to make it, fully fifteen minutes after the final whistle.

When everything has calmed down, we realise we have to go and get Carl from the cop shop, where he has been spending the afternoon.

The Sergeant on duty insists he won't be released for at least a few hours, so Ray pipes up, "If you don't let him go soon, you'd better be prepared to call an ambulance." No, Ray wasn't threatening to run amok in the police station, ("I'll take as many of you lot as I can with me......."), as he continued, "I'm a diabetic and I haven't got any insulin with me. If I don't get home in a couple of hours I'll fall into a coma and it'll be your responsibility......"

Whether this was the truth or was just a marvellous ruse we didn't know at the time, but whatever, it worked, and within ten minutes Carl was back amongst us. He did, though, have to return to Darlo a few days later, where he was handed a £50 fine for a breach of the peace.

It was only the Fourth Division, but it was by far the most enjoyable season I've ever had watching the Blades.

Where Were You When....? (5)

Rusty Old Blade

MAY 1981 - Due to family commitments, holidays in the eighties had to be arranged well in advance and come April/May, holiday booked, United were struggling to stay in the Third Division. Last home match, Walsall, but I am in Torremolinos. I still remember phoning home that evening to be told that United were down. What a miserable holiday that was.

Go forward to May 1984. Same resort, same hotel, this time with United needing that result from Burnley for promotion. This time the answer to my phone call was, "We're up!" Great holiday.

Ready...steady... go! The aftermath of the 4-0 win over Peterborough in 1982

Relegation Recollections

The Way Forward

Denis Wilkinson

I don't know what you did when you left Stamford Bridge but I left quickly after the match to be alone with my thoughts. This was the second time I had seen Chelsea deliver the coup de grace over the Blades in three relegations from the top flight. The previous time had been in 1968 when a stupid careless defensive error had the same dreaded result.

As I walked along I could see the lights of the stadium and the rear of the stand and I could hear the roar of the Chelsea fans as their team did a pre-Wembley lap of honour. I felt a loathing of the place that almost surpassed my thoughts during my flight from Sheffield 6 back in January. This was the sixth time I had been relegated with the Blades and I have known lower times but not many; perhaps that penalty miss that tumbled us from obscurity into oblivion in 1981 was the lowest point. The whole matter was just a big joke to the Chelsea fans. It didn't matter to them but to us it was a tragedy.

I wandered towards Earls Court bare headed in the pouring rain, through Brompton cemetery, and I came across a black marble tombstone. I don't know why I stopped to read the inscription. It told of some poor sod who had lost two daughters before they were five, his wife before she was thirty, two sons on the Somme in 1916 and his own life in 1918 from injuries suffered at Passchendaele. Perhaps it is a comment on my state of mind at the time but the thought came to me, "This man knew how to lose in a big way.

I bet he was a Blade!"

Three months later and I feel like a man who has had a leg amputated. I know it isn't there but it still itches. My anger at the Blades is unabated. How could they be so unprofessional, so uncaring, so incompetent, so bloody complacent? I blame them all.

Firstly and mainly, I blame Dave Bassett for allowing the team to enter the ground without the realisation that the consequences of the day were deadly serious. We could not afford the attitude that prevailed, "Chelsea won't be interested lads and everybody else will lose anyway."

What was going on? Why was Jonas Wirmola, a very adequate centre back, allowed to go back to Sweden and leave us so short of cover at the back that our competent left back had to fill in? Why was a left winger playing left back when we had a £300,000 left back on loan at another club? Surely if he was worth that sort of money in the first place he must be worth his wages to give the best cover we can get for a match of this importance.

The second person I blame is Brian Gayle. I keep reading what a fine natural leader he is. Well, all I can say is it is a pity he didn't show it on the pitch. If you are 2-1 up with fifteen minutes to play and all you have to do to stay up is not lose, what tactics do you employ? In my view eleven men behind the ball in our half hoofing the ball over the main stand wouldn't have been a bad start. After all hadn't we done that for an hour only four days earlier at Oldham? This wasn't the time to impress on the media that we can play football; they have

photos: Andy Greaves

At the Southend away game in October 1995 anti- and pro- Bassett Blades fans almost came to blows. Here police step in to quell the trouble.

already decided we can't. Instead the leadership needed was not shown, the goals were conceded and those fans who deserved so much got less than nothing.

The rest of the team don't deserve much better. They should not have needed DB to tell them what was needed; in fact he can't, once the match has started. They should have had a much better instinct for survival. The fact of the matter is that most didn't care enough, certainly not as much as those of us who support them every season.

So come on, let's remember that the Blades are all that matter and the Blades are not the board or the lads on the pitch. They are you and me and fifteen thousand others with new generations to come.

Where Were You When....?

Colin Richards

Question: What was so significant about Saturday May 7th 1994?

No prizes for guessing the correct answer. It was, of course, my wife's 40th birthday. As a treat for her, my son and myself I'd arranged a special weekend away in a country cottage on the Welsh border. This was well before it became apparent that the bit of a match down at Stamford Bridge the same day might become somewhat significant itself. Not that I'd even entertained the idea of going to Chelsea - the last occasion was the quarter final a couple of years earlier. That day must rank as the most unenjoyable away match I've ever been to. Crap journey down, crap ground, crap atmosphere, crap performance, crap journey back - in a word.......

Anyway, back to the Welsh border. To take our minds off the match we set off on a long walk in the Black Mountains, during which my wife had ten minutes on Lord Hereford's Nob (well it was her birthday). Stop tittering and look at the map.

From three o'clock onwards every look at the watch was coupled with thoughts of the events 150 miles away down the M4. At 4.45 we were trudging along Offa's Dyke. I remember thinking, "Surely the lads can't have cocked this one up" and set off down the hills reasonably at one with the world.

We were back at the cottage just in time to catch Channel 4 news and sport at seven o'clock. Footage of Everton fans celebrating didn't, at first, alarm me too much. After all, every other result would have to have gone the wrong way.

Then he said it......"Oldham, along with Sheffield United....."

My immediate feelings were quite mixed really. I was (and still am) philosophical about it. Throughout the season I'd had an uneasy feeling that this was one campaign too many. Dave Bassett's subsequent "Russian Roulette" remark just about summed it up. In a nutshell, I've had worse relegations. The most galling aspect about this one was the cruel finale and the thought that Everton had deserved it more than us.

To take our minds off it, the next day we trotted off down to the South Wales coast. We ended up at Barry Island, a sort of Welsh Disneyland without the attractions. Around noon we were sitting on a headland contemplating the Blades' demise whilst watching an enormous black cloud heading our way (which seemed entirely appropriate).

As is usual in these secluded, tranquil settings, the local village idiot appeared, asking us meaningful meteorological questions about this big black cloud such as, "Do you think it's going to rain?"

As is also usual, as soon as a traveller from Sheffield opens his gob, the reaction of the natives is always the same. First there is the look of quizzical disbelief while they try to work out what you've actually just said, quickly followed by, "Where are you from then?"

Upon my concise but geographically correct reply "Sheffield", all I got back was, "You bastards, you've just cost us £200,000!!"

Whereupon he buggered off.

And then it rained.

We shall remember that weekend.

The village idiot's response was a reference to the fact that had United not got relegated they would have had to pay Cardiff City a further instalment of £200,000 for Nathan Blake, bought earlier that season from the Welsh club.

Disaster Day

Glen Parkes

The day started pretty well. I awoke before noon (which isn't bad for a student!) and I was sitting watching television in my shared Nottingham house, with Radio Five blasting out. I've always sworn to never listen to football on the radio, due to the commentators' nerve-wrenching over-enthusiastic shouts when the ball is on the half way line. But I thought "Sod it! It's not even us on the featured game" (as ours wasn't a major concern in the relegation struggle!).

So there I was sitting smugly on the settee, explaining to my 'Leeds' flatmate how United only ever go near the bottom for a bit of excitement. The goals were flying in for Wimbledon at Goodison, United go one up, life is good. I even did a week's worth of washing up (whistling as well!). All thoughts of exams, lack of money etc. went out of the window; in fact for a moment I even thought there was world peace and the whole world lived in harmony. Life was bliss.

Then an awful thing happened. The Radio Five commentator stated that "Sheffield United are now safe." That worried me a lot. Then my bliss was tainted. Goals started (slowly) to go against us. Of course I shrugged it off but my annoyingly cheesy grin was replaced by a not-too-confident smile. Goals continued to go the other way, but still .... Blackburn had to score soon .... didn't they?

Then I worked it out that if two more goals went against us we may go down (go down? Ha!). The next ten minutes will be etched in my memory forever, worse than the penalty miss that condemned us to the Fourth Division. Another goal went against us......jeez, this was no fun anymore. Then the radio link went to Stamford Bridge for the final whistle. There were people cheering like mad. I thought we'd done it and it was our fans cheering. Then the reporter uttered the word "goal". Oh no.....it was 50-50.......up or down. I sunk to my knees and didn't move for ten minutes, while my Leeds 'friend' tried in vain to console me.

You'd think that in that situation I'd be upset, but I was more angry. With what or whom I couldn't say - I was just fuming. I borrowed a tenner, went to the corner shop and bought two bottles of wine and a four-pack, got smashed and ended up walking through the city centre with a bottle of wine in one hand and my United shirt on my back. I went to the bus station, where I asked a bloke where the Loughborough bus went from, whereby he looked at me sympathetically and said how unlucky we were. As far as I can remember I told him to "Eff off".

Found the bus and went to see a fellow Blade at

Loughborough University and bundled into his bedroom where his girlfriend was naked in bed finishing her post-coital fag and Bob was getting dressed. I slumped in the corner, drank the other bottle of wine and stared into oblivion.

Later we went to the Union bar where I proceeded to get semi-conscious, which was good because an Everton fan said how unlucky we were (git!). The next thing I knew I was fully clothed in a smelly pond nearby (apparently there are photos!). I think it was just after this that I passed out.

Going home the next day I went through Nottingham past the City Ground. They'd just been promoted, a year after we sent them down. Irony or sheer bloody bloodiness?

Coincidences?

Rusty Old Blade

Seasons 1967/68 and 1993/94......

Both seasons.........

We played in white shorts.....
We drew 3-3 at Southampton.......
We beat Liverpool at Anfield but drew with them at the Lane.......
We lost 3-0 at home to Manchester United......
We lost to Chelsea last match of the season......

We were relegated......

The Horror Of Stamford Bridge

Alex Atherton

I realise that nobody will want to be reminded of this fateful day. I could have stayed next to the radio for the afternoon but I didn't think I had much choice. I didn't care how much it cost, I was going to make this one if it killed me.

And to think that it all looked so promising. Ever since the 1993/94 fixture list came out I had thought (pessimists that we are) that if we needed to win our last game to stay up then Chelsea away was as good a fixture as any. I'd been telling everybody for months that if we had to win at Chelsea then we would. And having played like that to beat Newcastle I really thought that we were going to do it. Everybody

who knew me more or less said the same and laughed at my nerves, which had taken enough of a battering as it was.

The idea was to get the 9.30 train from Manchester but my travelling companion didn't quite make that for one reason or another so we caught the 10.30 and we hit London around one. I always like being in London on a Saturday; there are scarves and flags all over the place, everybody getting ready for their game. I reckoned that the best way to prepare for this one was to stay in the pub as long as possible, which is a reasonable tactic for most fixtures. But we overdid it a bit, because getting to Stamford Bridge on time when leaving the pub outside Euston at 2.30 is much harder than the journey from the Sportsman to the Kop at 2.55.

While changing tubes we met Labour MP Tony Banks and even he said that we would stay up. Fulham Broadway is normally where you get hassle from Chelsea fans but we forgot all about that as we ran out towards the ground. This was not all together a fine idea given what had been consumed on the train and in the pub, so halfway up the three thousand steps to the top tier I felt exceedingly sick. Then there was a cheer from the crowd. I dashed up the rest of the way expecting to see something like Nathan Blake raising his arms to the crowd. I was confronted by a lot of people with their ears pressed to radios explaining that Everton were one down.

I'd never been in such a strange atmosphere at a match as this one. It was as though everybody just wanted to get out (having avoided relegation) as quickly as possible. Then Jostein Flo scored and if it stayed like this we were safe. The season before we'd let in two stupid goals against Chelsea and Jakob Kjeldberg's header was another one. Everybody went back to the radio and were still fiddling with the dials when Glyn Hodges scored. The weight didn't quite leave my chest but I felt that if we kept singing to the end there was no way that even the Blades could let Chelsea score two. Chelsea were not playing well, they didn't have the commitment and they all seemed to be thinking about the cup final. That was until Glenn Hoddle came on and made a few pointed comments towards players who had taken their Wembley places for granted. Suddenly we looked tired and nervous, just as we had in the semi-final against Wednesday. The only player who didn't was Brian Gayle but he was injured and it was beginning to show.

I started to do my calculations. I had looked at

the table at least twenty times a day since Christmas and I knew that defeat did not mean automatic relegation. Southampton hadn't been doing too badly but it was Ipswich that we needed to lose and they weren't showing too many signs of doing so. With about fifteen minutes to go I was hoarse from shouting and the alcohol drying out my throat. Having looked as though we were going to score again and make the game safe we didn't look as though we could keep the ball out of our half for more than a few seconds. They scored again - it looked dodgy but there was nothing we could do about it. There were only a few minutes of a wretched season left and we had to cling on. The seconds and minutes dragged past and we were holding out. I kept looking at the referee urging him to blow his whistle but he hadn't done us any favours in the match so far and I didn't expect him to start now.

And then it happened. It was strange but as soon as Denis Wise crossed the ball I knew what was going to happen, just like in a film when, at the crucial moment, the action is slowed down to maximise the tension. The cross beat everybody including Simon Tracey, who I'd never seen play worse for the Blades, and Mark Stein scuffed it into the net. Everyone knew that was it and had seen it in the same slow motion.

I knew that relegation was not the end of the club but when the whistle went I was absolutely gutted. The adrenaline that I'd built up before and during the match completely evaporated and I began to feel ill again. I sat there completely stunned for a few minutes and then leaned over with my head in my hands trying to make the day start again. I'd forgotten what a horrible thing relegation is. After a bit I felt a hand on my shoulder. It was a policeman politely asking if I could leave the ground. I looked up and there were only about three people left in the top tier and my watch said five o'clock. I was probably a bit pissed as well, which didn't help. I'd drunk to calm my nerves before the match and to maximise the pleasure that safety would bring, not to make me look like a big girl's blouse at the crucial moment.

I decided that the best thing to do was to get away from the ground as soon as possible and go back to the pub. By the time the last train got in to Manchester it was 1.30. I'd forgotten that we'd gone down. It was only the next day when I really remembered the details.

That Chelsea feeling

James Slack

I left Stamford Bridge feeling destroyed, dejected, useless and frighteningly psychic. In the days following the 1-1 draw at Boundary Park I was told by friends from many corners of the country, with varying football allegiances (which, incidentally, included Everton and Ipswich), that the Blades were safe.

Indeed, many questioned my judgement in making the six hundred mile round trip to London from my temporary home in Lancaster, mid-finals, to watch what they expected to be a mundane and inconsequential game of football. I knew it would be far more than that. My head kept forcibly telling me that we could not possibly go down. After all, Mr Hill had stopped taking bets on the issue and Mr Hansen felt that it was "either Ipswich or Everton" for the drop, yet I knew in my heart of hearts that we were going down with Swindon.

Those feelings grew progressively stronger during the walk to Stamford Bridge, and as I took my seat in the sky I felt as if I had just taken my place as a member of the cast of some tragic disaster movie, which I would be made to watch time and time again. Even when we led 1-0, and later 2-1, and Everton trailed 2-0, I knew. I wanted to stop the confident ones from singing songs of thanks to Wimbledon because I knew that they would fold and kick their creator Harry Bassett in the teeth, and, to me at least, cries of "We are the Blades and we are staying up" sounded half-hearted and smacked of the bitterest irony. I knew.

The last ten minutes of United's Premiership swansong moved in what can only be described as slow motion, like the few seconds that precede the inevitable car crash, and when the final whistle blew I wiped the tears from my eyes and looked around at the puzzled faces of those who were still pleasantly oblivious. While those around me clung forlornly to the hope that numerous transistor radios and Alan Shearer provided, I knew, I'd known since Tuesday. It didn't make it any easier though, and whilst I don't know if anyone else experienced the 'Chelsea Feeling', I know that I personally don't ever want to go through it again.

United were relegated after losing 3-2 at Stamford Bridge on May 7th 1994. For the Blades to go down they had to lose, Everton had to win and Southampton and Ipswich had to avoid defeat. All four results happened.

Blades Shorts

Painting A Pathetic Picture

Floella

A 'top' soccer journalist describes an early moment in Andy Scott's footballing career........

"And it's going to be poked home by Andy Scott! It may only be two inches, but it's all important to him!" (Simon Clarke, United v Chelsea, 1992/93 season).

Never mind Andy, you could have ended up working for Radio Sheffield!

Andy Scott scored his first goal for United in the last game of the season, a 4-2 win over Chelsea on May 8th 1993. The other scorers were Paul Rogers and Dane Whitehouse 2.

Overheard At The Lane (1)

Steve Haythorne

1st Blade: If I were Bassett I'd sell Corky.

2nd Blade: What would tha do wi' t'money?

1st Blade: Buy a hot dog.

Overheard At The Lane (2)

Steve Haythorne

Jostein Flo makes an innocuous but clumsy challenge on an opposing defender. A free kick is awarded against him.

1st Blade: No way referee!

2nd Blade: Errr.......actually mate I think you'll find it's pronounced NORWAY.

Great Commentating Moments

Steve Haythorne

"Vitesse Arnhem have a Gilhaus, Norwich have a Culverhouse, Sheffield United have a Whitehouse and Sheffield Wednesday have a Sh.......eridan." We know what you meant, Dave.

Overheard At The Lane (3)

Steve Haythorne

1st Blade: Gerra grip, Beesley, tha must be on drugs!

2nd Blade: If he is, it's not speed!

Overheard At The Lane (4)

Steve Haythorne

First Blade: I'd rather see Littlejohn up front than Corky.

Second Blade: I'd rather see Elton John up front than Corky!

The Wonder Of You

Chesterfield Charlie

Some years ago now, whilst being detained after the final whistle at Old Trafford to allow the Man U fans time to head home for Cirencester and all points south, a Blade regaled the assembled throng with a classic piece of seventies kitsch. It was a solo rendition of a number whose lyrics captured perfectly the essence of being a Blade. So start scoffing the jelly beans and burgers, on with the shades and the white sequinned suit and take it away.......

"No-one else can understand me,
da da da da,
Everything I do is wrong,
da da da da,
And I'll never know,
The reason why,
I love you like I do,
That's the wonder,
The wonder of you."

Overheard At The Lane (5)

Steve Haythorne

Voice from the crowd: "Keep up with play linesman, you fat git!"

Linesman turns and smirks in direction of voice, which adds, "And stop bloody laughing."

Well, I thought it was funny.

Overheard At The Lane (6)

Steve Haythorne

1st Blade: I see Spurs are hammering Marlow.

2nd Blade: I'm not surprised. What chance has one detective got against eleven pro footballers?

Overheard At The Lane (7)

Steve Haythorne

As the referee was in the process of sending off Adrian Heath in the FA Cup tie against Burnley: "Nay ref, don't show him the red card, show him his UB40!"

This was January 2nd 1993.

Oo-Err Missis!

Anon

Those who had to make do with the radio commentary when United played at Blackburn in October 1993 were treated to the innuendo of a Radio Hallam presenter's gaffe. During the broadcast came the line, "Wirmola. Right up the rear of Shearer."

Pause, then an embarrassed, "Erm.....sticking to him like glue."

This match was on October 18th 1993 and ended goalless. Wirmola was United's Swedish centre half Jonas, while Shearer is, of course, the famous England international.

Strike A Light

Steve Titterton

In an early edition of 'Flashing Blade' a competition included the question "How many light bulbs were broken on the Football Special train that ran to Watford for the third round FA Cup match in January 1968?"

Now I am not a sad individual who has spent countless sleepless hours during the intervening period researching the answer. However, whilst reading through some old programmes I discovered the answer in a letter from the Divisional Manager of British Rail at that time. His letter is in full in the programme for the fourth round tie against Blackpool on February 17th 1968: "350 supporters travelled on the train. At the journey's end three fire extinguishers were missing, eleven light bulbs were missing or broken, seventeen light shades were broken, four tables had their vinyl covers torn, four toilet seats were broken and handles removed from the basin, six toilet handles were broken, the lino was torn in several places and coat hooks in the toilet were broken off."

A spokesman for Midland Mainline said today that they hope to have the repairs completed soon and apologise to any passengers inconvenienced while using these carriages.

United won 1-0 at Watford, who had future Blades Tony Currie, Keith Eddy, Stewart Scullion and Terry Garbett in their side and who were managed by future United manager Ken Furphy. The game took place on January 27th 1968 and United's winner was scored by Mick Hill.

Overheard At The Lane (8)

Anon

During a game against Coventry City, directed at City's diminutive Scottish striker: "Speedie, tha's gorra face like a bulldog chewin' a wasp!"

Blades Beginnings

Yarmouth Years

Graham Adcock

My family has been supporting the Blades for over a hundred years, going back to my grandfather before the turn of the century.

He actually saw United win the FA Cup in 1925 against Cardiff City. The rattle he took to the 1936 final against Arsenal is one of my most prized possessions. My father has been a fanatical Sheffield United supporter all his life, although since he suffered a stroke some years ago he has been unable to attend matches. However, I did manage to get him to the 1-1 draw with Palace over the Christmas period a few seasons ago, which will unfortunately prove to be his last game because of his condition.

This was on December 28th 1991. Jamie Hoyland scored.

My father was actually born on Bramall Lane and under the influence of his dad followed United from an early age. He attended the school on Duchess Road, not far from the ground. Eventually he joined the army and while in Great Yarmouth on leave he met and married my mother. They settled in Yarmouth and had a family.

I have been a diehard Sheffield United supporter all my life and reckon I've got slightly more Yorkshire than Norfolk blood coursing through my veins. I didn't have holidays by the seaside when I was a lad - I did the reverse. I spent my holidays in Sheffield during the football season.

I can remember going to matches with my grandfather and standing in front of the old cricket pavilion and waiting until we saw which way United were kicking and then we'd either walk to the Bramall Lane end or the Kop end. Then at half time we'd wander round to the other end, hoping to see Doc Pace score. There were some good players when I was a kid. Hodgy, Joe Shaw and Graham Shaw and a bit later, Mick Jones, 'Sherman' (Alan Birchenall) and of course TC.

While at school in Great Yarmouth I converted several of my mates to supporting the Blades, albeit on a temporary basis in all but one case. We all had red and white striped shirts, although not quite the replica shirts you can buy these days. We even used to make programmes for fictitious matches, copied on the school printing machine, which I remember being of a primitive nature. We substituted our names for some of the players and of course did the pen pictures of ourselves.

Every year we won the domestic treble, the European treble and the World Club Championship. I can just imagine any United fan on holiday in sunny Yarmouth being completely bemused seeing a bunch of Yarmouth boys playing for the Blades on the sea front. When we got to the cup final we played on the bowling green, which was a very satisfactory substitute for the lush Wembley turf, although I seem to remember the bowling green attendant wasn't best pleased when he saw the result of pounding boots on his pride and joy. Mind you, I don't blame him - he never realised we were playing a cup final and I recall we had to finish that particular match on the nearest playing field.

Anyway, all this goes to prove that all we needed in those days was was a vivid imagination and a football. I feel that if the kids of today didn't have computers etc. they might just discover their own imaginations.

My two sons Neil and Lee have followed the family tradition and are Unitedites through and through. My youngest son Lee goes to a school where 99% of the boys support the other United from across the Pennines, but he proudly wears his red and white striped shirt, showing he has the bottle not to be a sheep and follow their bandwagon. His ambition is to play for United and follow Nudger Needham and lift a trophy above his head.

Over the years I have had some great moments following the Blades. Beating Manchester United, Arsenal and Wednesday, Darlington away, Leicester away 5-2, Forest away 5-2. There have been plenty of lows too; the relegations, the cup defeat at Chelsea when I really fancied us to do well. The Wembley defeat against the other lot and, of course, the Mark Stein goal at Stamford Bridge, which I don't think Harry ever recovered from.

All in all though, I've been glad to be a Blade and I tell my two sons that they were always going to be Bladesmen - there really was no choice; it's our destiny to support the Blades in our family: even my wife has seen United.

Recently I have started a Norfolk branch of the Sheffield United Supporters' Club. The branch is still in its infancy and membership is still under twenty. However, the members are from this immediate area and Norfolk is a big county, so I believe there must be plenty more out there somewhere.

Living where I do I miss the banter that you Blades in Sheffield must experience with other Blades, and, let it be said, the other lot. I hope to partly rectify this situation and run a coach to selected matches when the membership is bigger.

I have been travelling to matches all over the country with my two sons for years, but the price of three tickets and petrol is making it a very costly day out. All my matches are away matches, apart from the Norwich game and possibly Ipswich, although even this is a one-hundred mile round trip. So hopefully in the foreseeable future a coach full of Blades will be running from Norfolk.

Germany Calling

Cynthia Titterton

My dad first started taking me to the Lane when I was about seven or eight, to the reserves before any first-team games. I can remember he used to carry me in until as I was nine as kids in arms were free (at school I was always the smallest in class), all to save about ninepence.

One of my best memories is from about 1951/52 time. Jimmy Hagan and Harold Brook had a sports shop on London Road, nearly opposite the end of Hill Street. I had a pen friend come over from Germany on a school swap and we took her to the match.

Anyway, when I was going over to stop with her she wanted a picture of Jimmy Hagan taking across. So I called in his shop and asked him and he said yes. He got this big box of photos out, which was full of Harold Brook's pictures but hardly any of himself. He had to look right

No.48 Bishopscourt Road, where impressionable youngsters once tried to catch sight of Alf Ringstead and Tony Currie, but maybe not of Barry Hartle and Steve Cammack, who also used to live there.

through them to find one, because he was that popular.

Teen idols are definitely nothing new. I can remember vividly a friend and myself traipsing up and down Bishopscourt Road hoping to see Alf Ringstead as we passed his house. We'd walk to the top and then cut round the back of the houses by taking a path that led behind them. We always hoped we'd catch a glimpse of him in his garden.

Autograph-hunting of footballers must be as old as the game itself. All generations have done it and we were no exception. We used to stand in John Street waiting for the players and once, what really left my dad dead chuffed, was when a small boy came up and asked him for his!

By far my best memory was of us beating Wednesday 7-3. I was still at school then. I can also remember going away to Leicester and they drew 5-5 and I remember going to Grimsby when someone kicked the ball and it hit the ref on the head and knocked him out, and no-one knew what to do. So Jimmy Hagan kicked the ball out while the ref got some attention.

United beat Wednesday 7-3 on September 8th 1951, before a crowd of 51,075. The match at Leicester took place on November 3rd 1951.

Sharpe Blade

Peter Sharpe

I was showing my newly-born daughter to my auntie's family at their home in Parson Cross on the day the Blades visited Meadow Lane in March 1995. At half past three it was time for me and my family to head for home in Chesterfield so that I could put on Ceefax and press for page 305. The half-hour journey was frustrating for me as I wanted to know the latest score urgently. We do have a radio in our car but it is no use to me to switch on the commentary from Radio Sheffield or Hallam (I don't know which is the best!) because I am profoundly deaf.

While I was stuck in the traffic on Queen's Road, I spotted a car with a Blades sticker in the back window and I was very tempted to wind down my car window and shout at the people in the car to ask if they knew the score but I didn't want to look like an idiot - not because of my desperation for the latest at Meadow Lane but because the lads in the other car would wonder why I had not switched on my own car radio!

This game was at Meadow Lane on March 11th 1995. United lost 2-1 with Paul Beesley equalising Devon White's goal before Simpson lobbed the winner for County.

Between 1970 and 1973 I was at most of United's home and away matches so it was hardly any trouble being updated about how the Blades were getting on, apart from being on holiday in late August in both 1970 and 1971. I remember being at Ayr in 1971 at the dancing hall in the Pontin's camp watching my family and other campers enjoying themselves dancing, but the most important thing on my mind was Arsenal v Sheffield United many miles away. At 9.15pm I dragged my dad from the dance hall to the TV room to catch the result on the news. We had just missed the results announcement so my dad asked one of the viewers for the Highbury result. He turned round to me saying, "Arsenal nil, Sheffield United one!"

You can imagine my joy because of the Blades' brilliant start to the 1971/72 season - four wins out of four, beating Southampton then thrashing each of the 1969, 1970 and 1971 League champions.

United began the 1971/72 season, their first after promotion, by winning their first four matches. They beat Southampton 3-1 (Alan Woodward (pen.), Geoff Salmons, John Flynn) at home, then Leeds United 3-0 (John Flynn, Bill Dearden, Eddie Colquhoun) at home, Everton 1-0 (Alan Woodward) away and Arsenal 1-0 (Stewart Scullion) away.

In August 1973 I started residing at a boarding school near Newbury after passing exams to gain scholarship. It did not really hit home that I would not be able to watch United as regularly as I had.

As the school year started in the third week in August it meant that I had to miss the opening fixture of the 1973/74 season, at home to Burnley. On that Saturday at kick-off time I was in the Manor House (all schoolgirls and first-year boys resided there). I was thinking of my dad in his usual place in row A, seat 85 of the Bramall Lane Stand (yes, I was very homesick!) and I noticed that some partially-deaf pupils had their transistor radios glued to their ears listening to the football. I had no luck in obtaining the score from Bramall Lane because the listeners were more concerned about Manchester United, Liverpool and Leeds, even though most of them lived many miles from their favourite club. They remind me of Chesterfield people who'd rather walk in town wearing a Manchester

United shirt than that of any of their local clubs. I got into the junior common room and saw two girls telling other pupils the half-time scores they had heard from the TV. I went up to them and said, "What's the half-time score for Sheffield United?"

One of the two girls said she had missed that particular score and the other said, "We're not interested in Sheffield United." Charming!

I decided that the only alternative was to go to the other hostel, the Mansell House (where the second year and onwards boys resided). I had to seek permission from a teacher or a matron to go to the Mansell House. It was near full time when I finally got permission. As I entered the television room I approached a sixth former who had the news I was waiting for, but I got a nasty shock to learn that United had lost 2-0.

Burnley won the first game of the 1973/74 season, beating United 2-0 at Bramall Lane on August 25th 1973.

Ten days later, on the night of the Blades v Arsenal match, there was no chance for me to know the result of the match until the next morning because, as a first former, I had to get ready for bed at 7.45pm and the lights went out at 8.15. I got up and got myself dressed quickly after the 7am waking call and went straight to the corridor linking the Manor House with the school, leaving the others in my dormitory still in torpor. One of the school rules was that you were only allowed to enter the classroom after breakfast, which finished at 8.15am, otherwise you would be grounded with no privileges for a period of time decided by the staff. I was waiting for the paperboy to deliver the 'Daily Mail' into my classroom (1M) and also my preferred paper, the 'Daily Express', into another classroom (1K). As soon as the paperboy had gone I decided to take the risk and break the school rule by going into classroom 1K. I turned over the 'Daily Express' for the important back page and then my mouth dropped open at seeing the print - Sheffield United 5 Arsenal 0, and a photo of Jimmy Bone scoring the fourth goal. After that I sneaked back to the dormitory (no, no-one caught me!) and screamed for joy! Sadly, I had missed seeing Tony Currie's 'revenge' on Alan Ball by sitting on the ball.

In 1971/72 Arsenal had beaten United 5-0 at Bramall Lane, but the Blades gained revenge by winning by the same scoreline on September 4th 1973. Bill Dearden, Alan Woodward, Tony Currie (2) and Jim Bone were the scorers.

I continued the trend of finding out the scores of the previous night's matches before breakfast a few more times until after I discovered that United had lost 3-0 at home to Ipswich in March 1974, when I was caught by a senior matron, resulting in having to lose my privileges over quite a long period of time. During the punishment I had to miss the annual talent contest (which every pupil either watched or took part in) on my birthday, and I had to go to bed half an hour before the others.

Due to the power workers' strike the game against Ipswich was played on a midweek afternoon on March 12th 1974.

Sunday walks from 2pm to 4pm were compulsory for all pupils except the sixth formers, unless there was heavy rain, so we were unable to watch 'The Big Match' on ITV. In my six years at the school there was hardly ever a downpour on a Sunday in Newbury! On a Sunday morning in September 1973, the day after the Blades' 2-1 win at Chelsea, I read in the newspaper that United would be featured on 'The Big Match'. Miss Sissons, my kind class teacher from my old school in Sheffield, had already made arrangements to take me out for the afternoon, as her parents lived in Thatcham, near Newbury. When Miss Sissons and her boyfriend arrived at the school I explained to her that United were going to be on TV that afternoon. She knew my devotion towards the Blades and agreed that I could watch the match at her boyfriend's house, after which we would all go out. I came back to school afterwards and told my envious friends (who had to go for a Sunday walk), that I saw 'The Big Match'!

United won 2-1 against Chelsea at Stamford Bridge on September 1st 1973. Tony Currie and Alan Woodward scored.

Throughout the six years I was at school my dad would post me the 'Green 'Un' every week along with his own match reports, which my friends liked to read even though they did not support the Blades. A typical letter from my Dad would read something like "Dear Peter, Blades... blah, blah..." and end with "P.S. Oh, by the way, our house got burnt down!"

Between school holidays my dad would take me home for the weekend twice a term. I once asked my Dad how he managed to get enough petrol for his car to pick me up from school for the weekend to see a United match during the fuel shortage of 1974. He said he got petrol by siphoning it from his firm's van. Bless him! Also, about once a year he would drive down to the school on a Saturday and take me and two or three friends to an away match in London or Southampton, returning home after dropping us back at school after the match. In the holidays I would attend almost all the matches United played.

Entering the second form meant that I now resided in the Mansell House. Getting the scores was a bit easier. A Newcastle fan, three years older than me, would inform me of the score, but only if the Blades were losing! Before the final match of the 1974/75 season at Birmingham we all thought that a win would be enough for United to finish fifth and win a place in the UEFA Cup the following season. The match was played in midweek and I had to go to bed at 8.15pm, with lights out at 8.30. Earlier I had asked the Head Boy if he could look out for the result and he said I could go to see him the next morning after the waking up call at 7am. That night I was tossing and turning in bed, unable to sleep. I kept hopping out of bed pretending I needed to go to the toilet in the hope that I would bump into a senior pupil in the corridor and he might be able to tell me the final score. At 11pm I realised I would have to wait. The next morning I dashed towards the head boy's room, still in my pyjamas and dressing gown, only to be stopped by a prefect who doubted that I had permission from the head boy to enter his room to find out the important result. He told me to get washed and dressed and put on my school uniform before I could. I said OK, but I had a lot of unprintable words for the prefect. After I hastily got washed and dressed I ran back. The prefect was still there! This time he went into the room and asked the Head Boy for the score. He returned and said, "Nil nil." I sadly strolled downstairs to the common room and cried in front of the other puzzled pupils.

United drew 0-0 in the last game of the season against Birmingham City at St Andrews on April 29th 1975. A victory would have meant qualification for the UEFA Cup.

From the second year onwards I played in goal for the school team at all ages, and also for the first team. At away matches there would usually be someone listening to the radio on the coach - if not I would have to wait until we arrived back at the school. I suffered a lot of ribbing when United seemed to lose nearly every week in the disastrous 1975/76 season.

Fourth formers were allowed to watch the first game on 'Match of the Day' on Saturday nights. As soon as I discovered that the 3-0 home defeat by Luton Town was to be shown it was obvious

that it would be the second match. I pleaded with the teacher on duty to let me watch the whole programme that night and miss it for the next three Saturdays. The teacher nodded and informed all the prefects of the agreement we had struck. I know we lost the match, but it was important that I could see my heroes on TV.

United lost 3-0 at home to Luton Town on January 22nd 1977.

In February 1978 my dad asked my cousin to come with him to my school, pick me up and watch the Blades at Southampton. The problem was that I was selected to play in goal for the school's Under-15 team at Bearwood College (somewhere in Surrey) and it was the school's policy that a pupil had to play for the school rather than go out for the day. The week prior to the match had a lot of frosty weather and my hopes had risen when the sports master said that the match at Bearwood was doubtful. I wrote to my dad to tell him of the situation - he knew I would rather see the Blades than play for the school team. The decision on the match going ahead was taken on the Friday night after a discussion on the phone between the sports master and Bearwood College. The better weather forecast swung the decision - the match would be played. After being informed, I went upstairs to my dormitory for a quiet weep in the dark.

The next morning, when my dad arrived with my cousin, my sad face indicated to him that I had to play for my bloody school. Dad tried to gee me up and told me to do my best in goal - but I let in eighteen goals in the match! My teammates complained I wasn't trying! Did I try my best in goal? I leave it to your thinking!

United were beaten 2-1 by Southampton at The Dell on February 25th 1978. Colin Franks scored for United.

Teletext TV arrived in the school in 1977/78 and Ceefax had a latest score service, although it wasn't updated as regularly as it is now. In October 1978 the score on Ceefax was updated when Sunderland scored their first goal at Bramall Lane. I, along with the others, kept pressing the remote control for the scores every five minutes. At 4.45pm it was still Sheff Utd 0 Sunderland 1 and I was praying for United to score a last-gasp equaliser. We stopped looking at Ceefax and opted for 'Grandstand's' teleprinter results service. I prefer to find out United's results from the teleprinter as it is more exciting than the final results sheet.

The picture on 'Grandstand' switched to a

report of a game that would be shown on 'Match of the Day' that night. I instantly recognised the scene as Bramall Lane and was confused yet elated at seeing the caption "Sheffield United 3 Sunderland 2". I was trying to work out how four goals were scored at such a late stage. I reckoned that Ceefax wouldn't update the score because United were winning! A partially-deaf Charlton Athletic supporter listened to the report for me and said that Alex Sabella (my hero at the time, and I still can't believe that the skills the United team had that season were to condemn the club to the Third Division) had a brilliant match.

The problem was that I was on the last day of a two-week punishment and I pleaded with the teacher on duty to let me watch 'Match of the Day' - he paused and made an agreement similar to the one I had had for watching the home defeat to Luton two years earlier.

United beat Sunderland 3-2 at Bramall Lane on October 7th 1978 with goals from Peter Anderson (2) and Steve Finnieston.

When I left the school in 1979, despite United's relegation to the Third Division I bought a season ticket for the coming season (my dad declined to buy one for the first time in years). I believed I was going to attend every game home and away for ever. Instead I found myself playing regularly (not as a goalie!) on Saturdays because I was disillusioned with 'Happy' Harry Haslam's broken promises and because players who were well past their sell-by date were using to the club to earn fat wages. I did go to midweek matches, or if my team did not have a match on the Saturday or if our game was postponed then I went to the Lane if United were at home on the same day.

In 1988 I gave up playing to start going to the Lane again and it was because of the appointment of Dave Bassett as manager. It was a breath of fresh air to the club. Also it was good to see the whole team wearing the colours of Sheffield United with pride for a change. In November of that year on the Headquarters Branch Supporters' Club coach to a midweek away match at Aldershot I sat next to a man who was unwilling to talk to me despite my efforts to start a conversation with him. On the way back from the 1-0 defeat I asked him if he could listen out for the results affecting United's promotion chances for me. He said OK.

Then I could sense that the coach radio had started to announce the results because the supporters stopped their conversations and were shaping up to listen, then moaning and cheering. After twenty minutes of patience I asked him if the results had been on. He nodded. Then I asked him what the Third Division scores were and he said, "I can't remember."!

United lost 1-0 at Aldershot on November 8th 1988.

I have been on the HQ branch coaches to many away matches and nearly every time various people have cheerfully helped me with the results but on the coach to Coventry in March 1993 I got into a needless incident because of the coach steward's ignorance towards me (he had also been nasty to me on the journey to Spurs earlier in the season). I wondered if he was related to the man who sat next to me for the Aldershot trip!

United won 3-1 at Coventry City on March 24th 1993. Dane Whitehouse, Brian Deane and Adrian Littlejohn scored after John Williams had put Coventry ahead. The earlier game against Tottenham Hotspur was on September 2nd 1992. Spurs won 2-0. Teddy Sheringham and Gordon Durie scored.

On the day United were relegated in the last thirty seconds at Chelsea in May 1994 I was at Castle Dyke Playing Fields on Ringinglow Road, playing cricket in the Norton League. My cricket team consists mainly of profoundly-deaf and a few partially-deaf players. We batted first. I was out for a duck (yes, I was thinking about the match at Stamford Bridge!). At 3.30 I dragged my partially-deaf friend Kevin to my car. Kevin does have problems in understanding the reports fully. He got the scores at Chelsea and Everton but got confused with the scores at Ewood Park and Upton Park, saying that Ipswich and Southampton were leading 3-0 and 4-0 respectively. I had thought that Wimbledon were home and dry leading 2-0 and United were 2-1 ahead. I was cheerfully telling the United supporters in the team that we would be safe, and then Everton started pulling back and Chelsea equalised. I was hoping that Kevin was getting the scores wrong and then when Everton went 3-2 up he was saying that the commentator was reporting that United now simply needed a point, which did not make sense to me because I was thinking that Ipswich and Southampton were winning easily.

Just before the final whistle my cricket team had just finished our innings and our opponents (none of them deaf, of course) surrounded my car listening to the final scores. One of them, a Wednesdayite, said, "United's lost 3-2, Southampton are safe, Everton have won 3-2, there is only the final whistle yet to come at

Blackburn and it's 0-0 at the moment."

At that time it became clear to me that Blackburn had to score a last-minute winner to save United from the drop. A minute later the insensitive Wednesdayite screamed that United were down. I just sat in my car feeling numb.

On May 7th 1994 an unlikely combination of results was needed to relegate United. They all happened, as United lost 3-2 to a goal by Mark Stein thirty seconds from full time at Stamford Bridge. It was his second of the match, having earlier equalised Glyn Hodges' goal. In the first half Jostein Flo put United ahead but Jakob Kjeldberg levelled early in the second.

Now, with bringing up a family, the high costs of going to away matches meant that until I bought a new PC which included the Internet, I would have to stare at the Ceefax pages for the latest scores, or until my Dad's sad passing in September 1999, he would listen to the radio commentary for me at his house.

My Dad had become a Blade because he was in the same class at school as the son of Fred Jessop, a tough-tackling player who joined United from Derby in 1938, so if any of my three children becomes another Blade in the family, it will be down to Fred Jessop! I will always be grateful to my dear Dad, who was also a dear grandfather to my kids for bringing me so many happy memories by taking me to so many Blades matches.

Father And Son

Duncan Payne

My father, Don, was born on December 10th 1925, just 229 days after United last won the FA Cup. The day before his birth the Blades lost 3-1 at Newcastle but within a month they had recorded their biggest ever victory, 11-2 against Cardiff City. By the end of that season United had climbed from below half way in the First Division to finish in the top five. But let's not delude ourselves; my father's arrival on the scene did not herald a new dawn of Blades domination. We have only appeared in one cup final since - which we lost - and have yet to finish higher in the league.

Dad can vividly remember listening to that cup final in 1936 on the wireless at home on Rustlings Road and he recalls being devastated when Ted Drake scored Arsenal's winner late in the game. United have never been so close to winning a major trophy in his lifetime and

probably never will be again.

United's goalkeeper at Wembley, Jack Smith, played in the same side as my father many years later, in an exhibition game, but this time his role was as a scheming inside forward. Without doubt Smith could have reached a high level of football playing in this position; he only became a goalkeeper by accident whilst playing for Bolsterstone. Ernest Jackson, United's half back in the cup final, played in the same exhibition match and Jimmy Hagan was one of the linesmen.

Dad's footballing skills developed while he was at High Storrs School. At the time it was one of the best school teams in Sheffield and my father's year frequently won their matches by large scores. As a direct consequence of this the players would take it in turn to play in goal and were so adaptable that most could play equally well in any position. Ajax may well have based their total football philosophy on this system!

In the early 1940s my grandfather contacted Norton Woodseats FC and recommended that they give his son a trial and when asked what was his best position a shrug of the shoulders was probably the reply. My father, although more than happy in defence, also enjoyed playing up front as his eight goals in his last game for High Storrs testified.

Dad's first appearance for Norton Woodseats was at left back. The club had a reputation for being something of a nursery side for United and to play for them was to play for one of the top amateur sides in the area. But there was a drawback - you had to wear Sheffield Wednesday's cast-offs! However, if this meant a ticket to Bramall Lane it was a small price to pay. Many Norton Woodseats players progressed on to United's books and two of them, both of whom my father played alongside regularly, became Lane favourites. His partner on the right was Cec Coldwell, who joined United in 1951 and made over 400 league appearances.

During the late sixties Coldwell became United's coach, a position that he held for fifteen years, although he also had a highly successful spell as caretaker manager following the sacking of Jimmy Sirrel in September 1977. At centre half was Howard Johnson. He joined United six months before Coldwell and made almost a hundred appearances before a move to York City in 1957.

Alas, my dad's career as a footballer didn't reach the dizzy heights of this pair but he was a fine player nevertheless. He mastered the art of the sliding tackle to perfection and to such a degree that he claims never to have fouled an opponent in his life. His sheer pace and anticipation would not allow many outside rights a sniff of the ball. United's manager, Teddy Davison, was clearly aware of my father's ability and on one (but only one) occasion he paid a visit to my family home. Here he was to enquire as to the possibility of my dad turning out for the Blades at Chesterfield that afternoon but unfortunately my grandfather had to turn Davison away because Payne junior was out and could not be contacted!

United weren't the only club interested. Bolton Wanderers kept tabs for a while and Burnley actually made a firm offer for him. His chances of becoming a First Division footballer were quickly dispelled, however, when grandfather would not allow him to move to Turf Moor. In those days, of course, footballers' wages were no different to those of most other professions and my grandfather believed that he was better off staying in Sheffield and finding a proper job.

During his time as a player he once managed to get his name in the 'News of the World' and, like often happens today, they totally misrepresented the facts. The day after playing for Norton Woodseats against Walton and Hersham in the old Amateur Cup they credited him with an own goal. Naturally he hotly denies that he was anywhere near the ball when it crossed the line, although for the life of him he cannot recall which teammate committed the offence!

As time marched on into the 1960s my dad became known as Mr D.N.H.Payne (Sheffield), particularly in match programmes. On the terraces he was known by more unsavoury titles. He had become a Football League referee. Much as I would like to relate to you tales of numerous controversial refereeing decisions that my father made, I cannot because in reality they were few and far between. He once sent off Mike Doyle of Manchester City though, and he had the satisfaction of accepting the disgraced defender's red-eyed apology after the game.

By now I had entered the world. Up until the age of eight I detested football. For a start it took my dad away from home on Saturdays and quite often he wouldn't be home again until after I had gone to bed. Also I never got a kick of the ball when he took me into our back garden on Sunday afternoons. He used to laugh maniacally as he kept the ball away from me. He was Pele while I was an out-of-touch Dennis Longhorn. I was small for my age and was always one of the kids who wouldn't take part in the eighteen-a-side matches in the schoolyard with a tennis ball at playtime. More likely to become a jockey than a footballer. As it turned out I became neither.

With all this in mind my father performed his greatest achievement. He got me interested, nay, besotted, by football. His tactic was simple - he took me down to the Lane. On the evening of November 8th 1971 my life changed. As we got into the car to go to the match I was feeling excited, although this was probably more due to the prospect of a late night than the visit of Arsenal. The game itself is nothing but a distant memory; the history books remind me that it was a League Cup fourth round replay and the Blades won 2-1 with goals from Alan Woodward and Gil Reece. At the time I did not appreciate that United were in the top four in the top division and that a month earlier they were the most feared team in the land. I was far more appreciative of the gloriously green pitch gleaming under the floodlights, and how the cigarette lighters would flicker every few seconds. The mass of people, like one giant being, created an atmosphere that was scary, yet irresistible, to an eight-year old child. That night I climbed on to a rollercoaster that I have never been able to get off.

We didn't go regularly to the Lane until the 1973/74 season, which was the season when I first saw the Blades lose, at home to Manchester City, when Tom McAlister broke his leg courtesy of Rodney Marsh.

On October 20th 1973 United lost 2-1 at home to Manchester City. Bill Dearden scored for both sides. Alan Woodward took over in goal from McAlister.

Later that season, on January 1st, I made my debut on the Kop but I did not bring the team luck as Tony Currie's 24th birthday bash fell flat.

United lost 2-1 at home to Chelsea on January 1st 1974. Alan Woodward scored for United.

I rarely ventured away from the Kop on matchdays from then on, although I had my one and only season ticket for the South Stand for the 1975/76 season. Call me superstitious but I have never had a season ticket since. From then on, of course, the club went into decline but my enthusiasm grew even stronger. My dad was ditched in favour of mates and I began to travel to away games more frequently. Then in November 1980, as United were inching their way down the Third Division, I made my biggest mistake; I began to work in the retail trade.

Saturdays off were not always possible, alternate ones if I was lucky, but I still got to games when I could. I am grateful that I saw plenty of the Division Four campaign that took me to places like Halifax, Crewe, Tranmere, York and the town that holds many treasured memories, Darlington.

This pattern continued for a few years and during this time my mates and I formed 'The Three Bs'. The interests of this politically incorrect group were namely Blades, Booze and Birds. Copious amounts of the former pair were were imbibed by us all but, in my case, there was not much joy with the third!

Then in 1986 I was promoted - something that United were finding impossible at the time - and moved to Grimsby. I'm proud to say that I never once ventured inside Blundell Park during my two-year sentence. However, it did mean that I was not able to attend as many games and in particular evening kick offs. One exception was the Bristol City play-off disaster in 1988 when a Cleethorpes-based Blade, Nigel, drove like his namesake Mansell and whisked me off to the Lane. After the game I drowned my sorrows like a good 'un in the Royal Oak at the bottom of Cemetery Road and the following morning I had to contend with a mega hangover and United back in Division Three.

United drew the second leg of the promotion/relegation play-off with Bristol City 1-1 at Bramall Lane on May 18th 1988. Colin Morris scored in his last game for the Blades. Bristol had won the first leg 1-0 three days earlier so United were relegated.

The following season the revival under Dave Bassett began. The Blades led the table in the early part of the season and thrashed Newcastle United in a League Cup tie by 3-0.

First Division Newcastle were beaten in the first leg of a second round League Cup tie at Bramall Lane on September 27th 1988 with goals by Brian Deane (2) and Paul Stancliffe. Newcastle won the second leg 2-0 two weeks later so the Blades progressed 3-2 on aggregate.

A few days after this triumph I was on the move again. This time my job took me to Ilkeston in Derbyshire where the local football club, the Town F.C., were languishing in the Central Midlands League and were about to have their ground turned into a supermarket. United, however, went from strength to strength, and won successive promotions to earn themselves a place back in the top flight for the first time since 1976. My appearances at United matches were becoming rarer but I was one of the fortunate eight thousand or so Blades who were able to get to Filbert Street to witness one of United's most remarkable performances ever.

United needed to win the last game of the season away to Leicester City on May 5th 1990 to ensure promotion to the First Division. After Gary Mills gave Leicester an early lead, United went on to win 5-2 with goals from Paul Wood, Brian Deane, Tony Agana (2) and Wilf Rostron.

It is somewhat ironic that, with the Blades back amongst the football elite, I rarely got to go and watch them play. The travelling distances, working Saturdays and a mortgage conspired to make me only an occasional visitor to the Lane. On the times I did watch them they never let me down; one of my favourite matches ever was the 5-2 win at the City Ground, when United outpassed and outclassed Cloughie's boys.

United won 5-2 away to Nottingham Forest on February 1st 1992. Mike Lake, John Gannon, Ian Bryson, Carl Bradshaw and Brian Deane scored for United, Roy Keane and Stuart Pearce (pen.) for Forest.

The team did well on other occasions too. I only ever saw United lose twice in their four seasons at the top! Shortly after the Forest game I began watching football live more frequently, but it wasn't the Blades. I had an affair. I started following the fortunes of another team. Before you all start shouting "Traitor!" please let me explain. Like any affair I made sure that the two loves of my life could never possibly meet (if they ever did, I'm sure that I would do what most men do and go back to the one they have had a long-term relationship with), as the two teams were then five divisions apart. As if to further justify my actions, it should be said that at least I didn't take the easy option and follow Manchester United. No, I began to watch games in the Doctor Marten's League (Midland Division). I made many new friends standing at the New Manor Ground, home of Ilkeston Town F.C. and progressed from casual observer to ardent fan to joint programme editor - our programme finished third in he Southern League for the 1995/96 season in the annual Wirral Programme Club awards - and finally to author, when I penned the story of the club's fiftieth anniversary in 1995.

I do not feel guilty about this relationship and I get as much out of supporting the Robins as I do the Blades, but for very different reasons. I enjoy the freedom you get at the New Manor Ground that league grounds cannot provide.

The rush to the clubhouse for a pint before the half-time whistle blows, the friendly banter with opposing supporters (and goalkeepers!) and also to mingle and chat with the players and managers after the game. But despite all this the Blades will always be the number one club for me.

There have been very few links between the two clubs over the years. They have actually met three times, during the 1960s and 1970s and, not surprisingly, United won all three, by 8-2, 4-1 and 2-1. There have also been around a dozen players who have been on the books of both clubs, but only three of any note: John Tudor, a born-and-bred Ilkestonian, was a Town reserve who had only made occasional appearances for the first team. He moved to Coventry City in the mid-sixties before joining United, where he scored regularly before moving on to greater things with Newcastle United in 1971 (John Hope and David Ford joined the Blades in exchange for Tudor). Gary Hamson joined the Blades as a youngster after being spotted playing for one of Ilkeston Town's junior sides (at around this time Ilkeston Town had a deal with Jimmy Sirrel whereby they would recommend to United any outstanding local talent), and finally Alan Young, who came the opposite route and signed for Ilkeston in the late 1980s. Unitedites will be interested but not surprised to learn that his spell at the Old Manor Ground was interspersed with long periods on the treatment table.

By October 1995 the wheels of my football life had revolved full circle. I revisited Bramall Lane for the Derby County match. And just like in the very beginning I sat down with my father, I was in a three-sided ground and faced a vast open space; and like in the very beginning the game ended 2-0, but this time it wasn't United who won. Yet although I was saddened and at times angered with what was frankly an inept performance, part of me felt happy. For the Euro 96 Championships the song went, "Football's Coming Home". On that afternoon so was I.

United lost 2-0 at home to Derby County on October 7th 1995.

How I Became A Blade

Chas Ponsford

It was destiny but I never realised the glittering truth until a fateful day in 1988 when the Blades defeated a typically under-performing Wolves 2-0 at the Lane. On that crisp October day my

brother and I experienced what could only be compared to St Paul's experience on the road to Damascus. On that day, not on the road to Damascus but on John Street by a burger van, we became born-again Blades.

This was October 8th 1988. United's scorers were Brian Deane and Tony Agana.

The signs were there all my life even though I'd been (apparently) a through-and-through Manchester United fan for nearly twenty years.

Sign 1
My mother's side of the family were all from Woodseats, great grandad a foreman in the steelworks, grandad a small cutlery factory owner before the depression in the 1930s. As a kid I remember visits to Sheffield from our home in middle-class Cheshire in the 1960s. Standing at the bottom of grandad's garden on Cobnar Road watching the sun set (through the smog) over hills, factories and terraced houses - a sight that stayed with me until I was drawn back to Sheffield in 1988.

Sign 2
My dad's side of the family inflicted the name Ponsford on me ('fat guts' in French apparently - yes, my ancestors obviously ate all the pies). The name has only two saving graces: 1) it's the surname of the great Aussie Test cricketer Bill; 2) it's a famous snobby furniture company in the heart of Blades territory.

Sign 3
And finally, an uncanny experience that would have made an excellent episode for that crap Michael Aspel programme 'Strange But True' or whatever it's called (I await with eager anticipation the episode on Chris Woods).

I attended THAT game at Old Trafford as a 13-year old in 1971/72 in the October sun as a Manchester United fanatic - yes, that game, when Sheffield United were top of the league and unbeaten and who lost 2-0 to a much-shown George Best classic as he glided with seeming ease past five or six defenders before scoring, and a Bob Booker type effort from gangling Alan Gowling which is never shown on TV. A number of events in this match pointed to my future Bladesmanship:

1) Under my parka (not a fish tail and it had red lining, might as well have been an anorak) I had a white Umbro shirt with red trim that uncannily happened to be the Blades away top that year.

2) The game was 0-0 when I left the ground for

our Crosville bus back to Frodsham at the cricket ground thinking it was close to full time. My watch was wrong. I have never left a game before the final whistle since. Prophetic. Someone was making sure I didn't celebrate my future team's defeat.

3) Our windows were put in by some skinheads lobbing railway bricks - was this a warning shot from the infamous BBC about my then Mancunian leanings?

There then followed a bleak fifteen years or so of Manchester United supporting with a short interim while on teaching practice watching Blackburn Rovers, when they were a proper club of the people, under our one-time revered leader Mr Howard Kendall, as he cut his managerial teeth before creating his memorable Everton teams of the mid 1980s. Another sign?

And so it was, after seven years teaching in Guernsey (where that mercurial genius Matthew Le Tissier, then a skinny teenager, put paid to my school team's chances of the championship with two late goals in a 3-2 win for Mare de Carteret Secondary in the final game of the season) that I returned to my roots to realise my destiny. When I resigned my cushy public school teaching job in the Channel Islands for a two-term maternity leave post at Brinsworth Comprehensive some friends questioned my sanity. I glibly told these friends I wanted to get back to decent beer and football and hills but secretly thought it was a broken marriage and a political conscience that had pushed me to move to Sheffield. The latter, of course, was utter bollocks: it WAS for decent beer, hills and definitely football - I was destined to be a Blade.

A couple of desultory trips to Old Trafford told me the magic had gone out of the relationship and a quick perusal of the 'Red Issue' fanzine told me that the present day Manchester United fans seemed a sick, arrogant, smug bunch who had lost touch with the great Busby-inspired footballing heritage.

One or two trips to Hillsborough convinced me that I could never support those half-hearted boys in blue and white. My initial impressions still hold true. The majority of Wednesdayites are the biggest bunch of moaning, humourless, fickle, slack jaws I have ever witnessed (outside the south). They can't sing a song of more than two syllables, their colours and emblem are sad and their players exhibit as much commitment to the club as David Hirst does to a low fat diet.

So to Wolves, 1988. What happened nearly ten

years ago that led to my ownership of a season ticket on the Kop (with those brilliantly planned brick ladies' loos, brick gents' loos and brick snack bar crammed together with post-Hillsborough sensitivity)?

I enjoyed everything about the whole day: a couple of silky pints in the Noah's Ark in Crookes; a football ground that felt like it was in the heart of a city (not on the edge of some industrial Siberian wasteland one sheep short of Barnsley, like Hillsborough); a distinctive club emblem exhibiting pride in the heritage of Sheffield, not some bloody outline of a shortsighted bird dangerously suitable for on-the-pitch kiddies' mascots; a crowd ready to be critical but also full of wit, humour and some magnificent songs; a manager in Harry Bassett who gave and demanded 110% and who could wear his heart on his sleeve with players, press and spectators alike; and, in Brian Deane, a new hero.

As my brother and I left the ground that day nothing needed to be said - an exchanged meaningful look as we passed the burger van in John Street said it all. It was back to the Noah's Ark after the match to celebrate our new found religion.

Subsequent years of ups and downs have only matured that initial infatuation in the long-suffering but rock solid love of a true footballing marriage. When I stood up in 1990 and hurled abuse at Brian McClair as he notched the winner for Manchester United in the FA Cup at the Lane I knew I was strangely a free and fulfilled man.

This was the FA Cup quarter final on March 11th 1990. Manchester United won 1-0.

Even now a store of memories is there to be drawn on, and all worthy of detailed treatment. Suffice to say I have no trouble getting to sleep when I can, at will, call up such nostalgic nuggets as Deane's sublime chip over the stranded Grobbelar; the big man's shot through Chris Woods' legs and the only kind of double season that counts; the fairy tale goals of Brentford reject Bob Booker; the lime yellow shirts at sunlit Leicester City and the party that followed; the gutsy Mitch Ward brace in the cup against Blackburn; the magnificent if Waddle-flawed Wembley occasion; six v Spurs; Carl Veart's pride-restoring header versus Arsenal as the style finally matched the passion; Ireland's impeccable No.1; the balloons, the flags, the greasy chip butties......

And finally in this tale of a spiritual journey

from Warwick Road to Bramall Lane, has any-body else found the peace I have found as exhib-ited in this memory?

The night before the Wembley semi-final, bed and breakfast booked, ticket in pocket, alcoholi-cally settled in a London pub, with a handful of mates.....the rich anticipation of a great Blades occasion......this was one of the most contented moments of my life.

Sad bastard really.

My First Match... And Taste Of Champagne

Karen Keenan

Although I came from a United family, I didn't really take much notice of football until I was about eleven. My Dad, having worked for United in the sixties, was a regular supporter, and we have photos of my younger brother in a United kit circa 1968. He was a big fan of Alan Woodward, which was one of the few names that meant anything to me at that time. I'm sure that moving to comprehensive school in 1970 had something to do with my increasing awareness of football - people were either United or Wednesday - and it soon became clear that, in 1970/71 United were top dogs.

Unusually, the first United match I ever went to was an away fixture towards the end of that sea-son. Dad was a regular at the Lane, with his mate, my Uncle Roy. They also took great pleas-ure in going to the occasional away match - pre-sumably this gave them a good long day out, away from wives and children. When I discov-ered they were planning to go to Middlesbrough in April 1971, I pestered to be allowed to go. So, apparently, did Roy's daughter and his wife. Dad and Roy resigned themselves to the fact they would not be having a boys' day out and off we all went. The match was a 1-1 draw but I did not see Bill Dearden's goal as everyone in front of us leapt to their feet just before he scored. I remember someone hooting one of those klax-on-type horns all the way through the game and asking Dad if he thought it was on our side or theirs.

This was April 24th 1971.

Three days after this game, United beat Cardiff City 5-1 at home and the following Saturday pro-motion was clinched by a 3-0 victory over Watford. That night Dad and Uncle Roy returned in the highest of spirits ñ not least because Roy worked for a wine merchants and Dad had brought home a bottle of champagne. I don't believe that, at twelve, I had ever tasted alcohol before, let alone champagne, but I was about to have my first glass of bubbly. When the cork flew out it hit the kitchen ceiling and dent-ed the polystyrene tiles. Nobody minded.

I think that was when I became a Blade.

A Blade In Wolves Clothing

Derek Smith

You may wonder why someone from Wolverhampton is writing about United, so I'll explain. Until 1963 I lived at Beighton before I moved down here. Anyway, my earliest recol-lection of the Blades is back in 1943 during the War when we had a lot of guest players playing and I can remember some very good games and some very high scores, but I really became a true supporter when the Division One games started again in 1946. I remember the Lane with bomb damage and being at the match against Stoke City in January 1946 when the gates on Shoreham Street were forced and until a police-man on horseback paraded up and down the line at the pavilion side the crowd was virtually on the pitch.

During the same game, spectators climbed up on to the girders, which were exposed due to the roof of the Kop being blown off in air raids and suddenly a man standing next to me clutched his hands to his head and when I looked at him I could see a trickle of blood coming from under his cap. The only way we could get him to the ambulance men was by rolling him down the Kop over people's heads. I learned later that a piece of metal had fallen from a girder and had gone through his cap and hit his head.

In the 1945/46 season FA Cup ties were played over two legs. The match against Stoke City was the fourth round second leg at Bramall Lane on January 28th 1946. Stoke won the first game 2-0, United won the second 3-2 with Colin Collindridge hitting a hat-trick. The paid attendance was 50,809.

It was about this time that I began to collect autographs and chased many footballers down John Street, often fruitlessly, but one day going to Chesterfield (where I went to Technical College) I saw Charlie Thompson (centre for-ward at the time) and he agreed to take my auto-graph book into the dressing room after a match to get me the visitors' autographs. Our friendship lasted until he told me that his eyesight was failing and he was going to Hereford, then non-league, as a player and then groundsman. Many times he took me into into the dressing room, which to me as a young lad and United supporter was a great thrill. Meeting Jimmy Hagan (my idol) remains a wonderful memory and an unforgettable experience. I was very pleased to hear that Charlie Thompson is still living in Hereford and I recently got in touch with him again.

Several of my mates found out that after matches at the Lane and other local venues, visiting teams went to the Victoria Hotel, just outside the old Victoria Station, and we used to go up there instead of hanging about outside the dressing rooms. I was once up there after a match against Manchester City when the late, great Frank Swift, who had been kicked in the face and suffered a broken jaw, and Sam Barkas (full back and English international) came out. I asked Swift for his autograph, to which he replied, "Can't you see I've been injured?"

My reply was, "Well, you don't sign with your face do you?", and Sam Barkas laughed as he told Frank Swift, "He's got you there!", and they both signed my book.

Another time we got off the train at the Victoria on our way to the match and the Everton team was just coming out of the hotel on to the coach. We saw T.G. Jones (centre half and Welsh international) talking to another chap and he told us later that the man was Cyril Sidlow (Liverpool and Welsh international goalkeeper), who was playing at the Lane that afternoon. He walked down the station approach and we jumped on a tram for the Lane. Then we saw Sidlow walking towards Hunters Bar so we shouted to him and he got on the tram with us. As we walked up John Street with him all the lads collecting autographs ran up and were surprised we knew Sidlow. He told us to send our books to him at Liverpool and he'd get us all the team's autographs. This I did later, enclosing a stamped addressed envelope, but he never returned my book. So much for appreciating our help.

The 1946/47 season was very memorable as it was the first League season after the war and except for the game versus Brentford on Christmas Day (no buses ran from Beighton) I went to all the matches played at the Lane and saw all the cup matches. I went to Wolverhampton for the fourth round and remember paying 6d (2p) once inside the ground to stand on the terrace (where the John Ireland Stand is now built). There was snow on the

ground on the Kop end and when the mascots walked round the Wolves fans snowballed Bertie Blade, so the police took him off before the pitch became covered in snow again. Little did I know that twenty years later I would be living down here and dislike the Wolves as much now as I did that afternoon! Back to the game. Stan Cullis was kicking Jimmy Hagan all through the match and when Hagan retaliated just before the final whistle he was booked. In the replay the following Wednesday the opposite happened. Hagan played dirty, Cullis retaliated and was booked.

Stoke City were beaten easily and then we played Newcastle at the Lane in the sixth round, including Len Shackleton who had scored six goals in an earlier round against Newport County. After Newcastle had scored their two goals, somewhat against the run of play, the hardest workers were the ball boys, fetching the ball back from the cricket pavilion, which Newcastle tried to reach every time they possession, just to waste time.

The 1946 Christmas Day league match against Brentford was won 6-1 (scorers Jimmy Hagan 2, Colin Collindridge 2, Walter Rickett and Ernest Jackson). The cup match at Molineux on January 25th 1947 was a 0-0 draw but United won the replay 2-0 the following Wednesday thanks to Harold Brook and Albert Nightingale. Harold Brook scored as United beat Stoke City 1-0 away in the fifth round on February 8th 1947, then Newcastle United won 2-0 at the Lane in the sixth round on March 1st.

The same season we had played a friendly against Eindhoven of Holland and I had passed my autograph book into the team bus after the game. Before I could get my book back the bus started to pull away down John Street with me running at the side of it, pleading for my book. Thankfully before too long somebody threw it out of the window, much to my delight.

The friendly against Eindhoven was actually played by a team representing Sheffield, and was organised by the Anglo Dutch Sports Association. It took place on August 27th 1946 and Eindhoven won 2-0.

The next memorable season was 1951/52, mainly for thrashing Wednesday 7-3 at the Lane and 3-1 at Hillsborough. Another high spot I remember well was in the sixteenth game of the season when we scored our fiftieth goal. I can't recall many other teams or seasons when that has been done. Referring back to the 7-3 win against Wednesday, I was working down the pit with a chap called Walt, a real raving Wednesdayite, and I could see him standing on the terrace quite close to the Kop. When Wednesday scored after ninety seconds his cap went up in the air and he was jumping up and down. But as the game went on and we scored our third, fourth and fifth he gradually seemed to shrink further and further up the terrace. Then when the sixth goal went in I saw him disappearing towards the gate.

On the Monday morning following the game I went down the pit and saw that Walt was on days as well. "Hello Walt," I said, "how are you?", trying not to appear too cocky, but Walt thought I was taking the mickey and just grunted. Later he said that he may as well have his sandwiches and added that he had not had anything to eat since Saturday. Then he issued a mouthful of swear words and, as the snap tin flew past my head, he said, "I'll bloody kill her!"

Then I noticed his sarnies and laughed. Bacon sandwiches! Just imagine six slices of white bread with red meat between!

United beat Wednesday 7-3 at Bramall Lane on September 8th 1951. The scorers were Derek Hawksworth 2, Harold Brook 2, Alf Ringstead 2 and Fred A. Smith. The return was at Hillsborough on January 5th 1952 and United won 3-1 with goals from Alf Ringstead 2 and George Hutchinson. United's fiftieth goal of the season came in the sixteenth game in a 4-1 home defeat to Nottingham Forest on November 10th 1951. Alf Ringstead scored it. United managed only forty goals in the final twenty six games and Wednesday, beaten twice by the Blades, won the Second Division championship, scoring a hundred goals in the process.

Whilst mentioning Walt, I must recall the time after Derek Dooley's horrific accident at Preston. All the week following the game bulletins were issued at regular intervals about Dooley's condition and as Walt went down the pit early and I didn't go down until 10.20, he collared me every morning to tell him the latest news. Even though all genuine football supporters were genuinely concerned about the eventual amputation, Walt was inconsolable for days after and I'm sure if I'd tried to take the mickey out of him at that time he'd have hit me.

Many other memorable occasions spring to mind, such as the fantastic return from the obscurity of the Fourth Division to the short-lived term in the Premier League. Visits to Crewe and Darlington, where we had to win to become champions, will always live in my memory. The support was fantastic in those games, particularly at Darlington, where the ground was a mass of red and white.

In the club's only ever season in the Fourth Division, in 1981/2, United won 3-2 at Crewe on May 1st 1982 (scorers Keith Edwards, Jeff King 2) and 2-0 in the last match at Darlington to clinch the championship. The scorers were Bob Hatton and Keith Edwards.

The past fifty years for me have been full of highs and lows, climaxed by an invitation to visit the Lane and see the dressing rooms fifty years after I went into the old ones in the John Street Stand. As I sat beside the players of the day my thoughts went back to the players of old. And when I was introduced to Reg Brealey I recalled the day at Darlington and he remembered it as vividly as I did. Later in the directors' lounge, I met Jock Dodds and John Sheen and was amazed that Jock, even at eighty years of age, still remembered a goal I saw him score at the Bramall Lane end when he played for Everton. He even told me that United won 2-1 as well. I was amazed even more when John Sheen told me that Jock lived in Blackpool and still went out dancing quite often.

The Everton match must have been on November 17th 1928. United's scorers were Fred Tunstall (pen.) and Tom Phillipson.

My best eleven of the past fifty years are:

1. Alan Hodgkinson
2. Len Badger
3. Graham Shaw
4. Joe Shaw
5. Paul Stancliffe
6. Alec Forbes
7. Alf Ringstead
8. Jimmy Hagan
9. Brian Deane
10. Tony Currie
11. Derek Hawksworth

Manager - Dave Bassett (I can imagine what he would do with a team like that).

Forging A Blade

Gordon Hodgson

It all started for me in 1957 with my dad, United v Huddersfield in the FA Cup and, to start how it would go on, we lost! Dad told me later that Denis Law was playing for them aged sixteen. All I remember is trying to get what seemed an enormous rattle to turn two-handed but couldn't do it (I was only six) and the blaze of colour that is a match at Bramall Lane.

Gordon's memory is not quite right here as the game ended 1-1. It was an FA Cup third round replay on

January 7th 1957, played on a Monday afternoon. United's scorer was John Spencer.

A while later dad took me to a night match to see a man called Joe Shaw play again after breaking a leg. This was something else. The colour, the red and white stripes, the floodlights. "Look son, that's him, a great player." And he was. It had started. It was entering my blood. I was becoming a Blade.

My dad stood right to the top of the Kop, behind the white wall. I was left at the front wall, apparently in no danger in those days. I remember during boring times and during half time watching all the fag ends light up in random nature all round the ground, totally mesmerised. A lad stood behind me, who nowadays would be called an anorak. He used to give the rattle a quick burst for every pass, shot and corner and then bung it back under his arm very quickly, leaving the handle exposed for the next incident or goal, whereupon an absolute explosion of rattles went up from behind the Kop goal.

Rattles were lost forever in the early sixties with the onset of hooligans. They used to hit people with them! Also as a result of this element, the bloke who used to walk round with the scoreboard and the people who used to come round with the blanket collecting money at half time disappeared, due to morons sharpening coins and throwing them at 'em. A lot worse was to follow.

By now I was a veteran supporter of about five years. My first idols came. The one and only Doc Pace. He always seemed to be enjoying playing, as you should, paid or not. What price today for Doc? Hodgy in the net. Brilliant. Cec, Joe, Billy Hodgson. He had the same surname as me and I told all my mates at school he was my uncle. The kudos was great. Funny how gullible you are at ten and eleven years old.

We had a good team. Sixth round of the cup for four years on the trot, including a semi. Who'd have thought we'd have to wait thirty years for the next one? In the sixth round against Burnley I was only yards away from where the wall collapsed. There were ambulances, the job lot, on the cricket pitch. The match carried on. As always happens with United, what could have been a disaster off the pitch turned into one on the pitch, losing to one of the flukiest goals you'll ever see, from Ray Pointer. Gutted! I was only ten years old and was more upset about the result than the wall collapse. My mother knew how close I was. It wasn't as important as the result, was it?

This was March 10th 1962.

One of the sixth round matches was against THEM. I can see my dad now listening to the draw, twelve o'clock Monday, as it should be. The BBC voice says (rustle, rustle) "Sheffield United," (another rustle of the bag) "..... will play (pause)..... Sheffield........"

The next thing a piece of bread and tomato hit the kitchen wall behind him.

I actually lived in Sheffield 6 and went to Hillsborough every other Saturday with my dad or grandad, who was one of 'them'. I would wear my red and white striped shirt (which eventually, when I grew older, had to be surgically removed) and shout my head off for the opposing team, returning home unharmed (different days!) and as hoarse as I'd be if I'd gone to the Lane.

So, as you can imagine, Sheffield went berserk. There were team photos (some even in colour) and free rosettes. My 'friends' at school (Philadelphia, now demolished, just off Infirmary Road) tied me across the school fence. They tied my ankles to one side, bent me across and tied my wrists to the other, then kept hitting me to get me to shout, "Up the Owls!"

No way. I'd die first. It's too important. As usual United lost, and life was sheer hell for a while.

United lost 2-0 to Wednesday at Bramall Lane in the quarter final of the FA Cup on March 12th 1960, before a crowd of 59,692.

Then came a chance of red and white glory - a semi final. I can't stand it. Doc scores. Disallowed! By the second replay me mum's having to nail me to the bed to get me to sleep. Usual result, but it all comes with being a Blade. I've always been convinced we'd have stopped Spurs winning the double that year. We were a great cup side then. I don't think I'd know what to do if we ever won anything.

United failed to reach the FA Cup final in 1961, losing a second replay 2-0 to Leicester City after two goalless draws. The games were at Elland Road, Leeds, on March 18th 1961, at the City Ground, Nottingham, on March 23rd and St Andrews, Birmingham, on March 27th.

Then disaster. Dad says he's not going any more. Something he'd heard about "Maximum wage."

"Arm not goin' dahn t'pit fo' fourteen hours a

day ter get less than them fo' playin' football!",
and he didn't. The only match he saw after that
was Sir (as he called him) Jimmy Hagan's testimonial.

Until I was allowed to go on my own I had to get
an adult to take me, but I did go anyway. As
soon as I was old enough I began a spell of twenty three years of unbroken home games. I even
arranged my wedding day for when United were
away. We lost!

Through all the hooligan years I sat. I even sat
in the new Lane Stand on its opening day. Gil
Reece played a blinder. He was applauded off
the field....by the players! I remember Jim
Baxter playing for Sunderland that day.

*This was on October 15th 1966. United beat
Sunderland 2-0, with goals from Mick Jones and Gil
Reece.*

I went all through the seventies with me mates
on the Kop. Probably our best side. Tony
Currie, head and shoulders above anything ever
seen in Sheffield 2 or 6. Wonderful! Woody,
Badger, Salmons, Eddie Colquhoun. 1971 promotion. This was my third promotion already.

That last game against Watford. Scullion hit the
bar for Watford. He always seemed to do well
against us so John Harris got fed up and bought
him! I were absolutely legless that night. I still
have the number three from the cricket scoreboard that day in me garage.

*This was May 1st 1971. Gil Reece 2 and Alan
Woodward (pen.) scored.*

That first year in the top flight I went to fifty
nine of the sixty-odd games, including that one
at Old Trafford. The day of the flukey Best goal
they always show on the telly. Had Hemsley not
gone off he would never have scored that goal
that day. I still look for myself on the telly whenever they show it.

We used to be able to walk round past the pavilion at Bramall Lane. There was one match
against York in the cup when we were drawing
2-2 and an embarrassing replay looked likely
with a couple of minutes to go. We were just
going past the pavilion when Woody got the ball
just near the centre circle. Everybody shouted,
"Hit it!, Hit it!", and he did. The sound of the
ball hitting the net reached us a second after it
went in. What a weird place it were at t'Lane.
Even Woody remembered that goal at the end of
his career.

*This was a League Cup third round tie on October 5th
1971. Alan Woodward 2 (1 pen.) and Tony Currie
scored.*

Then Currie leaves. Leeds as usual. The South
Stand's built. Being United, we celebrate with
relegation and a dreadful decline sets in. I
acquire a son of my own. He arrives in time for
Happy Harry (the first one) to take us in typical
fashion - a last-minute penalty miss - to the
absolute depths. Was Don Givens invited to that
centenary do, when all ex-players were assembled, I wonder?! I still can't believe it, the
Fourth Division, I really can't. Again, life is hell
for a while. I faced the music in the club that
Saturday night, and many nights after.

*United lost 1-0 at home to Walsall on May 2nd 1981
and so were relegated to the Fourth Division for the
first time in their history. Walsall needed to win to
stay up, United needed to draw. Don Penn scored
from the penalty spot but in the last minute Don
Givens missed from the spot, his weak kick being easily saved by Ron Green.*

To cheer me up, I acquire a second son. That's
more important isn't it? He arrives in time for
Harry the Second. A great manager and an
optimist by nature. He wouldn't qualify to be a
Blade - only pessimists need apply! He takes us
all the way back, where we should be in
Division One. Then in our customary way we're
relegated in the most incredulous circumstances.
Why do these things always happen to United?
Weird. Just shattering.

Players come and players go. Managers come,
managers go. Chairmen come and won't go! I
still love going to the Lane, still love night
matches. Me sons are mega Blades, both of 'em.

Players are paid unreal wages, far removed from
the people who support them. The players and
managers leave but the supporters stay and pass
it on to the next generation. That's how it is.

I'm nearly fifty now and everything seems the
same. But it isn't. My dad, who was born after
our last cup win in 1925, passed away aged sixty
nine in April 1994 and I finally realised that it's
not that important. It is only football. Isn't it?

More Sixties Memories

Bernard Jones

The sixties bring back great memories for me
and I still try to relive them sometimes, even

though my wife no longer allows shoulder-length hair (my pathetic attempt to grow a pony tail one year was quickly squashed) and she has long since donated my 7/6 'bush jacket' and my 3/3 denim cap to the 'Help the Aged' shop.

One thing I remember was the tremendous amount of football songs and ditties that were around at that time (did people like Eskimo and Willie Ward pen them themselves or did they employ a team of script writers?). The instantaneous wit of football crowds in those days was very impressive. I remember an incident at Villa Park when the Villa winger McLoud was pulled back by Ken Mallender. Immediately the crowd responded with their own version of the Rolling Stones song: "Hey, you, get off of McLoud!"

Other fond memories of the sixties include Frank Barlow being allowed to get off the train at Mexborough coming back from the away game at Newcastle and Cec Coldwell having to put a word in for him with the lady ticket collector because he didn't have a ticket. I always felt sorry for the person who had to wear the No.11 shirt in those days as they were always the target of the boo-boys: Barry Hartle, Gil Reece, Len Allchurch, Bill Punton, Pat Buckley.

Yes, there were some great memories from the sixties: Joe Shaw's goal at Highbury, the 5-3 win over West Ham, two 3-3 draws with Spurs, a Doc Pace hat-trick against Birmingham, two Birchenall goals at Hillsborough, Tony Currie's debut goal against Spurs, Bill Punton's derby winner, the Gil Reece goal against Sunderland on the day they opened the Bramall Lane stand, when he beat every man in the Sunderland team twice, two policemen and Neville Pyne, the 'Star' photographer, before slotting the ball home.

I hope this will provoke more memories among we middle-aged Blades as we didn't win a great deal then (come to think of it we didn't win anything except the County Cup) but, my word, we did enjoy it in our own simple way.

Twenty Five Years

Matthew Bell

Anyone who regularly reads the 'Green 'Un' will know it carries a feature every week entitled "25 Years Ago", which, as it might suggest, looks at the sporting events that were hitting the headlines in the current week a quarter of a century past.

The "25 Years Ago" article in the 'Green 'Un' of March 27th 1993 carried the headline and sub-heading about United's 1-0 FA Cup quarter final defeat at Elland Road on March 30th 1968:

"BLADES CUP AGONY AS LEEDS MARCH ON - 13,000 travel for United's big FA Cup day out."

Reading the story it suddenly struck me - this was the first match that I was aware that Sheffield United were playing in. In fact, it was the first football match of any description that I had taken any interest in at all. I can't remember England winning the World Cup, Wednesday losing in the final the same year, Celtic lifting the European Cup in 1967, or even any of United's previous cup wins leading up to the tie at Leeds. I didn't know, either, that United were struggling to avoid relegation from the First Division that 1967/68 season - I don't think I even knew the league existed.

For some reason, we (my brother, my parents, my grandparents and myself), were visiting Matlock Bath that Spring Saturday (we knew how to live). I didn't sit in the car all day listening to the radio like I would do today, but when my dad bought a 'Green 'Un' I recall clearly my intense disappointment that United had lost. I don't know why, because, as I said, I had never taken an interest in the Blades before and I didn't know the names of any of the players. One other stupid thing I remember from the 'Green 'Un' front page that day in Matlock Bath was that I had to ask my dad "What does 'Brum' mean?" (Birmingham had beaten Chelsea 1-0 in another quarter final tie).

Suddenly, my interest in football, but not necessarily Sheffield United, was aroused. I couldn't wait to watch the cup final between West Bromwich Albion and Everton, eagerly buying a souvenir newspaper that showed colour pictures of all the players on the front page. Again, I didn't know any of the players' names but I was surprised and amused to find that West Brom had a player with a 'Q' in his name and I didn't have a clue how to pronounce it (little did I know he was later to captain the Blades to promotion). You can imagine my disappointment, therefore, when I read that he would miss the final because he had broken his leg or something. If you ever see a photograph of West Brom's cup-winning squad, look carefully and you will notice that Eddie Colquhoun is on parade complete with sparkling all-white kit and his left leg in plaster.

The fact that West Brom possessed a player with such a funny name, even if he wasn't playing, endeared them to me for that day at least, and I was transfixed as the match went into extra time, then I leapt with joy as Jeff Astle scored the winner. Consequently, the first footballers I knew were not Woodward, Badger and Hodgkinson, but Astle, Talbut and Osborne (whose team I subsequently always wanted to win on 'Quiz Ball'); Kendall, Morrissey and West. It had said in my souvenir newspaper that this was to be the first FA Cup final broadcast nationally in colour by BBC TV so, naturally, I was upset when my mum told me that we wouldn't be able to marvel at the greenness of Wembley's sward, or the brightness of Everton's gold shirts on our humble black and white set. I didn't understand modern technology back then.

I was blissfully unaware that Sheffield United had lost their fight to stay in Division One, because the next big football occasion for me was the European Cup final at Wembley (I thought all cup finals were played at Wembley) - Manchester United versus Benfica. I had heard of George Best and Bobby Charlton, but I hadn't heard of Denis Law, so I had no reason to be worried when he was declared unfit and 19-year old Brian Kidd had to take his place. I watched this historic match whilst on holiday in Wales (I was allowed to stay up specially). I held my breath as Benfica equalised, then forced a brilliant save out of Alex Stepney and nearly won in the last ten minutes. But Best, Kidd and Charlton scored in extra time to ensure Manchester United became the first English team to win the European Cup. I can still name the team today, off the top of my head: Stepney; Brennan, Dunne; Crerand, Foulkes, Stiles; Best, Kidd, Charlton, Sadler, Aston.

Summer 1968 saw my interest in football wane somewhat (probably because there were no big matches) but when in the 1968/69 season my dad decided me and my brother were now old enough to actually go to a match, we didn't need asking twice.

It was Manchester United at Hillsborough, but, fortunately, we didn't arrive in time and we were locked out. I say 'fortunately' because had I witnessed Wednesday come from 4-2 down to win 5-4 I might be writing for 'Spitting Feathers' now. I do seem to think though, that I did go to Hillsborough before I went to Bramall Lane (dad's influence, with Wednesday in the First, United in the Second, don't forget). Wednesday lost 1-0 to Spurs, but we missed Terry Venables' (or was it Alan Mullery's?) goal because, again, we didn't get there early enough. The only things I remember about this game were how boring it was, how dirty Alan Gilzean and Mike England were and standing at the front right in the corner and being able to touch Colin Dobson as he took a corner.

Despite not yet having been to the Lane, I still had more interest in United than Wednesday and whilst at a relation's wedding I was pleased to see in a 'Green 'Un' that some thoughtful soul had bought that United had won 2-0 at Bury, John Tudor getting both goals on his debut. This was, therefore, the first United league match where I consciously looked for the result. I was now a United fan, no doubt about it, and I was devastated when the Blades lost 2-1 against Mansfield in the third round of the FA Cup. Note how cup games were still infinitely more important than league matches - I hadn't been unduly concerned a few weeks before when United slumped 4-1 in the league at Cardiff. I probably didn't even realise the match had taken place.

The Bury win was on November 16th 1968, the Mansfield cup match was on January 4th 1969 (John Tudor scored), the Cardiff defeat was on November 30th 1968 (Colin Addison scored).

Finally, at last, my dad deigned to take us to Bramall Lane. It was April 16th 1969, Barnsley in a County Cup semi final replay. Even now, I think we only went because my dad's mate, and my mate's dad, Roy Ironside, was supposed to be playing in goal for Barnsley. In the end, he was probably glad he didn't as his deputy Brian Arblaster (another name I'll never forget) saw the ball flash past him nine times. Denis Clarebrough's book reminds me it was Tudor 3, Staniforth 2, Colquhoun 2, Buckley and Tom Fenoughty who scored, but it was Tony Currie who struck me with awe. In the pre-match warm up he hit a shot that smacked against the bar from what seemed to my young eyes to be somewhere near the half-way line. I was hooked.

But it was still a while before my first league match - Hull City, 3-0, (Currie, Woodward, Tudor), October 4th, 1969. I was still more of a TV and newspaper United fan because my dad had more important things to do on Saturday afternoons, and I therefore had to rely on the occasional showing on Sunday afternoon, in the days even before Keith Macklin - Danny Blanchflower was the commentator then. I remember watching a 4-0 win over Blackburn when the electricity failed in the cricket pavilion, the cameras couldn't operate and they missed a goal, then the 2-1 FA Cup win against the mighty Everton, when Alan Woodward hit the bar and it was still shaking at half-time.

The Blackburn match was on November 1st 1969. The scorers were Tony Currie, Colin Addison, Alan Woodward and Len Badger. The Everton cup win was on January 3rd 1970, with Gil Reece and Colin Addison scoring.

As Nick Hornby says in his brilliant book 'Fever Pitch - A Fan's Life', isn't it strange how things you would otherwise forget stick in your mind because they are associated somehow with football matches? Just like I recall being in Matlock Bath when United lost 1-0 to Leeds, I was at my uncle's poultry farm in Lincolnshire when we were beaten 3-0 by Derby in the 1969/70 FA Cup, and, in 1969, England lost 1-0 to Yugoslavia at Wembley the night Arnold Laver's burnt down.

But I digress. 1970/71 was to be the season when I became really emotionally attached to Sheffield United FC. I heard United had beaten Aldershot 6-0 in the Watney Cup when I was on holiday in Holland and we were driving back from the ferry somewhere outside Dover on the first day of the new season when the result came on the radio - Orient 3 Sheffield United 1. Mark Lazarus scored one (or maybe even two) of the three, and not having had the remotest of religious upbringings, it wasn't until I first did R.E. at secondary school that his surname meant anything to me other than as that of the Orient footballer who had helped defeat United in August 1970. In fact, that's still the case today. If anyone should mention the name Lazarus, my first thought is not of someone who rose from the dead two thousand years ago, but of the man who convinced me that United were not going to win promotion because they had lost the first game of the season.

Tony Currie 2, Alan Woodward 2, Colin Addison and Gil Reece scored in the 6-0 win at Aldershot on August 1st 1970. Addison scored again in the defeat at Orient on August 15th 1970.

1970/71 was also the first season that I found an ally who was as interested in the Blades as I was. Fortunately, so was his dad, so I no longer had to rely on infrequent visits with my dad. Me and Stuart and Stuart's dad went to quite a few games and we (but not his dad) were able to fuel our now increasing obsession by walking slowly past Tony Currie's house on Bishopscourt Road every night on the way home from school in the hope of catching a glimpse of the great man. We even knocked on his door a couple of times to ask for his autograph but his wife said he wasn't in. He probably was, but he must have been fed up with snotty schoolboys interrupting his afternoon nap.

In those days TC owned a 1950s white Ford Pop, registration number 777 PPP (what would that plate sell for today?), but he soon went more up-market with a brand new H-reg Ford Cortina Mark Two. He still walked to the shops round the corner though, and I couldn't wait to run home and tell my mum when I saw him buying some onions in the Co-Op.

I wasn't allowed yet to go to night matches, unless they were in the school holidays, so I went to the 2-1 home defeat by Hull City (half term - with my dad this time and, surprise, surprise, we were late, so we missed Gil Reece's goal), and we spent the rest of the evening watching from the cricket pavilion as Chris Simpkin and Ken Houghton kicked the United players up in the air at every opportunity, but I missed the 5-1 against Cardiff that virtually sealed promotion. But I did sit with my head sticking out of my bedroom window, listening to the roars of the crowd (Bramall Lane was a good mile and a half away but the noise generated by the 42,963 carried easily to Norton Lees) and I could tell we were winning. My mum confirmed it by coming upstairs at half past nine to say she had just seen on the news that it was 5-1. I was too excited to sleep that night.

I persuaded my dad to buy me a season ticket for the 1971/72 season, costing £3 and instructing me to enter by turnstile No.18 (John Street) or turnstile No.54 (Shoreham Street). It also contained a load of orange sticky labels with which to apply for tickets for cup matches but seeing as we lost 3-1 at home to Cardiff in the third round, none were required to be used.

This was January 15th 1972. Ian Mackenzie scored.

It did say, though, that stand season ticket holders (not me) need not apply for tickets for home cup games, because they would be sent automatically, along with an account, which should be settled immediately. However, if the tickets were not required, they should be returned along with the invoice. Were United really that trusting, and were people that honest that they wouldn't use the tickets or sell them to somebody else without paying for them? Strangely, this system applied to home cup ties, but not home cup replays.

By now I was gripped by severe bouts of apprehension before every home match and I even feigned a headache so I wouldn't have to go to the Stoke match (we lost 3-2, a week after our unbeaten run was ended at Old Trafford).

The Stoke match was on October 9th 1971. Alan Woodward (pen.) and Tony Currie scored.

Other memories of that season include my dad telling me to stay put while he paid an extra 10p to transfer from the Kop to John Street (long before the advent of the Westfield Health Enclosure) to see if there was any room on the terrace because the Kop was so packed for the Leeds match. There wasn't and he had to clamber back over the turnstile and we watched United win 3-0 from right down in the bottom corner. I then remember feeling really important because our next door neighbour (a policeman) got us in for nothing for the Spurs match (despite the fact that, with my season ticket, I, or rather my dad, had paid for the match already) and hearing the crack as Trevor Hockey broke his leg against Manchester City. I left early when United played Coventry and missed Alan Woodward's second goal in a 2-0 win. I have never left a match before the end since, and to this day I cannot understand why people do.

This was November 13th 1971.

It's funny how little things from your childhood, seemingly unremarkable at the time, stay fixed in your mind for the rest of time, and I apologise if I've indulged myself a bit here, but thirty-odd years is a long time to maintain an interest, or perhaps even an obsession, in something, don't you think?

My Life With United

Marcus Geiss

Generally speaking my life with United can easily be divided into three entirely separate parts, and each of these parts is characterised by different routines, needs and necessities. And when I look back at them in greater detail I am always amazed by the strange timing and the rhythm of it all.

Mostly my story is about someone supporting a team from afar. I was born and raised in Germany and have lived there for most of my life, and from that alone it seems fairly obvious that I had a football life long before I had a life with United. My parents did not take me to see the Blades when I was seven; in fact I mainly grew up on TV football.

At this point I think it might be helpful to take a look at my background but also at German society, its attitudes and its peculiarities because I feel part of my hopeless addiction to United - a team from abroad, an English team, an unfashionable team - can be linked to some German post-war trends and can be explained not only on a purely personal but also a social level.

I am white (somehow we all are...we were neither any good at colonialism, nor ever ready to welcome people from abroad or share with the less wealthy), middle-class male from a rather well off academic background, born in 1968. And because we lost the war and were constantly reminded of our sins by teachers, newspapers and television, it was totally unfashionable to be proud of your nationality. No hymns, no flags, no anything, and it wasn't as if we were consciously missing the hoo-hah of national pride. Nationalism and patriotism only became fashionable after the unification with the East in 1989. By then, it was too late for me. The change didn't affect me at all. I was twenty one years of age and my attitudes were firmly established. I was into all things English and was a fierce opponent of most German club sides and most definitely the national team.

Our parents had compensated for the lack of national identity, pride and symbols by taking great satisfaction from our economic rebirth after the war. My generation was rather bored of that. We took wealth and prosperity for granted but at the same time we rebelled against the shallowness of a national psyche that is mainly based on economic strength and success. There was very little that was German that we could take pride in or be confident about. All we were left with was escapism in one way or other. I guess that's why insecurity is so endemic in Germans (take the beef scare: your cows may be mad, we stop eating beef altogether) but also why we are the world's greatest travellers and Europe's keenest Europeans (unless, of course, Europe threatens the stability of our currency and our cherished wealth). At heart, most Germans aren't really Germans at all; they're cosmopolitans or Europeans or......and most people have a favourite country somewhere else where the food's nicer, the people are more kind-hearted and more relaxed, the grass is greener and where they are truly welcome. Dream on.

Knowing all that, somewhat pathetically, Sheffield United are still my team. And what I may lack in God-given legitimacy I compensate for by pure commitment.

I was raised on dubbed American or British films. The music I listened to was British; in fact I have a complete collection of all the Smiths records ever released and when pressed I could still quote their B-sides and catalogue numbers.

So, if music, the movies and sport are what a young boy's life is made of, is it any real surprise that I subconsciously chose a football country that was already thoroughly tested and found suitable in the other two key areas?

To begin with I started my 'fan career' as a hater of teams other people liked. I hated the national side at the age of six when they beat first Australia and then Sweden in the 1974 World Cup. If I remember it correctly, I chose Sweden and Australia as my teams because they played in yellow, then my favourite colour. And I did (and still do) hate Holland because of their unspeakably ugly orange shirts. Somehow Brazil slipped my attention, maybe an indication that I was only allowed to watch the Germany games.

Fifteen years of agony followed, hoping for German teams to drop out of European competitions and for the national squad to be stuffed, mostly in vain. An alternative theory as to why I chose British teams as my favourites might hinge on the fact that they were actually the only ones you could trust. Invariably, English teams eliminated Germans in those heady pre-Heysel days (e.g. Liverpool-Moenchengladbach, Forest-Köln, Forest-Hamburg, Villa-Bayern). I can still recall the acute pain I felt when Northern Ireland edged past Germany 1-0 both at Windsor Park and at Hamburg in the European Championship qualifiers in 1984 but still managed to finish below the Germans, level on points but beaten on goal difference.

To shorten a long story (and the temptation to let memory wander and go into unnecessary detail is always there), it was only in 1989/90 that I was ready to actually follow a team I liked and no longer go against a batch of teams I hated. By then, I had gone to university and lived away from home.

And the team I inexplicably chose was Sheffield United. I'd been to England on numerous occasions with 'Inter Rail' or just for a weekend, but never to Sheffield. But, a bit like 1974 when shirt colour proved decisive, it was a mixture of strange phenomena that led me to the Blades.

For one, my music had somewhat predisposed me to like northern industrial towns and my 'Inter Rail' trips had actually strengthened my soft spot for the north. I somehow had this feeling that nothing could beat canals, rain, industrial wasteland, brick warehouses and little two-up-two-downs without front gardens. To travel on a train from Manchester Piccadilly to Bolton was my idea of heaven; a trip to the heartland of indie pop but at the same time, with a little

imagination, back in time to the age of the Industrial Revolution.

In 1989 I spotted United riding high in the old Second Division, and that's where it all really began. Sheffield sounded appealing to me, very working class, industrial and all that. And maybe The Clash's "This is England, this knife of Sheffield steel, this is how we feel" played a part too. I somehow presumed Sheffield was all red brick, and I generally preferred red 'Uniteds' to 'Cities' or 'Towns'. Despite knowing and loving Manchester, I had enough common sense not to go for Manchester United. They had a German ring to them, lots of money, lots of hype (though not success at that time). My musical likes and my minority taste in football had turned me into a lover of unfashionable, small-time underdogs.

Whenever I read English newspapers I always looked out for United's results and was really happy when they made it to the First Division at the end of that season. In late autumn 1990 the 'Observer' ran an interview with Dave Bassett after United's bad start to the new First Division campaign and I really loved the things he said and his quiet, optimistic assertion that not only would United fail to record the worst ever First Division record but that we'd also eventually beat the drop.

Later that year I saw United on French TV. To this day, I don't know what match that was. I only remember that the Blades played in yellow shirts and red shorts, and I think the opposition was French. A friendly, I suppose. Does anyone, by any chance, recall the occasion? Or did I dream it?

This was probably a friendly against Auxerre on January 6th 1991. Jamie Hoyland scored in a 2-1 defeat.

By then I was going to the university's English library every week to look up United's results and scorers. The sap was rising. I still remember beating Derby 1-0 but on the other hand a 4-1 defeat at Arsenal after being a goal up at half time sticks out (the highlights were on German TV). And then there was the famous unbeaten run, and the first and probably most spectacular of the Houdini escape acts was completed.

The Derby match was on January 26th 1991 (Glyn Hodges scored), while Ian Bryson put United ahead in the defeat at Arsenal on December 29th 1990.

In the following seasons I always watched the Blades live when I was over in England (away to Arsenal 2-5 and home to Notts County 1-3 being my first ever games) and it got to the point where waiting for the scores in English or German papers wouldn't do any more. It meant waiting until at least a day after the game.

United lost at Arsenal on September 21st 1991 (scorers Tony Agana and Clive Mendonca), and at home to Notts County on September 17th 1991 (scorer Agana).

I needed Teletext. As our TV was quite old and didn't have it I had to look for a VCR with Teletext included. It seemed to be quite an unusual desire (unhelpful shop assistants permanently told me to buy a new TV with Teletext and then a 'normal' VCR would do) and in the end it cost me quite a bit, which was entirely United's fault. However, the shop assistants' favoured solution would have been even more expensive.

The next seasons were followed on Teletext. Once I remember watching a whole match on Teletext. Everton against Sheffield United went something like "-:-" for ninety minutes as the scores from abroad are obviously not updated while the game is still in progress, only being given as final scores about ten minutes after the final whistle has gone. But the little flash and the "0-2" that followed were well worth the wait and the sweaty hands and the nerves.

This could have been either April 11th 1992 (scorers Ian Bryson and Alan Cork) or May 4th 1993 (scorers Carl Bradshaw and Glyn Hodges) as United won 2-0 at Goodison Park two seasons running.

Well, that fateful day at Chelsea has been described by many others before. Suffice it to say the relegation meant a clear-cut end to that first phase of my United fandom.

The Birth Of A Blade

Anon

I have been a Blade for more than thirty years. I had seen them before that but couldn't really call myself a supporter until 1965 when I started to work Saturday mornings and the obvious thing to do after that was to go for a few pints and a match.

I must confess, and may God forgive me, that I alternated between God's five acres in Sheffield 2 and that other place. I tried to convince myself that the game is the thing but a derby at the Lane fairly early in the season showed me the light and I have been hooked ever since. At the time I thought it was the fact that we had a class act with players like up-and-coming young-sters Len Badger and Mick Jones in the team that converted me but as the years went by I inclined more to the view of divine intervention.

I had seen United a number of times before and I can remember my father taking me to Leicester for some crucial match, the significance of which I forgot years ago. Suffice it to say that United were promoted or relegated almost every other season in the mid fifties, so one of these must have been involved. I had a Subbuteo game at the time and mine was always the team in red; I didn't realise the significance at the time.

I remember my first visit to the Lane with an adult. I can't remember the score but we lost heavily to Luton on Boxing Day or thereabouts. I stood on the Kop, it rained incessantly and poured in through the roof all over the place. I was the last to get on a tram at the corner of Shoreham Street and John Street and my mate had to walk, but the trams were so slow he still got to Victoria Station before me!

This must have been Boxing Day 1955 when United were beaten 4-0 at home by Luton Town.

I was at the City Ground for the 1961 semi final but I don't have too many vivid recollections after that, apart from seeing a cup match in about 1963 when Keith Kettleborough was sent off for burying his boot nine inches up a Villa player's backside!

This was actually on January 30th 1965 and was a 2-0 home defeat to Aston Villa in the fourth round of the FA Cup.

The years 1965 to 1968 were great. We had the blossoming talents of Badger, Jones, Alan Birchenall, Bernard Shaw and a youngster with tree trunks for legs who was to become one of the greatest Blades of all time - Alan Woodward.

We had finished above you-know-who for the first two years and in the third we were above them for most of the season but a disastrous run when we lost the last few matches sent us to relegation. Even then we went down with thirty two points: in any of the previous two seasons that would have been enough to stay up.

In a macabre way I recall the Blades car stickers for that season; "Sheffield United celebrate fifty years of First Division football". Talk about tempting fate. The last match of the season was against Chelsea and a draw would have been enough to stay up. Even now I can see Bernard Shaw fluffing a back-pass to give Chelsea the winner.

This was May 11th 1968. Mick Hill scored in a 2-1 home defeat that sent United to Division Two.

The seasons in Division Two were poor at first but as time went by we became conscious that John Harris was again building a superb side. Promotion was missed by a fair margin in 1970 but they did enough to mark United as a team to watch. At the end of that season I had one of my happiest non-United matches. Wednesday had to beat Manchester City to stay up and I went. City did everything they could to help Wednesday but 'unfortunately' nobody took the trouble to explain to a young City winger called Ian Bowyer, who won the match with two thunderbolts from twenty five yards. The ground was packed with 54,999 and it hissed down permanently throughout. I learned that it was possible to be lonely in a crowd when I was the only one of ten thousand in the North Stand to cheer my acknowledgement of City's goals!

1970/71 was magnificent, not just because it saw the resumption of the derby matches, with a win at the Lane in the autumn and goalless draw at the other place at Easter. It was the first time for three years that we had been up against them on a level basis. During those three years I had to suffer the insults and superior posturing of those poor misguided souls and it set me on a loyalty to the Blades and a hatred of everything blue, which I have never overcome. The writing was on the wall before the season started when I sat in the Leppings Lane Stand for Gerry Young's benefit match. United came out like lions and stormed into a three-goal lead within ten minutes with, I believe, Billy Dearden's first appearance and goals for the club. Somebody must have explained that you are not supposed to win matches like that and the Blades conspired to let in a few soft goals to leave with an honourable draw.

The 0-0 league draw at Hillsborough was on April 12th 1971, while the Gerry Young benefit match was actually at the end of the previous season, on April 25th 1970. Bill Dearden had made his debut in the previous game, the County Cup semi final against Barnsley, but did score his first goal in the match at Hillsborough, along with Tony Currie and Dave Staniforth.

After six wonderful years the best was yet to come. We had already developed a side with a mixture of experience and youth in 1965 to a team of youth and brilliance and, under the guidance of John Harris, the best manager we've ever had, the sky was the limit. I acknowledge Dave Bassett's contribution without reservation but Harris did all of this at the highest level on

less than a shoestring, made a profit every year, which kept the club financially secure, and produced some of the most exciting Blades players of all time. The years from 1971 are another story, but I won't push my luck by eulogising over those times!

A Posh Unitedite

Simon Proctor

Many people refer to followers of United as 'Blades'. That is the favoured term and I have no quarrel with that.

However, unless I am mistaken, in my early days in the late 1940s and early 1950s, we small boys talked about Unitedites and Wednesdayites, though of course we knew the team as the Blades. Therefore I continue to use the term 'Unitedite' because it seems to me to more accurately reflect the thoughts of my generation. I trust the youth of today will forgive the old such an indulgence.

And posh is what you are if you are born with a plum in your mouth, or whatever the phrase is, and if you go to private schools and live in middle class suburbs. Once it was something to feel moderately guilty about - in the days of Harold Wilson and the Labour government of the 1960s, the working class man or woman was the hero, and that was possibly right. Indeed, anyone who has had the luck to meet someone like Barbara Castle, as I once did briefly, will know that that view is absolutely right. But that does not mean that now, in the fullness of time, there is anything for the middle class to apologise for - or at least not much.

I suspect there are quite a few middle class supporters of United. They might not seem particularly numerous but they are there nonetheless - one cannot ignore one's history and one's upbringing, over which one has no element of choice of course. And if it's true in Sheffield, it is sure as eggs is eggs that it is true for the rest of the country.

In 1948 my parents, my brother and myself, then aged seven, came to Sheffield, where my father was born and where one line of the family traces itself back to the 1850s when one Robert Proctor had a shop at No.20 Fargate, and a store - quite a big one - with our name on it remained there until the 1960s. We went to live in a four-storey semi-detached house in Ranmoor, a posh suburb sandwiched between Broomhill and Fulwood. I was sent to Birkdale school, a fee-paying institution that my father first attended in 1923.

I can probably, if I do the requisite research, date my support for United from a specific time on a specific day. All I need to do is consult the records of Birkdale School to find out what was the first day of term in September 1948 and at what time the boys had their morning break. Then I could look up the 'Sheffield Telegraph', a morning daily newspaper of the time, or 'The Star', and find out what the weather was like that particular morning, just to complete the picture.

Most people probably became aware of their affection for a particular team from some event, like going to their first match or following the passions of their parents, fathers in particular. I did it because United, in the school yard at Birkdale, were the underdogs. So what's new, I hear people say with a chuckle. Nothing, I can only reply. But it does mean that I have supported United for over fifty years.

We dream of past glories. Was it in 1925 that we last won the FA Cup? Was it in 1936 that we last appeared in a final and lost 1-0 to Arsenal? Didn't we briefly, in September and October 1971, top the old First Division until Old Trafford, in a match no-one who was there will ever forget, when George Best, at his most supreme, scored one of the goals of the century, and Alan Gowling hit another against us?

My passion for the underdogs in life dates from my birth, and taking in United at the age of seven was probably no big deal.

Anyway, Birkdale is still going strong today. In fact it is the biggest private school in the city and possesses a tremendous reputation for scholastic excellence. I still remember my first day. Wearing a bright blue blazer, which they still wear today, and grey shorts, I went outside into the yard at the mid-morning break. The yard was then a sort of elongated triangle in shape, with a small single door in a wall at one end and another door, also in a wall, at the other. The doors or part of the wall represented the goals.

The yard was cobbled and across this area there roared hundreds of small boys, or so it seemed, all chasing a tennis ball. The figures might have been in the range of two hundred Wednesdayites against forty Unitedites, or perhaps it was closer to 80/20. Whatever the case, the odds had to be of the order seen in the Battle of Britain.

So on the spur of the moment and in the heat of prospective battle, I joined the good pilots there and then and tore into the Wednesdayites, all of us after the tennis ball. For ten or fifteen minutes we raced around chasing the ball, which was kicked wildly in one direction or the other, only generally towards the opposition's goal. When it was trapped by one or two boys between their feet, a sort of stand-up scrum would develop and the ball would only come loose when the numbers of one side overwhelmed the other - usually in this case when the Wednesdayites shoved the Unitedites off. Every so often, the ball would get near one of the goals and be held underfoot by an intrepid defender, who would be quickly surrounded by others, both defenders and attackers.

A goal was not scored by a clean, incisive shot with the foot or by something similar from the head. Not even a gentle flick. It was scored by sheer weight of numbers. The ball was pushed against the door or wall by a heaving mass of seven, eight and nine-year olds, who all shouted with glee on scoring and flattening the opposition against door or wall. I don't think anybody got hurt and it must have been quite fun.

There was, on reflection, none of this nonsense about being born into a United family. My father could not have cared tuppence about football, let alone United, and my mother came from an English family that had lived in North Wales for years. In the fifties she eventually took an interest in United but she was not a fan. She seemed to be much more interested in meeting Alf Ringstead, United's famous and much-loved winger in the 1950s, on the golf course than in actually seeing him play. Both parents much preferred to go horse racing on Saturday afternoons, rather than go to Bramall Lane.

So I say to myself, mockingly, that I supported United from the outset because they - the team and the other supporters - needed me. The odds were stacked against them. They still are, but supporting the underdogs, whether they be Henry's men at Agincourt, the Battle of Britain pilots, Sheffield United, and even the Labour party today in Sheffield, is part of the delusion we, every man jack of us, labour under.

I cannot remember seeing my first match at Bramall Lane (I probably went with two other boys, James Morris and John Gregory, when I was ten or eleven in 1950 or 1951) but I do recall that moment of chasing the tennis ball in the yard at Birkdale and of forming from that time a devotion to United that will never leave me.

Pig Tales

Confession Time (1)

Pete Moxon

We all harbour dark secrets lost in the depths of our past, don't we? Sometimes the soul needs baring to exorcise all the ghouls that lie gnawing away deep within.

Most, if not all, true Blades fans will tell you that the team they hate most, that they wish all ills upon, that the very mention of their name provokes teeth-grating tension is, of course, Sheffield Wednesday. I am one of these people and cannot for the life of me understand the 'it's good for the city if they both do well' types: I dislike Wednesday and their fans with a venom and nothing gives me greater pleasure or softens the blow of a Blades defeat more than to hear of another loss for them. So, what I am about to relate here is an exercise in the cleansing of the football soul. An incident stands out whereby my loyalty to United and disdain for Wednesday were open to question. It happened in early 1979.

Was it the Beer?
It was a cold, grey early January day. All local football had fallen victim to the weather. This included the team that I played for, although we made it to the ground only for the referee to deem the pitch unsafe to play on. So all the lads, dependent on who they supported, were making plans to travel to either the Lane or Hillsborough when we heard that United's game against Aldershot in the FA Cup had also fallen victim to the weather. However, Wednesday's match against Arsenal, also in the Cup, was on

due to the under-trotter heating, installed even then at Chez SWFC. The thought of seeing Arsenal giving the then Third Division Owls a good stuffing tipped the balance in favour of going to Hillsborough with my teammates instead of a potential shopping trip.

All the best-laid plans of mice and men...... Wednesday actually held the Gunners to a draw and my abiding memory of the game is the snowball bombardment of Pat Jennings by the Kop and Jack Charlton's appeal to the fans to stop, for which he also received a shower of snow.

This was January 6th 1979. United eventually lost 1-0 to Fourth Division Aldershot after a 0-0 home draw on Tuesday 9th.

Still, at least they would get well stuffed in the replay at Highbury, thought I. But it was not to be and only a late Arsenal equaliser saved what would have been something for Wednesday fans to gloat about for many a year.

In those days cup ties were played to a conclusion - none of this one replay and penalty shoot-out malarkey of today - and the Owls and Arsenal were to replay at Leicester, who were then experimenting with a huge warm air-filled balloon covering the pitch. It must have worked as the game was replayed during the week when nearly every other match was called off.

Now here comes the first point of shame! My brother-in-law, an avid Wednesdayite, asked if I fancied a trip down to Leicester as he was stuck for someone to go with. Again the thought of a night out witnessing the slaughter of the Owls

The Shoreham End at full throttle

photo: Andy Greaves

seemed quite appealing so I agreed to go. We arrived in Leicester on a pig (no pun intended) of a night to be confronted with a huge crowd trying to get into the ground with only a few minutes to kick off. As we forlornly trudged round looking for a small queue it appeared that we were either not going to see the kick off or even get in at all.

Amidst all the confusion and disorderly queuing I noticed one turnstile without a queue and kept my eye on it for ten minutes or so. What I noticed was the odd person being allowed through but the majority turned away. I moved closer, trying to distinguish just who was and wasn't allowed in there. After a few minutes' observation all was revealed - Leicester City, in their concern for their own fans, had reserved the Leicester City Supporters' Club pen just for them at the production of some sort of membership card to a steward by the turnstile, who then gave the thumbs up to the turnstile attendant. Special rate of £1 applied as well!

Most people who were going through appeared to merely flash some sort of wallet at the steward and he waved them through. Nothing to lose, I thought; may as well have a go at masquerading as an official Leicester City supporter. A quick word with my brother-in-law and he agreed it was worth a try. Out came the wallet

(containing nothing remotely resembling a membership card) and in my best Leicester accent I barked "Leicester City supporter mate" to the steward as we confidently marched to the turnstile. "In here boys, just £1 tonight", he said as he turned away some Arsenal fans behind us desperately trying to get in.

We were in! When we got on to the terrace it was a lovely spot right on the corner flag, a sort of special corner that Leicester Supporters' Club obviously used at their home matches. It was complete with its own food bar and, would you believe, drinks bar as well. Seeing as there were only about a hundred people (all Leicester fans) in this little quadrant, we were in comparative luxury compared to the rest of the fans who were squeezed in far too tightly around the rest of the ground.

As the match unfolded and the beer began to flow I was beginning to enjoy myself, especially when Arsenal took the lead. Even when Wednesday equalised I wasn't too upset as the atmosphere was great and I was confident of the final outcome. Again the Gunners went in front only for Wednesday to peg them back once more. By now I was really into the match and we had got chatting to some Leicester fans who were also enjoying themselves, fuelled by several pints, and when Arsenal swept into the lead for the third time we all jumped up to celebrate (except my brother-in-law, of course, who buried his head in grief!).

This is where the second and most shameful moment occurred. Wednesday, to their credit, refused to lie down and went in search of a third equaliser and as they peppered the Arsenal goal I noticed that my reaction was similar to that when the Blades were striving for an equaliser - was it something in the beer that was making me behave this way? Then it happened.....Wednesday equalised for a third time near the end of extra time, the Owls' end of the ground erupted, the neutral Leicester fans went wild, my brother-in-law was jumping up and down in a mutual hug with someone...... and that someone was.......ME! I was celebrating a Wednesday goal........an unforgivable sin.......why was I doing this? Was it the beer, was I going down with some terrible tropical disease that evoked uncharacteristic behaviour, or had I just completely lost my marbles?

To this day I'll never know why I even went to the match, let alone show some sort of favour to Wednesday and when the game ended at 3-3 and we were on our way home I realised what I'd done and quickly shoved it to the back of my memory bank. I've often thought about it over the years and wondered why I behaved in such a fashion. Deep shame is the only feeling I've ever felt about this and maybe, more than twenty years on, the need for me to ask forgiveness from fellow Blades for this single indiscretion is part of the therapy needed to help me come to terms with what happened and eventually go to meet my maker with my sin absolved. Say three Hail Marys........

Blade In The Woods

Anon

Andy is a Boston Blade. Boston, Lincolnshire that is. One of Andy's big hates is when former Wednesday goalkeeper Chris Woods is reported as also being from Boston. Apparently, the man with the Swarfega gloves is from Freiston, which is one of the little villages outside Boston, and the difference really matters if you're a Wednesday-hating Bostonian. Which is why it must have seemed strange to those that know him when Andy went along and queued with a few others to see, meet and acquire an autograph from 'Flapper' Woods when he was once guest 'star' at a sports goods promotion or some such, which was taking place at Oldrid's, which is Boston's largest department store.

Andy queued for some time, with as much dignity as was possible in such a situation, along with giggling schoolgirls, 'Ooh young man!' adoring old ladies and pre-pubescent boys who didn't realise how crap this local-born star was. As he got closer to the 'celeb' he could hear the embarrassed, shy requests for a signed photograph or an autograph and could that see our butter-fingered friend was enjoying every minute of it.

At last. It was Andy's turn and when the hapless juggler looked up he sensed nothing untoward, although his smile began to wane to a quizzical frown as he saw Andy's Blades shirt.

"Could you sign me this please, Chris?"

"Er, sure," replied Swiss-cheese hands with now slight trepidation.

Our fellow Blade then thrust in front of him a copy of 'Match' magazine, dated from some time just after that famous November Sunday in 1991, back page uppermost, which showed a picture with the caption 'The Last Shot'. The picture was of Deano's shot going through those Wicker Arches legs. Woods signed it with both pen and bewilderment.

"Cheers pal!" said our grinning hero as he wheeled away in triumph, leaving a dropped jaw, a deflated ego and a ruined day, and had the clown-like 'cat' been using a pencil, Andy would also have left the sound of a lead point snapping.

A Christmas Apology

Steve Titterton

No doubt you have all experienced the problematic question of what to buy your nearest and dearest for Christmas. It's nice to feel that no expense should be spared, but of course, unless you happen to have won the lottery, most of us are limited in our choice of gift by financial constraints.

Then there is the added problem of what do you buy for the person who has everything? This usually entails a detailed search of the packed malls of Meadowhall, or competing with the tumbleweed on the streets of Sheffield city centre, hunting for that unusual, novel, but useful gift. I have not forgotten, of course, the Lane Souvenir Shop, but the person I had in mind already has most of what they have ever sold.

This particular year I solved the problem of what to buy my brother early, obtaining for him a gift that has a multitude of uses, that was reasonably priced, and the profit of which benefited a worthwhile cause, not the overladen pockets of some mega-rich tycoon.

Whilst helping my son's scout unit to prepare for a jumble sale I spotted the very item. There it was, calling to me, Our Kid's Christmas gift, just waiting for me to purchase it. I considered the item. Would it make a useful gift? Would he appreciate it? Would it be value for money? Would he ever speak to me again?

Deliberating over the above, I could see the endless potential for this gift. It could be used to wedge open doors, balance any wobbly furniture (particularly apt in view of Our Kid's penchant for DIY), it could chastise my nephew by way of a rap around the ear or the threat of a bedtime horror story. It could be shredded for cat litter, although this would require the further purchase of a cat.

For those, such as my brother, who are into toilet reading, this could be the ultimate article, especially if there was no bog roll.

Further examination clinched the matter. The requisite words 'Sheffield United' appeared in the said item.

After handing over my hard-earned money, I realised that the only thing he would never do is actually read 'The Wednesday' by Keith Farnsworth.

So, Kev, please accept my humble apology. I hope it didn't spoil Christmas dinner too much and please don't bear a grudge. It was only a joke. Anyway, I was doing a public service, removing such an offensive publication from the streets, especially when it could have corrupted the minds of the young and vulnerable.

Besides, you know I'm a tight get and the 10p did go to a good cause.

The Owl Next Door - Two Hundred Miles Away

Andy Cowell

Fate can undoubtedly be very cruel. An exiled Blade, my quest to earn an honest crust has obliged me to live in Derby, Somerset and now on the south coast. In both Derby and Somerset I was happy to find fellow Blades living in the area; indeed a small coach travelled up from Taunton for that memorable day at Leicester in May 1990.

My latest 'posting' was to Barton-on-Sea, a small seaside town most notable for an abundance of old people's homes, batricars and a smattering of fickle Bournemouth supporters.

Our criteria, as we searched for a house, were simple: not too expensive and close to other children with whom my son could play football and, of course, who he could indoctrinate into becoming Blades. In Barton both these features proved difficult to fulfil but finally we settled on a humble home on a small, but very exclusive, estate.

Soon after our installation, the Bramall Lane derby was due to take place. Unable to make the trip, but now the proud owner of a Sky binlid, I settled down to watch the Blades stuff our friends from Hillsborough on TV, when there came a ring on the doorbell.

A tall, dark stranger, clutching an armful of beer cans, was standing in the doorway. To my horror, he was a Wednesdayite, he lived next door and having seen the dish and the stickers adorning my car, he correctly concluded that here was an opportunity too good to miss. Tempted only by his beer, I let him in and subjected him to an abandoned display of ecstasy when we took the lead. My regret at having so generously allowed this infidel into my home grew as the match began to slip away and finally the inevitable happened and they equalised.

United and Wednesday drew 1-1 at Bramall Lane on November 8th 1992. Adrian Littlejohn put United ahead but David Hirst equalised near the end.

For the record, the Wednesdayite is now a firm friend and, anyway, he hasn't been to Hillsborough since the days of Vic Mobley and Gerry Young! Typical!

Confession Time (2)

Pete Moxon

All good Blades bring their kids up in the same fashion........after the obligatory first words of "Mamma" and "Dad" the next are usually related to football and Sheffield United. I was no different and my two sons were quickly initiated into the rituals of supporting Sheffield United and hating Sheffield Wednesday and all things blue and white. Maybe the incident I am about to relate was some sort of divine retribution from the football god on high for my indiscretion at Leicester several years earlier.

This was the time when replica kits were not quite as widespread and obtainable as nowadays and Blades kits were somewhat hard to come across. My elder son already had a Spurs 1982 Cup Final strip. This was the change strip of pale blue and just about the only one I could get a two-year old that came close to fitting him. He wore this regularly until he'd outgrown it and the time came for another kit. He was around six by now and had been joined by another male addition to the family, three years his junior and twice as awkward!

I was now looking for two kits and heard of this place in the market that did full strips for a tenner, so off we went in the hope of finding two Blades kits for a six- and three-year old. We arrived at the market and found the stall, only to discover that the kits were those of First Division clubs and England (the Blades were a pretty poor pre-Dave Bassett Second Division side at the time). My lads were not to be denied and despite being schooled in Sheffield United, really only wanted a footie kit to play in the garden and mimic real-life heroes.

As they scanned all the kits on display I'd decided that apart from the obvious one they could have any they wished and my elder son, true to his easy-going, conformist nature, chose a Manchester United strip of white shirt, black shorts and black socks pretty quickly. I was not too concerned by this, but my younger son was playing rather more choosy and despite several suggestions of England, Southampton or Liverpool from me, his gaze kept going back to the dreaded blue and white stripes of you know who!

Finally, after a prompting from his mother to make up his mind, the unthinkable happened.........he uttered the words "I want that one" and pointed to the kit that brings all Blades out in a rash!!

"Any one except that one!", shrieked his now frantic father but the tiny mind was made up and he placed his hands on his hips, trembled his bottom lip and dug in. I began an exercise in damage repair by suggesting they hadn't got his size, but the stallholder (who must have been one of them) quickly despatched that idea by proclaiming that he had it in all sizes. Well, if he insisted on blue, then why not have a nice Everton kit or a Manchester City one......what about England or one like your brother's.......please, anything but that one. By now he was beginning to attract a crowd with his wailing and his mother was getting just a little impatient as Dad desperately pleaded with the young dissident not to bring shame upon the family. But his mind was made up and the kit was duly purchased to guffaws from the stallholder who had sussed that Dad was having great difficulty coming to terms with this.

We arrived home and the kits were duly changed into, a camera was produced and photos taken for posterity. Dad stood in the house surveying the scene, wondering what the neighbours would think and at a loss to understand where the genes that precipitated such behaviour came from. Maybe I should ask my wife where she was, who she was with and what she was doing three years and nine months earlier!

However, shortly afterwards he realised that young Blades just don't wear the kit of the sworn enemy and it quickly found its way to some jumble sale or other but the photos remain to this day and, when produced, my younger son, who is an ardent Blade and Wednesday hater, cannot understand why I allowed him to have it. He says that when he has kids there's no way he would relent in the same situation and hates it when I get the photos out and show them to strangers!

So I have now confessed these two tales of shame for all and sundry to read and I hope that some degree of understanding and, ultimately, forgiveness, will emerge from this.

Late eighties, fighting outside Saltergate, Chesterfield

Tempers flare at Sunderland

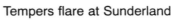

photos: Andy Greaves

Looks like Trouble...

Bristol Booby Trap

Anon

Once when we played at Ashton Gate in the late eighties we passed a park near the ground and we saw about half a dozen Blades playing football, just having a kickabout. By the time our coach had dropped us off at the ground and we'd got our programmes we heard sirens that signalled something was happening close by.

We found out later, both from the police and through terrace rumour, that a mob of Bristol fans had charged through the park sweeping through these lads, who were obviously caught unawares, kicking and punching, and one of the Blades just fell to the ground after a shocked pause.

Word was that one of the assailants had a carpet knife and had just slashed his victim across the back. From what we were told it was a pretty horrific injury requiring many stitches.

Motorway Madness

Anon

I can remember once in the seventies our coach pulling in at some motorway services, pre-'no football coaches' ban, at around the same time that supporters from elsewhere (if memory serves they were something like Burnley fans) were at the services on the opposite side of the motorway.

Of course, some fans ran across the footbridge spanning the six lanes to do battle but some from both parties ran down their respective embankments and across three lanes to meet in and around the central reservation. There were brief exchanges and scuffles and for the few minutes it lasted there was a bit of running backwards and forwards.

It had to be seen to be believed and even now it seems impossible that no-one was killed. God knows what it must have seemed like to view the melée from inside an oncoming vehicle.

Trench Warfare

Dave Shields

When United were away to Bolton in 1977 we hadn't booked on a coach but we went to the Lane and somehow got on to the 'Eds' coach (remember them?), even though it was only for under-sixteens and we were seventeen.

When we got to Bolton there was trouble near the station. I was wearing one of those long trench coats that were in at the time and I don't know how I didn't get run over as I struggled to run across the main road to get away from the fighting.

On the way back we had to stop at the services on the M62 so the coach could fill up with diesel. A coachload of Hull City fans stopped there as well and some of them attacked a group of United fans in a Mini. They must have pushed one of the windows out as suddenly there was this Blade chasing after them brandishing what looked like a complete pane of glass!

Car Trouble

Anon

Travelling on a coach to a game years ago I heard some lads reminiscing about a match at Blackpool in the mid seventies. One of them had borrowed his dad's brand new Morris Marina and after the match there had been lots of trouble. Heading from the car park towards the front to find a watering hole, these lads had found themselves trapped in non-moving traffic with a giant mob of Blackpool fans swarming around. They began thumping, booting and then rocking the car. The Blades couldn't even try to get out and fight back.

The next thing they knew was that the rocking had turned to rolling and they were upside down, with the last few kicks raining down on them before the mob was dispersed by other Blades who'd appeared. Hanging upside down, shocked and cursing, they suddenly went quiet when the driver said, "Shit! Me fatha's gonna fuckin' kill me!"

After a pause they all exploded into uncontrollable laughter and the police who'd just arrived were bewildered as they helped drag these lads out of where the windows had been and they were all just rolling about in hysterics.

The Grassy Knoll

Roy Young

After a match at Manchester City in the seventies we were driving through Belle Vue and a teenager came running out of like terraced back-to-back houses about a hundred yards into the path of the coach and you could see he had a rifle. I imagine it was an air gun and I actually saw him raise it towards us.

The pellet went straight through the window, just missing the driver. It shattered the glass and the next minute he was tonning off down a gennel. The driver were as quick as owt. He was first off the bus. Altogether there were about half a dozen Blades got off as well and gave chase.

Those watching from the coach saw that they'd caught him and he was getting a right pasting.

A kicking and a pasting, then the police came and took him away.

Boston Stranglers

Anon

After the FA Cup match at Boston in the early eighties we were heading back for the car and were literally stepping over prostrate bodies in the street as we tried to dodge the fighting.

We nipped round a corner, where a policeman was hiding, or so it seemed, from the trouble, waiting till it had all died down before intervening. As we passed him Dave remarked, "I think you're needed round there pal!"

This was after the FA Cup second round match against non-league Boston United on December 11th 1982. It ended 1-1, Keith Edwards scoring for United.

Uh-Oh. We're In Trouble

E.B.

I suppose this subject could be a little taboo but I'm sure there are loads of readers who will be familiar with it. I'm not trying to glorify violence in any way - I'll just tell it like it was.

In truth, lots of people (me included) got a big kick out of football hooliganism - unfortunately a few still do - so here's a piece of advice kids. Support your team as colourfully and as noisily as you can, but leave those weapons at home, OK?

As a teenager, me and my mates used to follow the Blades all over the place. Whether it was a pre-season friendly in Edinburgh or Newcastle, an Anglo-Scottish cup match away from home, an FA Cup tie against Burscough or in the league at Gillingham, we rarely missed a game. Our heroes weren't Deane, Kelly or Gayle. They weren't called Currie or Woodward either. No, our heroes had names like Dougie Brown, Jeff Bourne and Bob Hatton.

So how would you have recognised me and my mates? Team shirts, red and white flags, woolly scarves? Certainly not. I'm talking of course, of the early 1980s where any teenager that counted wore their hair neat and their clothes expensive, listened to Northern Soul and Spandau Ballet and was usually a football hooligan of the highest order.

None of my mates are violent now; it was just a case of what was 'in' at the time. Teenagers are very mindful of peer pressure and this, combined with the serious buzz it gave us (there wasn't any Ecstasy in those days), made us pretty nasty, naive and dangerous people.

The first match I can remember seeing trouble at was Boxing Day 1979. A few Blades had managed to infiltrate Wednesday's Kop, one of them being my school friend Phil. Even though I was on the Leppings Lane end I could recognise his green jacket a mile off. I spent most of the match whirling my arms over my head like a demented windmill. After the match we were marched to a massive line of creamy-white buses which were duly stoned by our Wednesday friends while still stationary. The braver Blades piled off, formed a crew and went searching for their lot clutching bricks and bottles. I jumped off the bus shouting "Shoreham Aggro!" as you do, then ended up running up the street on to another bus.

United were beaten 4-0 at Hillsborough on Boxing Day 1979 in the first League derby since 1971.

Still, it was a start. Back at school I exaggerated my part in the 'massacre' (they might have won on the pitch but.....). What few Wednesdayites there were at our school were chased, beaten and bashed whilst our fighting tales continued throughout the day.

This was the first season I'd been allowed to go down the Lane with my mates and while on the footballing front things were going from bad to worse, the better we young Blades became at being hooligans. We'd latched on to a mob a few years older than ourselves who used to organise incognito transport (mini-bus or removal van) to away games. Everyone had nicknames for obvious reasons and if Dodger, Jasper, Herman, Cooperman and Mitchell ring any bells with anyone (they're probably all accountants or working in the Town Hall now), well, there you go.

Anyway, around that time the Blades were regularly taking seven thousand to places like Hull, Blackburn, Grimsby and Blackpool, and I'd guess maybe half of this lot were into trouble, or at least, as Elvis says, they wouldn't run. Third Division stadiums were being destroyed with increasing regularity and the Shoreham Boys (SRA or Barmy Army - the BBC came later) were beginning to get a reputation as one of the hardest crews around. We prided ourselves on being the first Blades to arrive in the town

before an away game, usually before the pubs opened, so a 3am start from West Street after the Limit closed wasn't unusual.

Once in the centre of a foreign town we'd hit the off-licence or settle down discreetly in a pub while a few of the younger lads did a little reconnaissance work. Next on the agenda could well be a tour of the sports and casual shops on the high street, or possibly a little graffiti. We also had loads of other money-making schemes that can't possibly be mentioned here.

After drinking a lot the atmosphere would change. It was almost as though we could sense the confrontation ahead. Sometimes they found us first but we were always game and the results were often nasty.

Then to the match - for those of us who hadn't been nicked or hospitalised. We were usually under police escort by this time so the trick was to evade the cops and get into 'their' end. For some reason it was seen as a bit shameful to end up on the United end - as a rule you hopped the turnstile on to their end or paid to go in the stand nearest their end, ready for the pincer attack. Sometimes, seated areas (Colchester, Tranmere) were almost totally destroyed, sometimes stands were set alight (Blackburn), occasionally pitch invasions held up the game (Hull, Grimsby, Rotherham). All the time you could guarantee that a lot of United's following was more interested in what happened on the terraces than on the pitch. Given the state of the team at the time this wasn't too surprising.

If a match became too boring a kind of mass hysteria would take over. In its mildest form it could be a ninety-minute rendition of one song, a strange Indian war dance or a Can-Can. More serious were events such as the mass floodlight-climb at Leeds Road, Huddersfield. Not much had happened in the game until a sizeable minority of the six thousand or so on the away end decided that the best view was to be had from up on the top. Literally hundreds of Blades managed to be hauled up by their arms and legs. When the police arrived in sufficient numbers to commence battle with the hordes left down below, the floodlight pylon was leaning dangerously forwards.

Some time later, when some sort of order had been established below, an announcement was made over the tannoy. "We have a message here from West Yorkshire Police. Will all the Sheffield United fans on the floodlight get down now please. Failure to do so will result in your arrest."

Well, the police bluff worked. The euphoria quickly died and despite cries of "Stay up!" from the more seasoned floodlight climbers, a mad rush to get down ensued when it became obvious that the law, true to their word, were nicking no-one.

One particularly inebriated Blade was getting really upset at all the defections, complaining about his mates' lack of bottle. "Come on, what's wrong with you all?", he was yelling as yet more of his mates descended sheepishly into the arms of the waiting Bill. However, with true Yorkshire grit and more than a little Dutch Courage, our hero vowed to stick it out to the bitter end. Instead of climbing down he decided to head in the opposite direction, urged on by the crowd below.

The match was a non-starter. Far more interesting were the floodlit acrobatics being performed by the drunken, death-defying Blade. With half the West Yorkshire constabulary standing directly below, he pirouetted, swung and leaped around the steel girders. After about half an hour of this he had to take a breather. He sat down with his head in his hands to applause and cries of "More!!". I thought maybe he'd given up but in reality this particular Blade was yet to perform his coup de grace. As I told you, he'd had more than a few and he was faced with a problem. With no public toilets handy and fifty boys in blue beneath, what could he do? Well, inspiration came quickly and I actually saw one officer put out his hand and say, "looks like rain" before the truth of what was happening hit the ranks. Steamy rain? Sheer panic followed. If the law have ever been reduced to a state of total confusion, this was the day. Still, when you gotta go.......

Our hero stayed up there for the rest of the match and would probably still be there today had a rescue attempt not been launched. He dropped twenty feet into a dense crowd, swapped jackets with someone and made it as far as the railway station before being arrested as Huddersfield's Public Enemy Number One.

The season in the Fourth Division was arguably the best of the lot if you were a hooligan. Small towns were totally overrun by ecstatic Blades who finally had something to celebrate on the pitch. Surprisingly hard crews were found at Halifax, Stockport and Hartlepool, while places like Aldershot and Darlington didn't know what had hit them. My own particular favourite was the infamous trip to Torquay where about half the town's little fishing fleet was set adrift.

Mention the two words Sheffield and United to any long-term resident of the town and watch the reaction.

Taunton had the misfortune to be visited en masse by the "travelling hordes", as we were later described, and after leaving Torquay looking more like Beirut, United fans hit the local scrumpy bars in the Somerset town. The mini-riot that followed was more like a full-scale one in my book. Street battles with the cops went on into the early hours. The cops seemed intent on arresting anyone with a northern accent (including, so rumour has it, a certain Paul Heaton) and the Sunday papers took up the story the next day. Publicity was always very important to us hooligans, so to see a Sunday headline like 'Blades' Day of Shame' would round off our weekend nicely.

So why did hooliganism cease to be popular around the end of the eighties? There were still loads of unemployed young men with nowt to do - they just seemed to agree, in the main, not to beat each other up any more. For me it was a combination of things. Seeing a poor away fan surrounded by Blades suffering such a ferocious kicking that I felt he was going to die, that was one thing. He didn't - at least I saw nothing in the papers the next day - but that incident really brought home to me how ugly the whole thing was.

Of course a succession of football disasters did much to create solidarity between fans of different clubs. Facilities have improved - even if the all-seater idea is a load of rubbish it's pretty civilised not to have to stand in a pool of piss in the rain while you watch your favourite team. The only sure thing is that fashions come and fashions go and at the moment football hooliganism is about as fashionable as a pair of Chris Woods Sondico gloves.

Finally, a comment on Blades fans today. Although we can give ourselves a nice pat on the back for not attacking the away fans any more, I'd still like to see a bit more passion. It's maybe something to do with the demise of the Kop but we don't seem as fanatical as those Fourth Division days. Have we gone soft or what?

Forest Gumps

Dave Shields

When we played Forest away in 1976 we were going on one of the SUT coaches from Pond

Street. There must have been about a dozen coaches lined up ready to set off, but it was at the same time that the Wednesday fans were gathering for their home match that afternoon. At that time Pond Street was the place where everyone met up - especially football fans.

All the coaches left one by one - except ours. Before we could set off a small group of Wednesday fans came towards the coach and one threw a brick through one of the side windows. A couple of others somehow got on the coach and shouted down the aisle "Come on then!". Only a couple of Blades were brave enough to accept the challenge and got off the coach to chase the Wednesday fans, but not for very long as they knew there were loads more in the bus station. They soon returned to hear the coach driver saying, "Sorry lads, we can't go on this coach - we'll have to get a replacement from the depot."

The replacement wasn't long in coming but there was a problem, as the driver explained; "This coach has only got fifty seats, the other one had fifty-two. We need two volunteers to get off."

Me and Chris thought about it. We knew that with the Forest fans' reputation there would be trouble at the match, and assured that we would get a free trip on the coach to the next away match at Blackpool, we volunteered.

It was a good decision. There was trouble at Forest, and we lost 6-1!

Kopping It

Matthew Bell

In the early seventies there was often trouble on the Kop, usually when Leeds United or Manchester United were in town. I think Manchester were the only ones to actually 'take it', though.

By the late seventies the police were a bit more in tune with what was going on but I recall two particular games when there were problems. One was against Millwall when a group of fifteen or twenty Millwall fans infiltrated the Kop. They soon identified themselves and were immediately surrounded by Blades fans and then the police. There wasn't much actual fighting as the police managed to get themselves between the two sets of fans, surrounding the Millwall fans and escorting them to the other end.

Then when we played Wednesday in about 1976 there were loads of Wednesday fans on the Kop, but they seemed to congregate in one of the sections bordered by the white fences that used to run down the Kop. We stood way over the one side but one of the lads with us felt a sharp pain at the back of his neck, and then blood appeared. He had been slashed by a Wednesday fan with a Stanley knife, but he wasn't badly hurt.

The Millwall game was probably the one on March 18th 1978. United won 5-2, scorers Bobby Campbell 2, Alan Woodward (pen.), Mick Speight and Simon Stainrod.

The game against Wednesday must have been the County Cup semi final on October 12th 1976. United won 2-0 with goals by Paul Garner and Cliff Calvert.

Aggro Phobia

Kevin Titterton

As one of the world's biggest cowards and most pathetic fighters - I'm a cross between Blackadder and that bloke off the Mr Muscle adverts - as well as being anti-violence anyway, I've always tried to avoid physical confrontation and, where necessary......... RUN!!! Still, having followed football since the seventies, it has been unavoidable to at least witness violence.

One of my early visits to the Lane, once I'd reached the age where my parents tried to quell their fears and felt that I was old enough to go alone, led to my first experience of football-related violence at close quarters. While walking towards the Lane one Saturday and passing the Hermitage at the bottom of London Road, I noticed a fair crowd of people in around the doorway of the pub. They were all in red and white but I paid little attention as I'd not yet reached drinking age. I'd also not yet acquired that often useful 'sixth sense' that you gain after following football for some time, particularly in that turbulent era. Even to this day that extra sense has meant being able to tell when a situation or atmosphere changes say in a pub or on a sea front near a rowdy gang, when you can steer your family across a road or in another direction, even though your wife's seen nothing untoward.

Anyway, back to my naïve youth. The fact that we were playing Sunderland that day had not registered on seeing the red and white and as I went down the side of the Hermitage I heard a right rumpus going on inside but being too short to see through the side windows I carried on. When I'd gone a couple of yards past a window there was a loud bang and a shower of glass and I turned to see a bar stool bouncing around the floor at the spot I'd just been standing. To say it made me jump would be an understatement. In fact you could say I passed more than one stool on that occasion! Anyway, any natural inquisitiveness was far outweighed by natural cowardice and I didn't hang around to see more.

Another time I'd crossed Bramall Lane towards the old car battery sales place - around where the petrol station now stands - and as I was in the usual gormless teenage trance I just joined a swarm of red and white heading for the ground. As they burst into a chant their different accents brought me out of my slumber as it registered that they were (a) not of our ilk and (b) they'd begun to take the piss out of me. Luckily there was a fairly well-built Blade with his son walking at the kerb edge and he first threatened to sort out anybody who started anything and secondly said, "You'll be all reight son, walk wi' me."

Was I grateful or what, and although I didn't want to push my luck I just wished I had the guts to childishly gloat.

Two or three seasons later - and near the very same spot - came my first real altercation. I was just going to the match against Arsenal with my brother and we'd just turned right off Denby Street into Bramall Lane when I sensed that he'd dropped back a bit as he was no longer at the side of me. As I was about to turn to speak to him I heard what sounded like a loud popping sound and although it sounds daft I thought he had blown a bubble from gum, yet I knew he wouldn't be chewing bubble gum. When I turned round I saw that the popping sound had in fact been a punch to the side of his head. Everything seemed to happen in slow motion; he certainly seemed to go down in slow motion as I made towards him. This wasn't, I confess, any sort of brave action; it just happened naturally, and as speed and sound began to return to normal I saw that there were three or four Arsenal fans around him and one was trying to take his scarf. It was when this happened that my brother, who I'd always sneeringly thought of as Mr Sensible, flipped. I would have expected him to just stay down and let a piece of immaterial material go, but instead he fought back and wouldn't let them take it. I've often joked about him being a tight bugger but if he'd lost his scarf he would just have taken one of mine anyway. No, it was more than just financial loss.

This was such an incredible sight that I remember I started to laugh. It was probably shock and nerves but the whole situation seemed so bloody funny. How many times had I heard such phrases as "Why can't you be more like your brother?" Why not indeed? What a Blade! If I'd had more time I'd have been bloody proud of him.

Sadly I was snapped out of this surreal vision abruptly when my body was suddenly and violently jarred forward and the most incredible pain came from my arse. Punches followed that spun me round but I never felt them; I just wondered what the hell had happened to my ringpiece. Surely I'd been stabbed? But no, behind me was this, what seemed, immensely tall black bloke with a snarling face and a long leather 'Shaft' coat and he had just kicked me. His accuracy, though, seemed to suggest some medical knowledge!

It was over as quickly as it started and they all dispersed as the police ran over. My brother, who was himself a fairly recent recruit into the police force but was off duty, shared a few words with a sergeant he knew and we were back on our way. But I had to ask something along the lines of, "What the fuck did you think you were doing?" and he replied with something like, "Bollocks to 'em. They weren't tekkin me scarf," and as nerves subsided we both began to laugh.

Aggro On The A629

Anon

We were returning from United's 5-1 win at Halifax at Easter 1982 and had to stop in a queue of traffic, nearly all Blades fans, approaching the junction of the A629 at Grenoside. Coming the other way were loads of cars full of Burnley fans, who had just gained an important win at Chesterfield. Suddenly some of the Burnley cars stopped and people spilled out on to the road. It wasn't long before Blades fans were also out and fighting inevitably started.

Dave, who was driving, reached into his glove box and pulled out a couple of screwdrivers, in case the Burnley fans decided that we were easy prey. Fortunately they stayed away from us and we managed to negotiate our way through the bodies and stationary cars and escape.

No Boundaries At Boundary Park

Matthew Bell

When we played at Oldham one time in the seventies, before the game there was a most amazing sight.

I don't know if it was pre-arranged (I don't know how it could have been) but suddenly hundreds of Blades fans leapt over the perimeter wall (before the days of fences) and hared across the pitch towards Oldham's Kop. You could see the panic spreading through the home fans as they saw what was coming and most of them disappeared down the back before the Blades had completed the length of the pitch.

Some stayed to fight but by now they were hopelessly outnumbered and the match was played with more United fans on the home end than on the away end!

The Taking Of The Colours

Anon

On a Tuesday night in May 1976, with United already relegated, we 'entertained' Birmingham City at the Lane. The final score was 1-1 and I have a feeling that this result helped Birmingham secure First Division status. I can certainly remember their fans going barmy as if they'd just won something, so I presume it was escape from joining us that led to their celebrations.

Anyhow, at some point in the proceedings, Unitedites decided that a group of City fans standing on the Kop were, to say the least, not welcome. After a few scuffles they all seemed to appear down in the bottom right-hand corner from where, by nothing other than sheer coincidence, me and a few schoolmates were viewing the match. As they were part chased, part booted by Blades fans and part dragged by the police on to the perimeter track to be escorted round to the Lane end, one of their number fell backwards and although he received a few boots and bruises he was soon up and on his way.

He had, however, left behind a souvenir. Crushed underfoot, but rescuable, was a home-made cardboard blue and white top hat. I know this wasn't Wembley but it was the days of Slade, so home-made top hats were not that unusual. One of our party grabbed it from the floor during the scuffle and next day at school it was paraded like some sort of trophy, with probably a few exaggerations of both its method of capture and our proximity to the actual fighting.

The match took place on May 4th 1976; Alan Woodward scored United's goal.

Jeepers Speakers!

Matthew Bell

We were in The Aviary, that pub on the banks of the River Trent, before United's Easter Monday match at Meadow Lane in 1992. There was a DJ in one room playing loud music, so we went in another room where it was a bit quieter, although the music was still being piped through.

At about seven o'clock the music suddenly stopped and instead over the speakers we heard "thud, crash, bang" and the occasional voice shouting. We wondered what on earth was going on, but we soon learned that a gang of Forest fans had come into the pub, either to celebrate their win at Old Trafford that afternoon, or because they knew there would be Blades fans inside.

Fighting started and what we could hear was the sound equipment being turned over in the scuffle after the DJ had scarpered leaving everything switched on!

United beat Notts County 3-1 on April 20th 1992. Scorers were Paul Beesley, Glyn Hodges and Bobby Davison.

Fireworks before the 1997 play-off final against Crystal Palace at Wembley. The game, though, was a damp squib and, of course, United lost to a last minute goal.

photo: Kevin Titterton

It's A Funny Old Game...

Hee Haw!

Anon

After the match at Villa Park in September 1987 we were sitting on our coach waiting for everyone to get back on board. The coach was parked blocking off the end of a side street and someone sitting on the left hand side nonchalantly said, "Look at this soft c***!".

And when we all looked, there's this Villa fan facing our bus gesturing that he'd like to 'converse' with us, possibly with slight physical connotations. He didn't realise that his mates, after an exchange of verbal and signed pleasantries, had moved on to the next coach down. He began to do what all lads seem to do in these situations: kind of take one step forward and two or three slight hops backwards with both feet at once - Michael Palin as a street beggar in 'The Life of Brian' always reminds me of this - arms outstretched, palms upwards and fingers flicking towards himself, while silently mouthing, "Come on then!" Why do lads do this strange dance as a prelude to a scrap?

With his back to the side street he never saw the coppers approaching. While enticing him to stay with our own retaliatory juvenile gestures (actually if some Blades who'd wanted to get off had done, he'd have had the crap beaten out of him), we all waited with bated breath, silently praying that he wouldn't turn at the last minute and see the police, each of us whispering, "Come on! Come on!" under our breath.

His face when they grabbed him was a picture.

He was yanked backwards with some force (probably of the West Midlands variety!), his eyes almost popping out of his head with the shock, and his mouth was held in a giant 'O'. You could see the colour drain from his face before it turned beetroot as he was led away attempting to protest his innocence. We all exploded in a mighty cheer and his questions to the boys in blue of "What have I done?" were drowned out by our chorus of "Cheerio, cheerio, cheerio!"

The miserable sod didn't even wave back!

This was on September 26th 1987. United and Villa drew 1-1, with Colin Morris's penalty cancelling out a free kick from future Blade Kevin Gage.

Missile From Mars

Anon

In November 1976 I was allowed to travel to see United at Blackpool with my older brother. My dad had ordered me to stick with and listen to my guardian and had likewise threatened him not to let anything happen to me.

There had been much trouble already that day and once inside the ground the fans began to bait each other. Apart from a row of police, the only thing separating the rival supporters on the end where the United fans were massed was a mesh fencing. The problem with this was that it didn't go right up to the roof and so allowed missiles to be thrown from one section to the other. When things began to escalate, the volume of missiles started to increase and suddenly the

Blackpool contingent, who through experience of this type of warfare and having come well armed and prepared, were raining stones and coins down on us. Infuriated, the United fans ran at the mesh and a fight with the police ensued. A lad who was standing just to the right of us was leaning on a crash barrier and trying to raise himself up a little to see all the action when he was suddenly hit on the back of the hand by what was presumably a large stone. It certainly made a right mess of his hand and under a further barrage we all had to try to cover our heads.

Still, it was getting out of hand now but yet was proving irresistible to watch. It was during this second onslaught that I was struck, and there was no chance of avoiding it. Instantly my hands cupped the right temple where the object had found its target, the strange thing being that I'd felt no pain. I did, however, feel a sticky wetness that seemed to spread down my cheek, though before I had time to panic my brother had grabbed my head.

The first thing he did before checking my injury, though, was to say, "You daft twat. You would have to get hit!", followed by, "Me fatha'll go fuckin' barmy," and then once he'd taken a gander at the dark sticky substance spoiling my boyish good looks and given it a wipe with his hand, he announced that it wasn't blood. A quick look around on the floor revealed the most disgusting example of a semi-chewed-up Mars bar. Whoever among the Neanderthal clan on the right of the fencing had produced this had done a revoltingly good job in making it wet and gooey at one end, while maintaining a decent projectile shape at the other.

And while the Blades fans around us saw the funny side, my elder kinsman slapped me round the back of the head because I'd almost got him a bollocking back home!

This match took place on November 13th 1976. United were beaten 1-0.

Ale, Hoggies And Spice

Anon

Amongst the different culinary wares (and nightmares) that I've encountered and (not always) digested in an attempt to soak up some of the pre-match ale consumed at various away haunts, I have to say that the Cornish pasties (as opposed to other grounds' Cornish nasties) sampled at Exeter have to rank somewhere up near the very best.

When we played there in the late seventies it was my first encounter with the 'other' St James' Park and its wonderful pasties. The woman at the food kiosk said they were home-made "hoggies" and it showed. Even when manufacturers sell something as "home-made" they're all of a uniform shape and size. Not these ones. The edges had been pressed down by thumb; you could tell. And once tasted, well, your imagination and taste buds said it had to be a grandmother's thumb, a thumb of years of baking. Excellent.

The only problem was that they sold out in no time. They "didn't make that many" the woman informed us, as they "didn't normally get the crowds". But they had got some "ordinary pies". No comparison. It was like comparing hand-pulled Ward's with Watney's Red Barrel, or Michelle Pfeiffer with Janet Street-Porter.

Also at this game, sweets were handed out to some Blades fans by a policewoman. I can't remember whether it was before the match or at half time. Before, probably, when everyone was still half-cut. Anyway, she offered round the bag of spice in return for the Blades fans, at her request, to "say something". She said she loved the way we spoke and that she liked to hear the accent!

"What d'yer want us ter seh?" replied one Blade with his hand already in the paper bag being held out.

"Anything, just say anything. I love it. Go on and you can have a sweet."

One of the group known as the Barnsley Blades then enquired, "If tha gi's a spice fo' just one word, wot's tha gi forra sentence!?" and amidst much mucky laughter and cheering another retorted, "I'll read thi a bloody book if tha'll sit on me face!"

The WPC's face went bright red but she was laughing, as were her male colleagues, and she took it well - no pun intended!

True Love And Loyalty

Anon

Talking to a Blade before season ticket deadline day in the summer of 1995 he asked me if I'd bought mine yet. We were saying how crap the season just gone had been and, more importantly, how unambitious the club still was and of its lack of interest in the fans - other than their money of course - which was getting worse each year.

Anyway, I told him that no I hadn't but that, despite all the whinging, I would do. And it was no use my saying otherwise - one of the reasons as fans we never get anywhere.

I probably always will while finances allow, though this seems to get harder each year. Besides, I told him, I'd only go to them all anyway and that means it would obviously work out much dearer, I would never be guaranteed a certain seat and I would struggle to get tickets for big cup games (ahem, ever hopeful).

While nodding his head in agreement he mused, "Yeah, and besides, if I get one now I'll get it on our lass's Barclaycard and she'll pay it off with the other bills out of her wages. But if I go each week and pay it'll come out of my pocket!"

Quinny Cost Me Eighty Quid

Anon

This Blade (let's call him Brian, although that obviously isn't his real name) had this £2 bet on United to beat Reading 3-0 with Graham Stuart scoring the first goal, at odds of 40/1.

So when Gareth Taylor made it 3-0 with half an hour to go, Brian pleaded with United to play it safe for the rest of the match and settle for what they had got.

As the match entered injury time Brian's bet looked safe, but Quinny had other ideas. What a time to score your first goal for the club. Ten seconds later, full time, Brian £80 light.

This was March 14th 1997. Graham Stuart did score the first, Marcelo got the second.

Caught Underwears

Kevin Titterton

I can't remember what sparked off the insanity, though you don't have to be Hercule Poirot to suggest that maybe alcohol played no small part, but I remember one time at Bristol City when members of the Sheffield United contingent began to produce home-made bunting to adorn the perimeter fencing.

So what's so great about that? Well, nothing particularly remarkable were we talking of tying a few scarves together or maybe tearing up an old banner and joining the strips. No, the material supplied came from.....pants, knickers, kecks, call 'em what you will, but, yes, the whole thing was made up of underwear!

And, of course, as the idea spread it gained momentum. Most of the operation was carried out with people literally ripping their gear from beneath their trousers, leading to one or two eye-watering accidents with the undercarriage.

There were reports of one or two of the more

Caught underwears - the unusual 'bunting' on the fence at Bristol City

photo: Kevin Titterton

drunk debagging the first layer with little modesty and there were even some female garments, though cursed with the luck of Victor Meldrew I wasn't fortunate enough to be standing near any lady Blades as they clothed off. Of course there was no saying that these items actually came off female supporters and there may be a few Bladesmen who could well be in need of seeking some sort of professional therapy.

The whole thing was backed up by enthusiastic cheers and inevitably one or two choice comments were hurled, one of which was delivered in a brilliant 'Brucie' gameshow host voice when a pair on the fence was singled out with the call, "Oooh, all right my loves! Skidmarks out of ten!"

The police looked on justifiably completely bewildered but perhaps the thought of the day should go to the groundstaff, or whoever was unfortunate enough to cop for the clearing-up job, because judging by the state and colour of some of the contributions, the best rubber gloves in the world wouldn't have convinced me that my health would go unthreatened!

Linesman Lost

Matthew Bell

We were (un)fortunate to have three officials for the home game against West Bromwich Albion in February 1999. This Blade (we'll call him Paul) was walking towards the city centre on Attercliffe Common that lunch time on his way to the match when a car pulled up alongside him. The driver wound down the window and, whilst pointing to the floodlight pylons of Woodbourn Road athletics stadium, asked, "Is that Bramall Lane?"

"No," said Paul, "that's the athletics track but I'm going to Bramall Lane so if you give me a lift I'll take you there."

Once inside the car, Paul asked, "Are you a West Brom fan?"

"No," replied the driver, "I'm running the line."

As Paul was dropped off near the Lane and thanked the linesman for the lift, the linesman responded, "No, thank you, I would never have found it otherwise."

However, it would seem that the linesman's gratitude was not sincere. Otherwise, why would he persist in giving Marcelo offside when he never

was?

This was on February 6th 1999. United won 3-0 with goals from Marcelo 2 and Lee Morris.

Mortar Sponge Than Meets The Eye

Anon

In the early to mid seventies, at a Sheffield comprehensive school, a group of lads was leaving the playing fields after a games lesson. It was the time of year that most of them hated - little or no football. One lad in particular had his mind on a sport other than track and field. Why was it, he wondered, in fights between schools that missiles could be hurled over great distances and with reasonable accuracy, and yet in games lessons you couldn't get a discus or a javelin beyond how far you could spit?

Anyway, they were having the usual arguments about the city's best team and who'd fare better in the coming season. The group was going through the usual Blades/Owls banter as they passed near the large canvas high-jump bed and, because it often got 'help' from the pupils, some of its sponge contents were scattered around the field, both wind- and foot-assisted. There were pieces of various size, shape and colour. Some were identical in both shape and colour to those bricks with holes going vertically through them and had therefore been used many times to trick both car drivers and rival pupils on passing buses.

This lad, with his mind elsewhere, saw one of these 'bricks' just a few yards away and so, breaking away from the group and in an effort to show the Wednesdayites a truly brilliant player to copy, brought back his right leg, shouted "Woodward!" as loud as he could and swung his foot to contact as hard as possible. The thing was, to get these sponges to travel any distance you had to really welly them. He did.

Apart from the incredible searing pain, the thing that struck him most was how well the brick lifted and took off. After that he was only aware of seeing sky within a circle of laughing faces, and then blackness, followed by the sense of being chaired away by P.E. teachers. The part of his right foot that was not dead was feeling wet inside his trainer.

Later, as the story was being relayed several times over with great gusto, it seemed that the thing that amazed his mates most was that seeing as how crap he was at football, it had been the furthest and most accurate shot he'd ever made!

There's Some People On The Beach...

Anon

Blackpool was always a terrific away game to go to years ago. Loads of Blades would go a day or two before or would stay after the match and, of course, on the day hordes would descend on the town.

There were several visits in the seventies and eighties but I can't remember specific matches or specific dates (I can't think why!) and they've all merged into one from fragmented memories (or maybe I should say liquidised memories!). You'd meet other Blades who'd also gone for a couple of days with the lads. Not just in the pubs either. There'd be those gloriously ridiculous games of football on the beach, in all weathers. They'd start off reasonably sensibly with a decent orange plastic 'Wembley' ball, until punctured, or sometimes they'd be with one of those ten bob ones that even if launched from a Howitzer would still only travel a couple of yards in a line as straight as the Snake Pass. But the games would end with about twenty-a-side playing with a beer can, splintered shins and all.

Booking into a guest house was always something of an assignment that Anneka Rice wouldn't even manage. Coastal places have always been notorious for being wary of taking in lads in numbers greater than one anyway, and when they're football fans.....so you'd all end up in different digs, and the grottier places as well.

Over the years many footie fans must have woken up in the early hours in doorways or under piers, freezing cold from the sea wind, northern weather and the diminishing effects of alcohol. On one occasion two of us were booked in a backstreet place and after the game - a night match that we won - we met up with another mate who'd got nowhere to stay. In the pubs that night, and in the streets afterwards, there were even more Blades trying to cadge places to sleep with those that had managed to find digs and by closing time we'd got three coming with us. Five in a two-bed room, though there was a cot, and it was used. No-one cares as long as you're in somewhere. It's just a place to sleep it off. As happens when you're pissed,

we thought we were really quiet, and clever, and original, in sneaking them in, but the next morning on the way to the much-needed bog, I met the landlady on the landing.

"Morning!" she said.

"Morning, love!" I replied.

"Oh dear, you're not looking too well. Will you be wanting breakfast?"

"Oh God, I don't think so, love."

"OK, but what about all your mates? Will they?"

Rumbled!

This was on the night of October 3rd 1979. United won 3-2, with goals from Len de Goey, John MacPhail and Alex Sabella.

Another memory of Blackpool is, of course, the Pleasure Beach. There was once a mob of Unitedites (I think, if memory serves, they were Barnsley Blades), a couple of which were in a cable car, or some such ride up in the air anyway, while some of their party were trying their skills (hysterical after a gallon of ale) at a stall with bows and arrows, trying to gain a prize. After an exchange of jovial threats and expletives between cable car and ground, inevitably the weapons were aimed and fired skywards. The stall owner was going barmy, while the rest of us witnessing it were in fits; even the holiday-makers found it entertaining.

Also in the Pleasure Beach, at the top of a wooden walkway, was a pre-fab hut-type kiosk with a door at the side and a window in the front. From it a youth was selling teddy bears, on which were the names and colours of various football teams. The kiosk was approached by some Blades, one of whom was twinged with a sudden bout of romance. He decided to "Get aar owd lass one". The lad selling, who was obviously a student or something trying to earn a few extra bob in a crap job, not only said he didn't think they had a Sheffield United one, he said it in a questioning tone that suggested he'd never heard of the Red and White Wizards. He said something like "Sheffield who?" as he rummaged through his stock and he wasn't taking the mickey!

The fact that this poor sod probably knew nothing about, nor cared about, football anyway mattered not to the bunch, who began to shove and sway this fibreglass box until, with a final "Yo-oh heave ho!" it went over on to its side in which the door was. There were teddy bears and change all over the place as the unfortunate occupant crawled out of what had been the sales window, red faced and near to tears!

Cloud Nine - Vehicle One

Anon

This story is of an incident involving a Blade, which occurred the day after our famous, memorable, excellent, "I've died and gone to heaven" victory over Wednesday that clinched the double in 1991/92. It took place late in the afternoon of March 12th 1992.

Although any alcoholic content may have passed from this Blade's body, in one way or another he was still drunk on euphoria, and that's an important point to remember in this story.

Where he works, it's not far from Fitzalan Square in town and he usually went there to use a cash dispenser in the main post office. Obviously, with what he'd eventually dispensed of the night before, he needed to replenish his wallet somewhat. Usually he'd walk up to this cashpoint to withdraw money but as it was getting on towards home-time he decided to use one of his firm's vehicles he was out in at the time.

Anyway, he drove into Fitzalan Square, which is mainly buses and taxis only, chucked it on the double yellows, stuck the hazards on and walked the few yards to the machine. He got his money out and also bought a copy of 'The Star' off the seller who stood there. This paper seller was an old bloke, white hair and 'tache, he wore a hearing aid and never had a ciggie out of his mouth. What's relevant here though is that this bloke's a fellow Blade, and the two started talking about the previous night's match and looked at the brilliant pictures of the experience in the paper.

While scanning the photographs and reading the snippets between, with songs still ringing in his head, he turned to the paper seller and, while he laughed out loud sharing their enjoyment the old fella coughed a lung up, grinning and happy, and the Blade in question walked away.

About eight o'clock that night at home he received a phone call from one of the lads he worked with (names obviously altered to protect the innocent, the not-so-innocent and so as to not officially raise this incident again).

"Kev?!"

"All reight Andy! What's up?"

"Did you use (such and such a vehicle) today?"

"Aah. Why, what's up?"

"You went out in it?"

"Yeh?"

"Then what did you do with it?"

"I parked it up like usu.......oh bollocks!"

That's when it struck him - that he'd walked back to work as usual, reading 'The Star' on such a high - in fact you could say he'd floated back because he was walking about three feet off the ground - that he'd forgotten he'd left the vehicle parked in Fitzalan Square!

Through breaks in hysterical laughter, his workmate tried to convey to him the mayhem it had caused. He has never actually lived this down amongst some of those who found out - which to him seemed to be about half of Sheffield - and in the days that followed he heard all sorts of stories about the police going barmy, the congestion emanating from Fitzalan Square, blocking the city centre, Park Square, down to the Wicker and the Parkway coming in, right past Midland Station.

There were tales of bus and taxi drivers getting to blows as tempers flared and the company to which the vehicle belonged trying to find out why it was there and cover ups saying it had broken down (all this happened pre-Supertram works, so had all parties affected known what was to come in the future, things may not have seemed so bad!).

As stated before, though, this Blade had still been on cloud nine. I mean we all were. For a start it was unusual for 'The Star' to go to town on United as they did with the reports and the supplement and had we not just suffered years of being told how much better than us Wednesday were? And months listening to what they were going to do to us once we shared the same division? Then weeks of hearing how the Lane match had been a one-off and that they'd wipe the floor with us in revenge?

The thing is we'd flicked a few Vs at general opinion and expectation in both derbies that season, especially the performance and result that second game. Well that's his excuse anyway.

You've Got The Looks...

Len Strike

I had such high hopes that dismal grey day. Standing at the rear of a long queue in Pond Street's Nelson Mandela Building, awaiting an international film audition. With Sheffield United and Sean Bean being central themes in the potential blockbuster, originally named 'A Pint O' Bitter', I wore my brightest and loudest Blades sweatshirt.

I intended to impress, especially if interviewed by Sean himself. My obvious affinity to United would help. I filled in the questionnaire. Red ink of course.

"Availability?" Martini - any time, any place, anywhere. Good. A bit of humour. Might get me a leading part.

The American photographer, although I vehemently remonstrated against it, insisted that I pull back my jacket to reveal my United shirt. Things were looking promising.

An informal, very brief interview with a serious young man next. On seeing me his eyes lit up across the table, as if he'd seen the Mona Lisa or a beautiful cluster of diamonds.

"You've got the looks!"

For several seconds time stood still. With a subsequent rush of adrenaline, voices, sounds, happenings all occurred in slow motion. He was lining me up as either a Sean Bean lookalike or for a leading role alongside glamorous actresses. Wasn't he?

"You've got the looks we're after. For pit scenes, steelworks or pubs!"

After years of following Sheffield United FC I should be used to big let downs. But for several seconds, seeming much longer, I had really believed I was heading for super stardom and millionaire status. Worse was to come. After several days' celebrity status in my local, signing autographs and getting free beer, he rang.

"You've got a part for one day," he said. "Sitting at the back of a pub down Attercliffe. You must wear that old jacket of yours. It's ideally suited for an old, rundown pub."

It was my best coat!

Pee For Penalty

Anon

In October 1985 United were at home to Millwall and by the time me and the lads had secured our place at the back of the Kop I was ready for my first pee. Some people always astound me when they're drinking as they seem to possess bladders like the Tardis, whereas mine always amazes me because it always seems to release more than it actually takes in. This was, though, still in the days of standing so you didn't disturb people when paying visits during the game.

So there we were. A poor game, a small crowd and a weak bladder. The only saving grace of the day was that we'd had a skinful in the Lane Social before this suffering. It was during one of my visits to the channels that United decided to instil some excitement into the proceedings. While standing there with maybe a slight wobble, watching my wages spray back off the ancient tiles, I sensed the crowd's sudden change and as me and the only other occupant still in full flow looked up at each other we heard the crowd roar its approval. Others had just shaken, zipped up and run out.

It wasn't a goal though; you could tell, but before we had chance to think any further one of this Blade's mates came in and gave the answer to him; "Penalty! Come on!"

He had just finished and ran past me saying "Penalty mate!" as if he'd thought I hadn't heard his mate's announcement. I wasn't done, but I nearly was and in the milliseconds that followed I had to decide whether to stay and squeeze groin muscles for all I was worth or house my tackle and hope for just a few drops at most.

I went for the latter but as anyone who's ever knocked a pint over will tell you, what looks like a pint in a glass seems like a lake when it's emptied. As I ran out of the bogs, but not out of liquid, I could feel my leg becoming wet and warm. There were many people blocking my view near the rear exits and I had to partly lean on someone and partly jump if I was to see the penalty.

My timing had to be just right as I jumped and my calculations proved to be perfect. Sadly, the same could not be said of Colin Morris's calculations as I rose just in time to see his strike from the spot hit the post and rebound away. It was now that the full fruits of my earlier decision became evident and whilst muttering and cursing softly and shaking each leg in turn while trying to hold my jeans away from my skin, I inadvertently drew attention to myself, giving my fellow Blades their only laugh of the afternoon.

Jeff Eckhardt scored our only goal as United lost 3-1.

This was October 5th 1985.

Train Spotted

Kevin Titterton

I can never watch the film 'Zulu' without it reminding me of a trip to Notts County in the 1977/78 campaign. We played there twice that season but the match - or rather the journey to it - was in (I think) the Anglo-Scottish Cup competition, when we lost 3-0.

As was normal with the now-defunct football specials, travelling on the train had begun by boarding carriages that were used for the specific purpose of ferrying football supporters about - maybe with some justification on reflection of the past results of football hooligans' 'restoration work' - in that they were old, time-expired, basic, guts ripped out, virtual cattle wagons. As usual there were police to see us off, there'd be police to greet us and, just to keep us company, there were the British Transport Police on the train, one of whom I'll never forget.

Remember 'Zulu'? Well, it's been on the box enough. Remember the "Yes sah!", all-smart, all-saluting, never-question-an-officer type Colour Sergeant Major? The one with the well-groomed uniform and perfectly ironed moustache? Well in the late seventies he was escorting train-loads of football fans to away games.

The journey had been uneventful, save for some boisterous shouting and arguing that always ensues in games of cards, and we'd seen little of the Sergeant Major apart from the odd walk through the carriage when he might tell those getting carried away with Blades songs to get down from the luggage racks or some nutters playing 'chicken' with their heads stuck out of the window; "Don't be so daft lads!"

That is until we were nearing Nottingham and the train began to slow slightly. Then, following the first 'thud' of something hitting one or other of the carriages, he appeared, walking calmly through each of the carriages saying, "All right lads. No need to panic. Just lie on the floor or across the seats. Don't look through the windows and don't get up."

Of course, human nature being what it is, when you're told not to look at something then you've got to look, yeah? No!! Well not for long anyway. He had hardly finished his sentence in our particular section when the train, now being pulled at a snail's pace, came under a heavy barrage of missiles. Everyone dived for cover, expletives flying around and a well-timed chorus of "Bastards!" aimed at our invisible assailants.

But not our Colour Sergeant. He kept walking up and down the train, hands behind his back, head jerking forward every so often, stepping over head-covered bodies.

"Keep calm lads," (more thuds). "Heads down," (the sound of showering glass). "Not long now," (bang, crash, dent).

He kept this up for what seemed like ages until the train picked up a little speed again and the thuds and bangs became less, before they stopped altogether. As he passed through the carriage again a Blade remarked, "Tha must be fuckin' mental pal!"

In return he just smiled but I swear I thought he was going to say, "Do up your tunic lad. There's a good soldier!"

This was September 6th 1977. United lost 3-0 to Notts County at Meadow Lane in an Anglo-Scottish Cup play-off match after the two teams finished level in the initial group stages.

Mirror, Signal, Trusson, Manoeuvre

Janet Steer

I can live with myself no longer unless I get this off my ample bosom, so you'll have to bear with me.

The date was May 23rd 1982. The Blades had just been crowned Fourth Division champions. My other half was in a good mood so he agreed to give me a driving lesson in his new car. Things were going fine until I asked him if I could practise reversing. Behind my request was an ulterior motive as I knew that he'd suggest we practise on the road where my hero 'Hunk' Mike Trusson and one of his favourites, Paul Garner, lived and we might just get a glimpse of one of our heroes (well, it was a long time ago).

I positioned his beloved car ready to go back round a corner, off we went, and here things become a bit of a blur, but the next thing I remember is the car sitting squarely on a freshly turfed lawn and hubby sitting looking inside somebody's lounge admiring their cheese plant.

I was in a state of shock and my other half, in his usual kind and considerate way, requested that I move the car quickly or else. In my efforts to move the vehicle I first stalled and then did a racing start away from said lawn and house. To this day I have never driven a car at such speed as I did to get away from the scene of the 'crime'.

It was only when we pulled on to our drive that hubby shouted to me, "That was Paul Garner's lawn!!!"

And so Paul, if you ever wondered where the tyre tracks on your grass came from then I can only offer a belated apology and express the hope that the marks soon grassed over and I have your forgiveness.

Ticking Off

Kevin Titterton

At one time I kept my programme collection and other memorabilia (rubbish, wives call it) in the loft at our house. Apart from the space being needed elsewhere, it also appeased the wife, who had moaned about wardrobes and cupboards being full of them, and stuff falling out when she opened them. So, up they went.

This is until one day I was reading one of her magazines (erm, as fellas do, you know, and not just the problem page either!) and I came across this article about some microscopic mite that lives in houses. This did not signify any sort of squalor as they are normally found in clean houses. Apparently they particularly like places such as lofts and they eat their way through, amongst other things, carpets and loads of paper!!

All hell let loose. It was like a fire alarm had gone off. I had the ladder out and and went up quicker than season ticket prices following promotion. We formed a chain to get all the boxes down. Well, it was hardly a chain really. There were only two 'links', and one of them was sobbing quietly, handing boxes down, while the other was tutting and collecting them and saying

"Calm down" and "Don't be so bloody daft."

Anyway, thankfully there was no damage done and nowadays it's back to a bursting wardrobe with no room for clothes and the wife playing hell about it.

When One Door Closes...

Anon

When we played at Colchester on Tuesday August 21st 1979 it was one of those times and grounds when, because of the large contingent of Blades that travelled, we seemed to take over the place, pubs and all.

To the match though. After queuing for ages and after asking a most helpful copper if they sold programmes inside the ground - he said they did - we entered the ground to find that you had to buy them outside. There were two large blue wooden gates leading out that were obviously locked until the end of the game. One of the gates had a small wicket door incorporated within it. This old bloke stewarding inside heard us moaning about the programmes and so he said, "Go back through here lads. I know you've paid. Just knock when you're coming back in."

We were a bit surprised but also grateful, so we said "Cheers!" and went through the small door he opened for us. The queues of Blades still outside watched as we came out, bought programmes, knocked on the door and went back in, this time through the large main gate that the old fellow had opened. Our words of "Thanks again mate" and "You're a Blade pal" were drowned out by the racket of rap-tapping on the door. As we were walking away we turned to look back. Unbelievably he had opened it again! God knows how many got through before help arrived and they managed to get the gate closed.

Also at this game the tannoy announced that at half time all the Colchester supporters wishing to travel to the away game the following Saturday - I think it was Rotherham - should put their names forward at the special kiosk provided, so as to determine the number of coaches (or was it seats?!) needed. The kiosk was in easy reach of many Blades fans. I can't imagine that Colchester have ever really taken that many to away games, so the penny must have dropped when they filled their sixth coach!

United lost this game 1-0, their first ever fixture

against Colchester United.

Beware Of Sick Pockets

Anders

There's this well-known Blade called Andy who once, on a trip on the Sportsman coach to Middlesbrough, was feeling none too well after a heavy session the previous night. As the coach pulled up at Ayresome Park, Andy was looking distinctly green, clearly ready to throw up at any moment. He tried to hold it back until he was off the coach but try as he might, he failed.

Andy must be a really thoughtful fellow as he obviously did not want to foul up the coach for the journey home by vomiting on the seats or the floor, so instead he pulled up the John Burridge-style sheepskin coat he always used to wear and deposited the contents of his stomach into the pocket.

As if that were not bad enough, as the Blades fans entered the turnstiles they were being searched by policemen. Just imagine as Andy stood, arms widespread, being frisked up and down. "'Scuse me son, but would you please be so kind as to turn out your pockets for me...."

Who's Sorry Now?

Anon

With our coach stuck at some lights, or in some traffic or something, on our way to a match at Cardiff, we found ourselves right opposite a church where a wedding was taking place.

All the families and guests were milling around at various stages of the photo session. After someone on the coach had brought the scene to everyone's attention, all faces were jammed up against the sliding openers on the windows (they were old coaches), and heads were poking through the skylights. There were various comments shouted from individuals and a selection of United songs from all, when everyone started chanting, "You'll be sorry! You'll be sorry!"

Some of the guests, and even the bride herself, took it in good part and were laughing or smiling. Some even waved, but the groom definitely didn't look too chuffed. Apart from the fact that the poor sod perhaps felt that he was being manacled forever, and with his last moments of freedom slipping away, he certainly didn't want

the piss taking out of him as well.

Anyway, like a fool he turned and gave us a very nasty look and mouthed something; possibly requesting that we leave the area as soon as possible. Obviously this gave us all immense pleasure and made our efforts even more fervent.

Still, if he thought that his day was bad, we lost 4-0. At least he'd have 'scored' that night. I don't think United would have if they'd played all bloody night!

This was on April 21st 1979. It was Ian Benjamin's debut (as substitute) for United.

The Hot Dog Parade

Matthew Bell

Once, during half time of a game at Leeds Road, Huddersfield, we were being 'entertained' by a marching band. The band would march up and down, turning in perfect synchronicity as they reached the goalmouth, then go across the penalty area and back again.

As they approached our end for the second time and did their ninety-degree turn, one Blade decided to jump over the front wall and join in at the back. The problem is, he didn't have a trumpet or a trombone - he was eating a hot dog!

It was probably only a few seconds, but it seemed like several minutes, as we were rolling about laughing on the terracing, before the police realised what was going on and intervened and nabbed him. I hope they let him finish his hot dog before throwing him out!

A Bitter Film To Swallow

Kevin Titterton

When the news first broke about a film to be based loosely on and around United it was welcoming. Also, the fact that a well-known Blade and celebrity was going to take the star role could mean a world stage for Sheffield United FC. Hold on, I could feel a dream coming on.

Auditions for extras for the making of the film were held in the Nelson Mandela student union building in Pond Street. I work not far away and was working that Saturday morning so, while furtively looking around to make sure that no-one knew me, I went in. Metaphorically speaking I had a bag on my head but feeling a complete berk would be a small price to pay once I'd made it big.

After entering the building and passing the Mandela Bar you went upstairs to the concert hall. I remembered witnessing the great occasion of Nelson Mandela's release on television and felt slightly humble at what I was about to try to achieve. It also reminded me of a conversation I had with my brother some days after that historic event. My brother said that Mandela was "a lucky sod". When I asked him, "Why? Did you think they'd never release him?", he replied, "No, I mean for having all these bars named after him!"

Once there, you were given a form to fill in and had to queue with all the other sad hopefuls and have your picture taken holding up a number in front of you (ahem... a slight feeling of déja vu there). After waiting ages there was the briefest of interviews and that was it. A "don't call us, we'll call you", a verbal "Dear John". The end of a glittering career. The nearest I'd get to Hollywood anyway. I sense that it must have been looks, not enthusiasm, that mattered. I could have done Olivier's Henry V and it wouldn't have impressed. Probably Tom Hanks' Forrest Gump would have been more suitable.

There are two things I regret about the auditions for 'A Pint O' Bitter', now of course retitled 'When Saturday Comes'. First, that I could ever have imagined that I'd be successful in being chosen even for a small part - though if possessing a small part was an advantage I'd have been in with a chance! Ha! Ha! (read this bit in the style of Frankie Howerd).

Second, having told anyone that I went along to try, especially anyone at work and especially a certain fellow Blade by the name of Ken Simmons. I should have known better and wasn't too surprised at a bit of mickey taking.

However, a couple of weeks after telling this Blade of my attempts at entering the world of luvvies and Oscars I received a letter, on headed paper, from the producers of the film, which read:

"PRODUCTION REF: A Pint O' Bitter

LOCATION: Bramall Lane

Dear Mr Titterton,

I refer to your recent audition for the above production. Regrettably the specky-eyed Flashing Blade salesman is an unbelievable figment of the imagination and we doubt very much whether our viewing public could take the character seriously.

However, having viewed your photograph with hysterics, we are convinced that we now have a role in 'A Pint Of Bitter' for which you would be ideally suited. We are prepared to offer the you the part of a long streak of piss in a toilet scene!"

Fellow Blades - don't you just love 'em?

The Children's Christmas Party

Karen Keenan

In the mid sixties, my father was Assistant Secretary and Cricket Secretary at the Lane for three years. A favourite story in our family folklore trotted out at intervals and which my own children now find very amusing tells of how I let the family down at a Sheffield United Christmas Party.

Every Christmas, the club threw a party for the children of the players and the club staff. The story goes that Father Christmas made his customary appearance and handed out parcels that had been specifically chosen for each child. When my turn came I opened my parcel and promptly burst into tears in full view of everyone, including the lady and gentleman who had chosen the presents. I had been given a 'Doctor Who and the Daleks' board game, which I considered to by a 'boy's present'. Unfortunately I had seen another little girl shortly before opening her parcel to find a beautiful doll and this clearly influenced my reaction. Apparently, I refused to be calmed down and cried bitterly for some time, causing huge embarrassment all round, not least to my poor parents. Heaven knows what the young Len Badger and Alan Woodward - people I would later idolise - would have made of these scenes! Looking back, my Dad had probably been asked what sort of gift I'd like and, as I was never a 'girly' girl, a boxed game probably would have been eminently suitable.

Trust me to make a scene. I would have been five or six at the time. It would be another seven or so years before I became a real Blades fan. It may have been the first time that events at Bramall Lane drove me to tears, but it certainly wasn't the last!

Your Other Team's Lost!

Derek Goodison

Ever wondered why one silly phrase, on its own nonsensical, can set off a whole bar room of Blades into hysterical laughter?

Come back with me to January 4th 1964; the occasion a third round FA Cup tie against Lincoln City away. The Blades left Sheffield in good heart for what was to prove a very easy win over the Third Division side.

Here I must digress a little to explain certain social conditions that existed in the early sixties. Licensing laws were very harsh - strict closing time and no provision whatsoever for drinking up. On the plus side, however, it behove every licensee to open his premises on the dot (in Sheffield 5.30pm) and failure to comply could cost him his licence. Indeed, I often had occasion to find a policeman, point at my watch and request the constable to enforce the law.

So, 5.30pm found us outside a small backstreet pub near Sincil Bank, hammering on the door. After three minutes, a sleepy Mine Host opened up and, in surly fashion, began to serve us. Once again a little explanation. Then, no local radio, no electronic scoreboard and also, on our part, no desire to enquire how our city neighbours had fared, although to be honest we feared the worst.

For them, an easy match against Newport County, a club that now barely exists. Imagine, then, the scene at about seven o'clock, when Mine Host reappeared from the kitchen where he had been cowering, to utter the immortal words,

"I don't know what you're so happy about; your other team's lost!"

Absolute pandemonium. The look of incomprehension on his face as his pub was slowly reduced to kindling, started by an eighteen-stone steelworker giving an impromptu Russian Cossack dance on a tap-room table, was wonderful to behold.

Thus ends this tale, but for many years afterwards it only needed someone to say "Your other team's lost" to set off howls of Blade mirth.

United won 4-0 with goals from Barry Wagstaff, Barry Hartle and Mick Jones 2.

Kidnapped!

Matthew Bell

We were coming away from Ewood Park after a match there sometime in the eighties. It could have been the time we lost 6-1. We were driving along that little road that goes over the moors to Darwen, but we were still in the built-up area on the edge of Blackburn, following a mini-bus full of Blades.

We were just starting to go up a steep hill at a bit of a crawl when we passed a couple of teenage girls walking on the pavement alongside. Suddenly the mini-bus in front slowed down and three or four Blades jumped out and grabbed the young girls, dragging them back into the van.

The poor girls were obviously shocked and scared at being abducted by football hooligans, but they needn't have worried as at the top of the hill, about a hundred yards further on, the mini-bus doors opened again and the girls were let out unharmed, although we could see a dozen Blades rolling about in laughter inside the mini-bus!

United lost 6-1 at Blackburn on April 19th 1986. Keith Edwards got United's consolation - his two hundredth league goal. Future Blade Mark Patterson scored a hat trick for Rovers.

Epilogue

One of the best things about following a football team all around the country for years and years is that it allows you to meet people you would otherwise never meet and see places you would otherwise never see.

Many friendships, a lot of which prove to be long standing, and possibly even a few more intimate relationships, have been sparked by football, whether it be with someone you sit next to on the coach to an away match, a new colleague at work who you happen to be chatting to over a cup of tea, people you overhear talking in the pub or, more likely perhaps nowadays, someone you first encounter exchanging messages on the Internet. And under what other circumstances but at a football match would you willingly jump up and down and share a hug with an old bloke you have never seen before?

Whenever you meet an Englishman abroad, one of the first things you try to find out about him is not what he does for a living, what type of car he drives or how many children he's got, but which team he supports. The fact that the hostilities of the Great War were set aside for a football match one Christmas Day is as nothing when you consider that one of my best mates is a Wednesdayite I met at university, whose Owls sweatshirt was the subject of the first words I spoke to him. Twenty one years later we're still on speaking terms.

So we have ascertained, then, that football is a catalyst for friendships, relationships and conversations (and hugging) with strangers. Moreover, it is also highly educational. How else would you know the capital cities of Armenia and Azerbaijan except through their football teams? What better way is there to pick up a bit of Italian than by watching James Richardson on Channel Four on a Saturday morning? And a lot can be learned about the social conditions of certain eras by examining the influence of football on the people and their lifestyles. Then there's the insight into the intricacies of architectural techniques you can glean by a visit to the modern venues of Huddersfield Town or Bolton Wanderers, and the more classic style of Archibald Leitch at Goodison Park and

Ibrox Park.

I can get around virtually anywhere in Britain without a map because of the knowledge of roads and towns gained by travelling watching the Blades, and a trip from one side of London to the other, taking in the leafy boulevards of Maida Vale to the backstreets of Brixton is easy peasy.

There's the culture, too. I've seen the Golden Hind in Brixham, HMS Victory in Portsmouth and the Cutty Sark in Greenwich whilst on the way to football matches. I've visited the Whitworth Museum in Manchester to see those weird elephant dung paintings before going to Gigg Lane, Bury, and stopped off at the National Portait Gallery and the British Museum ahead of a night match at Loftus Road. A trip to the Manor Ground, Oxford, was interrupted by a walk through the grounds of some of the University colleges.

We know that football is much more 'acceptable' nowadays as the cosmetic surgery demanded by the Taylor Report and the slick marketing of Sky Television have made it an important fashion accessory for hundreds of budding actors, musicians and politicians. Every club now has its legion of 'celebrity fans', all eager to tell the world which team they follow, albeit usually only via the occasional visit to an executive box.

However, those of us who have been around since the days when football fans were treated either as lepers or cattle (or frequently cattle with leprosy) know the real score. We will be there long after the bandwagoners have found another hook to hang their careers on, following the Blades north and south, east and west, through thick and thin, logging into the memory bank for future recounting all those hilarious incidents, hairy or scary moments, times of anguish and despair, elation and joy.

Keep the faith, lads and lasses, and don't forget - UP THE BLADES!!

season ever. An exhilarating journey through the last days of the Wellington Road ground, via Crystal Palace and arguably the greatest Cup Final of all time, to the opening of Villa Park, then the best stadium in the World. Includes biographies of all the players and major backroom staff and offers a unique insight into the running of a 19th Century footballing giant, aswell as the lives of footballers before the days of multi-million pound signings, extortionate wages and television.

GLADYS PROTHEROE...
FOOTBALL GENIUS!

by Simon Cheetham with foreword by Graham Taylor
220pp A5 paperback ISBN 1 872204 10 4
£5.95 (+£1.25 p&p/Europe £2.50/Rest £5)
From the sun-baked terraces of the Maracana to the frozen teahut at Vicarage Road, supporters throughout the world love and respect Gladys Protheroe. Who discovered John Barnes (and Bruce Springsteen)? Who persuaded Alf Ramsey that Geoff Hurst was a better prospect than Jimmy Greaves? Who punched Ron Atkinson on live TV? And the astonishing truth behind Stuart Pearce's suicidal back pass against San Marino. Over half a century of football history and - sometimes shocking - revelations from inside the game. "Quite Brilliant ★★★★★" - FourFourTwo magazine. "A footballing masterpiece... kept me sniggering and dribbling to and from work for the next week" - Beesotted magazine. "We hope Maurice Johnston has a sense of humour" - Matchday magazine. As serialised on Radio 5. The football cult book to end them all!

FOOTBALL AND THE COMMONS PEOPLE

edited by David Bull & Alastair Campbell
320pp A5 paperback ISBN 1 872204 05 8
£9.95 (+£1.50p&p/ Europe £3/ Rest £6)
30MPs and former MPs describe their experiences of, and opinions on, 'the people's game'. Serious issues such as Denis Howell on the politics of the '66 World Cup and David Evans justifying his policies as chairman of Luton Town and Maggie's

lapdog! And fans-eye confessions: who indulged in the rather unparliamentary activity of "Taunting Rangers supporters" out of the car window (and not when he was a teenager either!). Was one MP really among the Tartan Horde ripping up Wembley in 1977? And which MP has an Irish Cup-Winner's medal - an Ulster Unionist playing for Derry City! Includes Roy Hattersley, Kenneth Clarke, Michael Howard, Michael Foot, Gordon Brown, Ann Taylor and more. Fascinating reading throughout.

EL TEL WAS A SPACE ALIEN

The Best Of The Alternative Football Press Vol. 1
edited by Martin Lacey
200pp A4 paperback
ISBN 1 872204 00 7 £5.95
(+£1.50 p&p/ Europe £3/ Rest £6)
GET YOUR WRITS OUT
Another Dose Of The Alternative Football Press
edited by Martin Lacey
200pp A4 paperback
ISBN 1 872204 02 3 £6.95
(+£1.50 p&p/ Europe £3/ Rest £6)
SPECIAL OFFER: Buy both the above for £10 post free (UK only)
Two classic compilations tracing the history and development of football fanzines, packed with features by, from and about the genre. Vol.1 covers the period from the conception of When Saturday Comes to the Hillsborough disaster. Vol.2 covers 1989-91. El Tel... was voted one of the ten most culturally significant sports books of the decade in Sportspages' 10th anniversary poll.